Wake up. Can you hear me? Wake up.

There was a weight on top her. Her eyes were open, she realized, but there was something covering them, covering her face.

Then she realized the pain in her head was caused by something cold and hard pressed firmly against her temple.

"Can you hear me?" the angry voice said again.

Carol didn't speak. She just nodded her head, yes.

"Don't move or I'll kill you."

His face, covered by a dark ski mask, was no more than an inch or two from her face . . . the gun remained against her head, but he shifted, pulling the sheet from her body.

"Why are you doing this?"

"I've been watching you for a long time . . . I've watched you through your window. I've been in your house . . . I follow you in your car and I think you are beautiful. I want to be your friend . . . and if you call the police I'll kill you."

Whispers of Romance, Threats of Death

*One Woman's Treacherous Ordeal with a Savage,
Seductive, Unstoppable Serial Criminal—A True Story*

Carol Cook
and
Ted Schwarz

BERKLEY BOOKS, NEW YORK

WHISPERS OF ROMANCE, THREATS OF DEATH

A Berkley Book / published by arrangement with
New Horizon Press

While the publisher and author have made every effort to provide accurate telephone numbers and Internet addresses at the time of publication, neither assumes any responsibility for errors, or for changes that occur after publication.

PRINTING HISTORY
New Horizon Press hardcover edition / March 2002
Berkley edition / April 2003

Copyright © 2002 by Carol Cook and Ted Schwarz
Book design by Kristin del Rosario
Cover design by George Long
Cover photographs by Photonica

ISBN: 0-425-18957-0

BERKLEY®
Berkley Books are published by The Berkley Publishing Group, a division of Penguin Group (USA) Inc., 375 Hudson Street, New York, New York 10014.
BERKLEY and the "B" design are trademarks belonging to Penguin Group (USA) Inc.

PRINTED IN THE UNITED STATES OF AMERICA

10   9   8   7   6   5   4   3   2   1

THIS BOOK IS dedicated to three women who took part in the process of my recovery, as well as assist in the recovery of thousands of other victims whose lives have been shattered by violent crime:

Patsy Day, founder and retired director of Victims Outreach in Dallas, Texas, and a board member for the state of Texas Department of Criminal Justice, an appointment she accepted from former Governor George W. Bush. Victims Outreach is an organization dedicated to providing grief and trauma counseling for victims and their families as well as protecting the rights of victims and giving them a voice in court. Patsy is the mother of a murdered child.

Raven Kazen, State Director of Victims Services for the Texas Department of Criminal Justice in Austin, Texas. Raven has worked diligently for over twenty years with several Texas officials and legislators to insure the passage of victims' rights laws to protect crime victims and their families.

Sharon Levine Ross, LMSW-ACP, of Dallas, Texas, the therapist who was vital in my recovery. I credit her with saving my life. Sharon stood beside me, day and night, during a long period of darkness. Without her support during the long months of reliving the story of the crime committed against me, I could not have brought my story to print.

CONTENTS

AUTHORS' NOTE

This book is based on the actual experiences of Carol Cook. The personalities, events, actions and conversations portrayed within the story have been reconstructed from extensive interviews and research, utilizing court documents, letters, personal papers, press accounts and the memories of participants. In an effort to safeguard the privacy of certain individuals, their names have been changed and, in some cases, otherwise identifying characteristics have been altered. Events involving the characters happened as described; only minor details have been altered.

ACKNOWLEDGMENTS

There are many people who have had a hand in this book and without whom it would not have been possible to finish it. My strongest supporter, my husband, Bob, stood by me as I questioned my purpose and worth while reliving and writing this story. Sharon Ross, the dedicated therapist who brought me from a living hell back to life, helped me during the writing process, assuring me I could, I would and I had to go on. Patsy Day, always there when I asked for help, spent hours in interviews with author Ted Schwarz as he tried to make sense of the complex criminal justice system in Texas and the laws in place to protect the rights of crime victims at the time the man responsible for my rape was arrested. Raven Kazen, State Director of Victims Services, offered guidance and support during the year-long process of researching and writing my story. Raven has been directly responsible for convincing legislators of the need for stronger punishment of violent criminals who destroy the lives of law-abiding citizens and their communities and for helping thousands of victims and their families find closure and peace. Chris Jenkins, an angel in disguise and the Victim Assistant Coordinator to the Dallas District Attorney's office, offered ongoing support and direction when I constantly bombarded her with legal questions. Sergeant Robert E. Rommel, a dedicated Dallas police officer and one of the officers who took the confession of the Ski Mask Rapist, patiently answered my constant questions with compassion and professionalism.

To Ted Schwarz, I will always be grateful for your work, the research you did to make sure the truth came out about my case, talking to the police and the hours you spent in research and interviews.

Most of all, to Joan Dunphy of New Horizon Press, who saw the act of violence perpetrated against me as one of the most shocking forms of betrayal in modern times and was determined to see my story told. My appreciation also goes to her staff, Joseph Marron, Lynda Hatch and Rebecca Sheil, who worked so tirelessly to see my book through from its inception to its completion. To Joan, Joseph, Lynda and Rebecca, your wisdom, intelligence, knowledge and ability to bring my story together were not only amazing, but indispensable. I shall be eternally grateful to all of you.

PROLOGUE

HE MOVED THROUGH the night like a mythical being, surveying the world as though he had been granted the pleasure of exercising his special powers from the pantheon of gods. The community was North Dallas, Texas, not Northern Greece, and his view was from that of a windshield in a sports car, not the heights of Mt. Olympus. Yet while there were differences, there were also similarities to mythic exploits. He had learned to manipulate many bustling, industrious North Dallas citizens. He had learned to enter their homes, possess their treasures and enjoy the bodies of the women, seemingly at will. He had befriended those who were sworn to protect them, gained favor with several of their elite and become so familiar a companion that those who should have known the real man were blinded.

A police helicopter flew slowly over the North Dallas area, crisscrossing a territory bounded by the LBJ freeway, the Central Expressway and the tollway. The searchlight used for hot pursuits and to expose hiding miscreants was turned off. Voices squawked from the police radio giving instructions. The officer/pilot and his companion squinted through binoculars, seeking the mythical night stalker. The ride-along companion was a man who also enjoyed the night, searching for a stalker, a thief and a violator whose deeds, if too widely publicized in the news media, could hurt the economic growth plans of the community at large.

That was one reason many of the officers in the police department were concerned about the growing problem that was shattering the lives of a growing number of bright, attractive and successful women in the area. That was why there was political pressure to find the perpetrator coming from real estate industry professionals and community leaders concerned with attracting new residents and new businesses to the area. That was why the man in the passenger seat of the helicopter was focused on the ground below, delighting in his participation in the hunt, which often brought him new insights into the frustrations, limitations and ongoing resolve of the Dallas Police Department. That was why his police officer friends appreciated his kind assistance with their seemingly impossible task.

Amongst the low, shadowed buildings under scrutiny was one in particular into which a once and future victim was moving. The beautiful blond woman's name was Carol Bryan, but she would come to be dubbed by the media and the police department, "Victim 23."

The number Carol was assigned was for the Dallas Police Department's records and, while it sounded quite specific, no one was certain it was accurate. Some of the attacks were probably never reported. Some of the victims may have been too terrified of possible retaliation by the man who had hurt them. Others may have feared the potential for publicity or that the police investigators would be callous in their handling of the rape report.

The fact that there was a "Victim 23" reflected how difficult it was for the Dallas Police Department to locate a man who had been assaulting women for weeks, months or possibly years. Worse, the Ski Mask Rapist, who claimed "Victim 24" within three hours of his attack on Carol Bryan, was forever shattering the sense of safety and self-reliance of his victims.

Mention "Victim 23" in a newspaper and she has no reality for the readers. She might be tall or short. She might dine on Big Macs and french fries, or she might delight in sophisticated European cuisine. She might be a marathon runner, confined to a wheelchair or forty-five pounds overweight. She might be the waitress who serves breakfast everyday at a popular coffee shop. She might be the electrical engineer who works in the next cubicle. She might be the police officer who gives out speeding tickets or the doctor who helps patients through successful treatments for life-threatening medical conditions. She could be anyone and that is why many people do not seem to care. Unless someone has a name, a face and a definable life, the public often finds it difficult to empathize with a victim's pain.

Use the proper name of "Victim 23" and everything changes. She becomes the person she always has been—a woman of flesh and blood, taste and accomplishment, an ex-wife, a mother, someone who has known love, death, childbirth, divorce and endlessly renewed hope as she moves through life. She becomes a neighbor, a friend, someone you pass on the street or the person standing in line with you at the grocery store. Make her "real" and you recognize your own vulnerability and that of your loved ones. Make her "real" and the failure to find the Ski Mask Rapist and stop the violent assaults creates terror. And it did . . .

CHAPTER 1

STALKED

IF ANYONE WAS aware of the man who had watched the moving trucks that first day Carol Bryan had come to Dallas and now was watching the very attractive blonde jogging along the golf course, the person's eyes would pass from his familiar figure to the woman he was watching. North Dallas, Texas, where the golf course was located, was famous for four types of residents. There were those who had made their living in the oil business. There were those who had become successful in banking. There were the individuals at the top of the insurance field. And there were women like the blond whose eyes shone with intelligence, whose steps were vibrant and purposeful, whose figures were trim and whose joyful auras came from being some of God's blessed. After all, why else would they have been able to live in the most prestigious section of one of the most exciting cities in the nation? And if the man was not watching this woman, not desiring to meet her, to know her better, to become as intimate with aspects of her life as her closest friends were, then there must be something seriously wrong with him.

The condominium complex in which Carol lived was a familiar one. The people who lived there—both owners and renters—were upscale, intelligent, usually college educated and drove expensive cars. They had the discretionary income that advertisers coveted, frequented quality restaurants and purchased high-end, off-the-rack and tailor-made clothing. Many had accumulated valuable collections—coins, stamps, jewelry and the like. They were not the super-rich with their multi-million dollar homes, but when they did buy a house, it was not unusual for them to go to one of the nearby neighborhoods and pay $500,000 or more for a suitable place to live.

Despite the costly rent, the complex into which Carol Bryan had just moved was somewhat of a transient community. The owner/residents reflected the greatest stability, rarely moving even though they often could afford larger, more expensive locations. Renters, by contrast, came and went based on their jobs, their degree of wanderlust and the vagaries of Dallas society. Married couples had children and some eventually felt the need for a larger home. Some arrived as entrepreneurs, working high-paying jobs while setting aside as much money as possible without sacrificing personal comfort. Then, when their bank accounts allowed, they quit their jobs and moved into whatever space was needed to both live and maintain a small office. Single tenants, who loved the location and the size of the units and planned to stay in the complex until they died, suddenly discovered Mr. or Ms. "Right" and moved into that person's home. Married couples blissfully planning "forever" found that one or both partners had been committing adultery and suddenly neither wished to continue living in the area.

The result was enough turnover in owners and tenants that no one questioned the presence of a stranger if he or she was well dressed, drove a top-of-the-line car and seemed comfortable walking about the complex.

Not that the man who observed Carol on the golf course was a stranger. He had spent extensive time in and around the community. He had friends and acquaintances in the area. When he was on the complex grounds, regardless of the hour, anyone spotting him just assumed he was there for a party, a date or to enjoy an evening with friends. All such assumptions had been true at one time or another, but the man had another preoccupation with the neighborhood. It was a periodic source of income and an outlet for a violent, occasionally overwhelming anger he acted out in the bedrooms of his unsuspecting victims.

The condominium complex was designed in a way that provided a false sense of security for the residents. There were light poles stationed around the grounds, but the light bulbs were positioned so they would never shine into tenants' windows and disturb the rest of some of the more important movers and shakers in Dallas. This left large, shadowy areas outside bedrooms and by patios. Most people walked on the paths where the light countered the darkness of the night. Few thought about the fact that all a "bad guy" had to do was step away from the paths to become almost invisible.

Numerous windows in the apartments gave a bright, spacious feeling to the rooms and all the windows had screens, again giving the illusion of security. Screens, however, could be easily cut or quietly lifted out by anyone who had even a little skill. The man who watched Carol and the other women was skilled and practiced, having been taught by professional burglars who conducted post-arrest "how to" seminars to pass the time while in the Texas state prison system.

Alarm systems in the condos were few in number, but even these could be easily defeated. He had learned all the tricks of the unsophisticated systems—from bypassing the alarm trigger while still outside to utilizing shaving cream to neutralize an external noisemaker. The placement of both the telephone and electrical lines had been designed for easy repair access within the complex, not for high security.

The most elaborate security systems available for Dallas homes included wireless devices connected to cell phones that alerted monitoring services. Although expensive, they could not be bypassed and, if installed throughout a home, would provide the best possible safety short of living in the midst of armed guards. However, those who rented the units often did not wish to spend that kind of money nor did they think it necessary. The exclusiveness of the area made them feel safe. It was a psychological weakness upon which the man preyed.

The items the man stole were often chosen before he entered the condominiums, houses and apartments he targeted. His approach was to "window shop," peeking inside when there was adequate light to see who had Rolex watches, gold coins, diamond earrings, expensive cameras and the like. When the glass was obscured by curtains or the type of shades made of multiple slats that could be opened or closed, he would look through the cracks between the cloth panels or through the holes that were used for the rope pull that opened and closed the blinds.

What the man stole varied with his desires. He had two fences, a local jeweler who was occasionally in the "recycling" business and a second jeweler in an upscale area of Los Angeles, California. The local jeweler was socially prominent and had a clientele that included some of the instant millionaire football players with the Dallas Cowboys. He allegedly would buy expensive stolen items, then alter them in a manner that would allow him to resell them, perhaps to the same victim seeking to replace what was lost. The distance of the California fence assured that easily recognizable, valuable items that could be spotted by the owners or investigators would disappear in a region where the victims would be unlikely to encounter them.

The man considered himself a professional. His polished skills had earned him few arrests and minimum jail time. He also prided himself on being a self-taught connoisseur of quality goods. He delighted in entering someone's home, walking through, looking at various items and imagining what it would be like to be the person who legitimately possessed such things.

No one is certain when the man went from collecting the luxuries purchased by others to claiming the most precious possession a female resident owned—her psychological peace of mind. Certainly, it was well before the time he targeted Victim 23.

It was a warm Dallas night when Carol Bryan locked the doors of her apartment, checked the windows and began getting ready for bed. She had been living in Dallas only a matter of weeks, but as strange as the city still was for her, the rented condominium in which she lived had a familiarity to it that brought her a degree of peace. She was a former military wife who had mastered the secrets of those people who must relocate often; "setting down roots" meant spending more than a year or two in the same location. Instead of viewing her life in terms of the neighborhood in which she lived, the art consulting business she had been developing, the stores where she shopped and the church she attended, she focused inward. Each time she moved, she carefully unpacked the accumulated personal treasures of a lifetime and arranged them on shelves in a familiar manner throughout her home. Here she would keep the Waterford, Baccarat and Lalique crystal, there the Wedgewood and Limoges china. Over in this area would be the photographs of family members and her daughters, the girls' images running the gamut from birth to the present, all of them now grown into lovely womanhood. Each small section of a room was a living memory, a present inexorably linked to the past.

In Carol's mind, the inside of her home meant peace, safety and freedom from fear. It was her sanctuary. Not that she was a stranger to grief. She had lived on and around military bases in war and peace. She knew of men and women killed in training missions and other actions taken by the United States military. She had lost friends in both. And she had seen some return from action alive, healed of all physical wounds, then slowly destroyed by memories they tried to drown in alcohol or promiscuous sex, ultimately losing those whose love had once sustained them.

Carol was not inexperienced in life. She was both a successful art broker and artist who dealt well with the realities of business. She just had never imagined how easily evil could penetrate the protected environment that had sustained her from the time she was first married and which she now created in this new city.

Now she was living in Dallas, where two of her three daughters had come, one to attend school, the other to work. She wanted to open a business and had brought substantial savings with her to accomplish that end. In other cities where she had lived, the business community embraced the small budget entrepreneur. Dallas was proving far less hospitable, business advisers more likely to criticize what she lacked than to want to help her work with what she had. The pressure had become great enough that she was restless as she prepared for bed, her mind reevaluating her decision to relocate to Dallas. However, as usual, sleep came easily in the comfortable, protected environment that was her carefully decorated home.

THE DIGITAL CLOCK in the bedroom registered 3:30 A.M. when Carol was jolted awake. In that brief instant between deep sleep and sudden wakefulness, she sensed an abnormal darkness. Carol thought she was dreaming, for she felt so heavy she could not move. She tried to rise, but her body was too heavy and her head hurt. She no longer could see anything, though there was always enough light coming through the curtains so the bedroom was never too dark to make out objects. Then she heard a man's voice and felt something or someone shaking her. That was when she felt certain she must be dreaming.

"Wake up. Can you hear me? Wake up."

She wasn't heavy. There was a weight on top of her. Her eyes were open, she realized, but there was something covering them, covering her face.

Then she realized the pain in her head was caused by something cold and hard pressed firmly against her temple.

"Can you hear me? Wake up," an angry voice hissed in her ear. It was a few inches from her ear. The breath was so foul it smelled to her like a rotting animal. Then she felt the bile rise up to her throat.

"Can you hear me? Do you understand me?" the angry voice said again.

Carol wasn't dreaming. There was a form, a body, on top of her, holding a gun to her temple. The person shook her, telling her repeatedly to wake up. She was awake, her eyes now wide open, but she could not see. The cloth or whatever it was covering her face was still in place. Yet her

mind was still groggy with sleep and she wasn't quite sure
what was happening.

*Am I dreaming? No, I'm awake. I left the television on.
It's a movie.*

For a moment, she felt relieved. Yet as she adjusted to
the darkness, she realized she could see the form over her.
Either the cloth had moved from her eyes or it was a loose
enough weave to allow a glimmer of light through. The reality of what was happening suddenly hit her.

*This is not a movie. A man. A black mask. He's holding
a gun!*

"Don't make a sound or I'll blow your head off. Do you
hear me?"

Carol nodded yes.

"Don't move or I will kill you."

Carol did not move. She could no longer see. She could
no longer speak.

What seemed like hours later, the man in the black mask
finally spoke his last words to which Carol barely reacted:
"I will keep watching you and I will kill you if you go to
the police. You may be sure of that."

CHAPTER 2

PAST HISTORY

THE BLUE-COLLAR TOWN where Carol was born is located along the Ohio River bordering Ashland, Kentucky, and Huntington, West Virginia. Carol's father, an ironworker, occasionally traveled to job sites to build bridges, skyscrapers and other large projects. He provided a good living for his wife and children, but nowhere near the quality of the successful farming family living nearby. Their oldest son, who left the farm community to join the Navy and see the world, came home on leave to find Carol had grown into a lovely young woman. He asked her for a date and by the end of her last semester of high school, Carol was planning on becoming his wife.

Women were not meant to have dreams of independence in the area where Carol was raised. Their world was expected to be marriage, home and family. She had long shown an aptitude for and interest in the world of art, but that had been limited by a lack of museums, books and educational opportunities outside of the instruction of her high school art teacher. She could pursue art as a wife and mother, perhaps becoming known for her paintings and handicrafts in church bazaars and state fairs.

Right after they were married, Carol and her husband

moved to San Diego where he was stationed. Once there, they bought a home in one of the newer suburbs that had expanded to serve the large Miramar Navy air base. The increase in military personnel brought new businesses to the area. Jobs were plentiful and new single-family homes were usually sold before they could be completed. They were well designed, well built and inexpensive enough that military families could afford them as readily as the business people who served the growing base-connected population.

For Carol, San Diego was a cultural delight. There were museums, art galleries, golf courses, clubs and resorts offering a variety of popular entertainment from which she could choose. She pictured herself happily raising the two daughters who had come along within the first four years of the marriage. Carol busied herself with her training in art, the raising of their children and helping her husband where she could.

A FUZZY, ROMANTIC notion of a life never experienced made a too early marriage seem both appropriate and certain to be triumphant. At the same time, the move to Southern California suddenly exposed the couple to unexpected temptations and the harsh realities of a strange new city.

The Hotel San Diego was a popular honeymoon and trysting spot located a stroll from the ocean and just across the street from a penny arcade that held a shooting gallery, pinball games and the other low-tech distractions of the pre-video era. It was also home to a huge military presence. When Carol lived there, San Diego was home to five military bases, including ones for the Navy Seals, the Marines and the Coast Guard. The city also housed the Navy's largest airbase, Miramar Naval Air Station, and the harbor held the largest fleet of ships in the Navy. Consequently, in addition to the arcades and other innocent amusements, the streets were hangouts for prostitutes and street hustlers. Sailors and marines on leave hid their uniforms in conveniently supplied lockers, changed into civvies, then walked the streets, acting cool, trying to pass as longtime residents. They never realized that their buzz-cut hair and shoes polished to a blindingly reflective spit shine were like neon signs flashing the words "on shore leave." They were instant targets for everyone seeking to seduce or con their money from them.

Drinking and carousing were considered badges of manhood among the virile young men on shore leave. It took five years for Carol's husband to succumb to the temptations, the paranoia and the immaturity of the insular world of young career Navy men. When it did, he left her and the children, an unfortunate but increasingly common San Diego military story.

The divorce left Carol with no resources other than her inner drive. Her parents and siblings were thousands of miles away. Her education prepared her for little more than menial jobs. Yet she was fortunate to be living in an area where upscale resorts and educational institutions abounded. She was also fortunate to have built a trusted friendship with an older Navy wife who was a tall, slender, carefree Meg Ryan look-alike. Marge, who Carol had first met at a party for some of the young career Navy men and their wives, had been a fashion model based in New York. She had given up her lucrative career and the future it might have provided in order to marry a career Navy man who was stationed in Southern California.

Marge claimed to never have believed in the "happily ever after" image of Carol's marriage. Her modeling career had left her sophisticated and street smart. She understood the temptations in life. Marge had seen the way people could hurt others in pursuit of their own goals. As she found herself enjoying Carol's company, she began treating Carol like a younger sister.

Marge knew Carol was blissfully happy in her marriage. After all, her husband treated Carol like a princess. He pampered her, gave her everything she wanted and spoiled her with a beautiful home, furnishings, a new car, clothing and just about anything she wanted. In addition, he was a good-looking man with blonde hair and green eyes whose charming personality and effervescent attitude drew people—especially women—to him like magnets. Yet Marge could also see before Carol did that the temptations of life were having a strong effect on Carol's husband. Thus Carol was stunned and devastated when her husband left her and their children. And it was Marge who came to Carol's side to support her, guide her and offer motherly advice.

Within a few months, the divorce was finalized and Carol was left alone with two babies. Her once devoted husband had simply vanished. After several weeks of watching her cry, Marge informed Carol that she had to get on with her life and get a job.

As a child, Carol and her best friend, Janice, had sold vegetables from a roadside stand owned by Janice's family. Later Carol had worked in an uncle's restaurant. Her job there had included wiping off the tables, making sure the salt and pepper shakers were filled and occasionally being allowed to ladle chili onto hot dogs. Where Carol would have claimed no experience for a real restaurant server's job, Marge showed her that she could claim that she had a background in both sales and restaurant work. Then Marge took Carol out to eat in several different restaurants in order to watch the waitresses at work. She showed Carol the ins and the outs so that she would not make major mistakes on her first day.

The ruse worked. Carol was hired for the morning shift at a luxury resort in the community of Del Mar. Marge helped watch the children and introduced Carol to a trustworthy Mexican woman who came across the border daily to work as a domestic.

Marge also encouraged Carol to enroll in San Diego State College's secretarial program. This was an odd hybrid—part solid business curriculum, part skills such as shorthand and part finishing school. The teachers taught the social graces along with the intricacies of the corporate world. The program was flexible, some of the students taking a full load of courses each semester, and some, like Carol, taking one or two at a time while handling job and family responsibilities.

After six months of being a working single mother and college student, Carol met a handsome Navy pilot named

Dennis stationed at the nearby Miramar Naval Air Base. He was tall, slender and extremely intelligent. A face full of freckles made him as youthful looking as she appeared and both were usually carded when they tried to order drinks.

The pilot began a courtship, starting with martinis and dinner in an expensive La Jolla restaurant. Carol hated the martini, stopping after two sips and rarely drank ever again. Dennis finished his, along with several cigarettes, his overt consumption stemming from nervousness. By the end of the evening they were laughing and joking like old friends, Dennis shocked to find that they were both of Irish descent since he drank and she did not, going against the stereotype of the Irish lass.

The courtship was slow and gentle, chaste kisses leading to enough of a hint of passion that the pilot felt himself falling in love with her. At the same time, Carol was pleased with his reserve, with the way he did not press her to be sexually active or to be anything that she wasn't. In fact, the only information she had not shared with him was that she was the mother of two little girls, a fact she was not really concealing. Marge cared for them whenever Carol had a date and the subject just had not come up. However, when Carol brought Dennis to her home for the first time and he saw the prominently displayed photographs of the girls, he quickly realized they were not Carol's younger sisters. With that, Dennis ended the romance.

The loss of the pilot came at the same time that the manager of the restaurant where Carol worked found himself shorthanded. He asked Carol to also work the bar in the evenings, an opportunity she embraced, because, after the Dennis fiasco, she had officially given up the idea of an adult social life.

Carol's experience with alcohol was limited to the martini she had sipped on her first date with Dennis. She had seen but never tasted beer and had no idea what the different brands were like. She certainly did not know the names or ingredients of the myriad cocktails requested nightly in the resort's bar. However, she was good-looking, always important in such a job, and she was willing to learn. Her strong work ethic had been proven on the morning restaurant shift so the bartender agreed with the manager to let her work evenings. The result was financial independence beyond any of Carol's expectations.

"It was nothing to earn $150 in tips in a day," Carol recalled. "I was able to afford to have the Mexican woman stay over at my house several days a week to take care of my daughters."

Rita, the Mexican woman, was typical of the household help available at the time. She had her green card, the work permit that allowed her to live in Mexico but cross the border to work in the United States. She spent part of the week living in Carol's home taking care of the children and part of the week in her home in Mexico. The dollar to peso ratio was so great that any Mexican national earning seventy dollars a week (U.S.) could support a large family in Mexico. Carol had no problem paying Rita what the woman requested. She earned more than enough to take good care of her children and pay for her college classes.

Carol also began pursuing art classes. Frustrated by her failed marriage, concerned about her children, tired from the long hours and aware that others might feel as Dennis had, Carol did not consider dating. Instead she focused on learning what she needed to know to find a better job and learning more about all aspects of art that interested her. In the years to come, wherever she lived throughout the world, Carol would attend short courses, semester classes and lectures by contemporary masters in all phases of art. Her work embraced every medium—oils, watercolors, ink, sculpture, etc.—and the teachers thought her quite talented.

Just as Carol was settling into single life and a satisfying routine, the naval pilot popped back into her life, ringing the doorbell one evening at nine o'clock. Dennis had felt nervous about coming to her home, frightened of his feelings for her. When Carol opened the door, he just stood there and stared. He was quiet and handsome, revealing his emotions on his face in a way that made her know she was truly loved.

* * *

WORK CONTINUED. SCHOOL continued. Dennis was her frequent companion, spending time with the children, getting to know them, getting to love them. Renewed friendship turned to passion and before long, Dennis proposed. Carol said yes, feeling that this time, she had the maturity and positive outlook to make the marriage last.

On Friday, July 3, Dennis had Carol take him to work so he could leave his car in the garage for minor repairs. He would be "flying" a desk that day, not going on a training mission. Everything would be routine. She would meet him at his home in La Jolla that evening, then they would have dinner together. Instead, when she pulled up to his house, she encountered a police car. The man to whom she had become engaged, the man with whom she had purchased a pair of wedding bands, the man with whom she felt she would find happiness for the rest of her life, had been found floating facedown in his swimming pool.

Exactly what happened was never known. He was an expert swimmer who was alone in the pool. Most likely there had been a mishap while diving, causing him to briefly lose consciousness when he was in the water. Whatever the case, the death was accidental and beyond Carol's comprehension. Navy pilots are supposed to die in combat. Or, perhaps they die in training accidents. Sometimes, they die while instructing new pilots not yet ready to fly solo. But once they are on the ground, they do not die except from old age or the slow ravages of terminal illness. To die as Dennis did seemed preposterous. Though his accidental death may not have been an unusual occurrence when home pool owners ignore such safety rules as not swimming alone, it was a loss Carol had not anticipated and had difficulty accepting. She was shattered and did not know how she would be able to go on without him.

Carol walked around in a daze. On the day of Dennis' memorial service, Marge found a pin-striped gray suit for Carol to wear and took care of Carol's children. For Carol, that period was all a blur. It seemed to her that one moment she was being told of Dennis' death and the next she was standing in the small military base chapel. Everything on the military base, including the chapel, was painted battleship gray. The only color in the chapel was the American flag draped over Dennis' casket. In the years that followed, Carol would attend other memorial services in gray military chapels. Eventually, she stopped going, because they always reminded her of the first and most painful military memorial service she attended.

PERHAPS SAN DIEGO was the training ground Carol needed to prepare for the future. Her childhood had been in a pastoral setting that looked like the type of rural community Norman Rockwell immortalized on the covers he painted for the *Saturday Evening Post*. Families worked together, rejoiced together, grieved together and sought spiritual guidance together in their churches. Love was unconditional. Life was a constant experience of planting, harvest, rest and renewal.

In San Diego, there were few extended families except within the military community and these were transitory relationships that often ended with reassignments to different parts of the world or the discovery of adultery by one or both partners. Carol had wrapped herself in family and wedding vows she thought were "forever," only to find herself betrayed by her husband and cheated out of her next love by unexpected death.

It was after Dennis' funeral that the dry-eyed, zombielike state of shock wore off and Carol finally succumbed to the overwhelming grief. She was home in bed, the children asleep in their bedroom. She was completely alone for the first time in days, looking at the door, knowing that Dennis would never again return. She wept then for the first time, her sobs wracking her body, making breathing difficult. She looked up and railed at God. "I would have given you anything if you had just not taken him!"

Gradually the intense sobbing subsided. Carol's emotions were spent. She thought of Dennis comforting her. She almost sensed his presence, as though summoned by the intense love they had experienced all too briefly. It was this thought that enabled her to fall into the first restful sleep she had experienced since she was told of his death.

The pain of the loss slowly diminished in the months and years that followed. Yet the love had been too great, the death too sudden, for her to ever completely heal.

However, in the end Carol realized Dennis had shown her she was still capable of deep love. And San Diego had proven to be a city that seemed to take all the pain someone could endure, shoving it into his or her face, then challenging the person to go on. It was also the city where Jim Bryan entered Carol's life.

JIM BRYAN WAS that combination of intellectual and roughneck seldom seen being bred outside the oil fields of Oklahoma where he was born. His ancestry was a direct line from Mary, Queen of Scots, to his Oklahoma-born, oilman father. Jim himself had earned two college degrees, become a petroleum engineer and then faced the draft. The roustabout life in the oil fields was probably not much different from being in the Army and that was something he did not want. Instead, he looked to the Marines and their reputation for being hard fighting men with the intellect necessary to solve any problem. Equally important, they had an air wing that reflected his thirst for adventure. It was while he attended Officers Candidate School that Jim achieved First Lieutenant status by the end of his second year with the Corps. He also decided on two things—that he wanted to be a career officer and that he wanted to wed the vivacious young woman named Carol whose challenged past did not prevent her from embracing life.

It was just six months from meeting to marriage and a move to a comfortable home just outside the El Toro, California, Marine air base. Jim had finished his basic flight training in San Diego before the move and Carol looked forward to the time they would spend together in their new home. She thought nothing of the evening in March when Jim told her his squadron was going on a two-week training mission. He packed enough clothes to last him two or three days, then left twenty-four hours later.

The story of the training mission was a ruse. Carol and the other squadron wives were unaware that anything was out of the ordinary until two weeks after Jim and his squadron left the air base at El Toro when the squadron commander's wife called all of the wives and invited them to a meeting in her home. The men were not on a training mission, she explained to the other women. The men were not returning home as expected; instead, they were on a real mission. Upon hearing the news, several wives began to cry. Carol picked up her purse and left without saying a word.

Decorated with a chest full of medals, Captain Jim Bryan returned thirteen months later. He was an ace, an experienced combat pilot who was sent to an East Coast base to train more pilots. Within eighteen months, he was back carrying out flight missions. Again, he returned safely after thirteen months with over 450 bombing missions to his credit. But this time Carol could clearly see a change. Gone was the youthful, exuberant young man whom she kissed good-bye at El Toro. She didn't know that the missions were intense, violent, emotionally draining experiences for the officers. Many returned in emotionally fragile states and began drinking heavily. Jim Bryan was one of many who was traumatized by the violence and felt both responsible for the lost lives of fellow officers and guilty for his own survival. The emotional walls he built along with his many long-term assignments away from his family led to a slow erosion of the couple's marriage. Still, for years they remained married even as they grew apart.

The deterioration of Carol and Jim's marriage was a slow process, not unlike that of many others who were career military. The couple had a child, another daughter, whom they both adored. They traveled together from base to base as Jim received continuous training and promotions and Carol treasured not only each new location but also the journey to get there.

She and the girls stopped at every scenic site, every historic marker. Carol tried to show them all the new and exciting things they were encountering. "I wanted them to experience the world as best they could, helping them learn that other people's lives could be vastly different from their own."

Carol also learned to take advantage of the different locations to increase her skills as an artist. Wherever they went, she discovered art schools, colleges and other training programs. She took courses in sculpture, in painting, in every artistic endeavor she could find. In her spare time at home she painted and honed her skills, learning that she had special gifts, special talents and a sense of self she had lacked when first married. For a long time she sold pieces of her work here and there through friends and art school contacts, but soon realized she could do much better if she started her own business. She opened an art consulting company in which she was both artist and broker and before long she tasted the fruits of success. At the same time, however, her personal life was rapidly falling apart.

The trauma of combat had so imprinted itself on Jim's mind that he built emotional walls to try to contain it. When that didn't work, he used alcohol to temporarily obliterate the past. He was unable to let Carol and the children inside the mental fortress he had created. He was unable to seek help because, in the macho environment of the military, seeking help could be seen as a sign of weakness and weakness could cost you your next advancement. What he failed to realize was that by not reaching out, his marriage would die. By the time the youngest child was in her teens, everyone knew the marriage was over. Divorce, for Carol an overwhelming tragedy after all she'd been through, ultimately seemed the only choice.

EVERYTHING MOVED SWIFTLY after that. Close friends tried to discourage Carol from moving to Dallas, where two of her daughters were living, but she wanted to be near her girls. Her friends knew Carol was ready to leave their city. They also knew Carol cared about them, going so far as to try to persuade her best friend, the single mother of a teenage son in his last year of high school, to go with her. But Carol felt she needed a complete break from the past. Certainly she needed time.

As for choosing Dallas, Carol's daughters were there and although they didn't need her as they did when they were small, the chance to be nearby to offer her counsel and guidance as they matured and grew into independent young women seemed important. This time in their lives, when they still looked to her for guidance and advice, would soon be over. However, they certainly did not need her constant attention anymore so it would also be a chance for Carol to exhale, to think, to make decisions about the rest of her life. Or so she thought.

CHAPTER 3

A SAVAGE HUNGER

HE WAS A soft-spoken, charming man. Of that most people were in agreement. Polite, generous, the type of individual who holds the door open for women, helps the elderly cross the street, gives money to the poor and goes out of his way to take care of someone having a problem.

The women who clerked in the menswear department of Neiman Marcus knew him by sight and always enjoyed his stopping by their counters. His purchases were few but luxurious, though not lavish. None of his shoes cost less than a few hundred dollars—five times the maximum price successful middle-management workers might pay in the less pretentious Fort Worth and Houston areas. The price of his neckties hovered around one hundred-fifty dollars each, again a mere ten times the price of silk ties whose look and feel were almost identical, but which did not bear the right designer label. And his choice of cologne was respectable—fifty dollars for a tiny bottle of his favorite, Obsession, a fragrance that, while not cloying, demanded attention the moment the wearer entered a room. However, in a store where cologne could cost as much as a top-of-the-line suit in lesser men's stores, the purchase brought only a moderate commission for the clerks; nevertheless, they liked his genial manner. He was a self-made success, although an undereducated man. His siblings delighted in telling anyone who would listen that he had been a petty thief as a small boy. By the time he learned that other people thought stealing was wrong, something his parents allegedly had not mentioned during his turbulent childhood, he found he enjoyed it. There was an excitement to shoplifting, to going joyriding in a stranger's car, to entering someone's home and discovering that the treasures they had so lovingly acquired over many years of effort could be easily his for the taking.

There had been a price to pay for that excitement. He had served time in jail. Now, having paid his debt to society, he was learning what he needed to know, was successful in business, had a spiritual side and reached out to others with kindness. He treated the shop girls and the Dallas socialites with equal respect and his approach to life seemed to be working. As his business prospered, his pockets bulged with money. He drove expensive cars. And he slowly acquired a wardrobe of custom tailored suits, personally monogrammed, made-to-order shirts and pairs of shoes appropriate for each outfit.

There would be other transformations, including lessons in elocution and practice in speech, along with the adoption of the upscale Anglo style of clothing, all in an effort to make himself more acceptable to the social group of which he wanted so much to be a part. The question he avoided thinking about was whether he sought respect from the rich and powerful who were his customers and casual friends or whether the respect he sought, the acceptance he desperately desired, was unattainable, because it could only come from within.

The Dallas jeweler the man patronized was a connoisseur, a professional who understood the subtle differences among gemstones regarding their clarity, color and cut. He could look at a ring or a brooch, a necklace or a bracelet and recognize both the quality of the workmanship and also what made one designer a genius and the other merely pedestrian. The jeweler bought and sold expensive watches as well—Rolex, Piaget and many others. But more than brokering such items, he knew what made one watch valuable because of the quality of the timepiece itself, the rarity of the design and the genius of its functions, and another watch desirable solely because of the way it was adorned with gold and diamonds. More important, he shared his taste and savvy with customers wealthy enough to pay as much for a timepiece as they would for a Rolls-Royce or a Ferrari.

The quality of the merchandise that passed through his store and his indisputable knowledge made the jewelry connoisseur successful. In one sense, he was little different from any other small business owner. His merchandise, however, was more glamorous and expensive than that of someone who sold office supplies or hair care products or stereo equipment. His sales figures were far greater per square foot of shop space than those of purveyors of more mundane items. But had the jeweler's product not been so extremely upscale, had he not worked with collectors, investors, devoted spouses, errant spouses, lovers and kept women, he probably would have been just another anonymous Dallas shop clerk. Instead, he partied with the elite, hobnobbing on a first name basis with many of the power brokers of the city.

The jeweler's problem was trying to locate enough quality merchandise. In the rarefied atmosphere of Dallas, sometimes it seemed that everyone who wanted another expensive item already had something very similar.

Not that Dallas was unique in its hunger for luxury goods. Other parts of the country were enjoying extremely strong economies. Los Angeles, for example, was booming and jewelers in that city also were being inundated with requests for merchandise they often could not easily obtain.

The solution for such ambitious jewelers was to buy quality pieces from anyone who had them, reselling them as they were where appropriate or utilizing the precious metals and quality gems to create new custom pieces. Gold would be melted down, for example. Diamonds and other stones would be removed from their settings. Everything would be altered in one form or another, creating new pieces of equal value but no longer recognizable as to their sources.

Sometimes the jewelers purchased items from estates. The elderly died and their heirs were more interested in the money obtainable from selling the possessions than in owning and wearing them. At other times, an individual came on hard times and sold his or her jewelry as a way out. Europeans who experienced World War II learned to put their money into precious gems and gold coins that could be easily hidden on their bodies and bartered anywhere in the world.

Diamonds were also used by drug dealers and others who laundered money in Europe, but then wanted to discreetly bring their newly acquired wealth back into the United States. They bought quality gemstones abroad, secreted them on their bodies or in their luggage, then sold them after passing through customs. Or they bought the stones in the United States, took them abroad for sale, used the money for new gems, then brought those back into the country for resale. However they did it, the criminals and those who helped them rarely got caught. And when jewelers in New York, California and elsewhere, including Texas, encountered the stones for sale, they were frequently offered by legitimate diamond brokers who did not know or if they did know, did not reveal their illicit sources.

The money-laundering scheme was illegal, but the buying and selling of the gems by jewelers lacking knowledge of what was being done was not a crime. They did not request that the money be laundered. They did not know that the money used to buy the stones was from a criminal enterprise. And they certainly did not coordinate the drug sellers, international diamond merchants and others whose efforts led to the gems being offered to them in their stores.

There was one other source for the high-ticket jewelry being offered by many respected jewelers. This additional purveyor was the burglar who specialized in robbing upscale homes, apartments and condominiums where quality gems were treated as fashion accessories and kept as casually about the bedroom as lipstick and perfume.

* * *

THE SOFT-SPOKEN MAN with a taste for theft understood the needs of the jewelers. He also understood their occasional greed. The man made contact with a California jeweler, letting him know that he would regularly have quality merchandise for sale for a fraction of its value. He then began visiting the Dallas jeweler, making certain his manner of dress fit the image of the shop. He would never be mistaken for someone who could buy the most expensive merchandise available, though even in Dallas those numbers were limited. Instead, he had the look of a man whose family might have the money to carefully invest in quality pieces in the same way that others acquired real estate investments. That was why he did not look out of place in the jeweler's shop. That was why the jeweler could buy from the man and not have anyone ask questions as to where the man obtained the merchandise he sold.

So far as is known, neither the genial man with the larcenous heart nor the jeweler with the elite clientele ever spoke the word "fence" during their early interactions. That term, meaning someone who knowingly buys and sells stolen merchandise, was reserved for the California contact the man also used. Yet either early on or as the months went by, the Dallas jeweler would succumb to his greed and profit handsomely by buying people's stolen jewelry without their knowledge.

What few, if any, of the jeweler/fences realized was how their seemingly non-violent, non-hurtful actions gave license to more insidious crimes. The fact that there was a ready, ongoing market for stolen merchandise also meant that there was a reason for a burglar to continue breaking into homes. A thief could fancy himself a businessman. He could fancy himself a professional. He could delight in the irony that some of what he was taking would eventually be returned in a circuitous route as the previous owner bought the same stones, settings or both from the jeweler who had paid for the stolen merchandise. The victim inadvertently would "ransom" his or her own possessions, never connecting the burglary, the jeweler and the new purchases.

The problem was that not only was the burglar given license to continue his crime spree, he was also being given an opportunity to indulge whatever other fantasies or desires he might have. For some thieves, this meant something as mundane as simply avoiding having to earn an honest living. For others, this meant encouraging them to return to homes where, when occupied, they could possess more than people's jewels. They could briefly possess the lives of the women who lived there.

As the soft-spoken man grew more experienced, he found that what he liked best was looking into other people's windows, experiencing their lives vicariously. Some people might consider such actions sex crimes. Certainly that's what psychologists were saying in Dallas and elsewhere.

He occasionally saw sex acts, of course. He saw naked women and naked men. He saw people changing their clothes, taking showers, whatever was visible through the openings that afforded a view.

The man had learned early on that the window blind holes through which the ropes were strung could be used as peepholes. If you pressed your face to the glass, scrunched up one eye and looked carefully, you could see as though you were looking through the eyepiece of a spyglass. Sometimes he saw empty rooms, letting his gaze wander from object to object, assessing what was of value to the person who lived there. Sometimes he saw single people doing whatever was appropriate in the room into which he could see. And when he encountered a sex act in progress, he knew the couple was certain they were safe from prying eyes. All the views were of equal interest. All the views made him an intimate in lives where he was otherwise invisible, existences he coveted more than the items he took.

WHAT THE SOFT-SPOKEN burglar did not realize was how angry he had become over the years. He hated those who had what he did not, whether that meant expensive jewelry or the love of a beautiful, intelligent companion.

The anger, coupled with his improving skills as a thief, meant that he could enter many homes at will and, as time passed, he could not stop at stealing a woman's treasures. He needed to possess her, an idea that both repulsed and compelled him.

The changes that came over time were so subtle that the man may not have recognized them himself. The first was a desire to truly enter the private world of the women whose lives he had observed from the shadows near their windows. He wanted to walk where they walked, touch what they touched, experience the myriad little treasures those rich women purchased. He wanted to put himself into their worlds, as intimate as a lover.

The anger, especially at the young ones, the pretty ones and the blonde ones with the high priced cars continued to grow. And he began, along with the rapes, to strike at the women he chose and to threaten them with death. He didn't like aggressive women. He didn't like women who held good jobs, who worked at those corporate levels he could only cautiously approach, hat in hand, to solicit business. At the same time he was drawn to successful, confident women, fascinated by them, wanted to possess them, caress them; he also wanted to shatter their egos in ways he called "seductions" and to violate them so they would become submissive.

His hostility was greater when they had boyfriends or husbands who fit the stereotypical image of the tall, super-rich Texan. Dallas had become a multicultural city, an international city, a place where Hispanics, Asians, Arabs, Indians and others all lived, though usually in their own neighborhoods. The strapping rancher, ranger or oil man—well over six feet, with calloused hands, a craggy, weathered face and arms sculpted from heavy lifting—no longer existed as the dominant resident, if such a man ever did. But height still mattered in Dallas. Most of the business leaders the man came in contact with were several inches taller than he was. And though they respected his accomplishments and appeared to see him as a success, he seemed to think that they might be mocking him, holding him back, looking at him with disdain when his back was turned. A successful woman involved with an affluent, confident Texan left him seething inwardly whenever he encountered them during his nights peering into windows from his secret hiding places.

The man would later see himself, when he tried to understand the rage that was increasingly building inside him, as having two equally powerful sides inching him ever closer to actions he did not want to take. One side had a foot in the church, the place where he sought solace and acceptance. The other side was walking with the devil and if his actions indicated his desires, he would soon become more comfortable with the evil than with the good.

In some other big cities the changes in his behavior might have been noticed, especially as the man had run-ins with the law. But Dallas, Texas was unlike most other big cities in the United States during the time when the man walked its streets. That was the reason his crimes would continue until, it was later rumored, some individuals had their lives snuffed out and at least one hundred women had their lives violated in ways that can heal, but only with scars that forever altered how they lived and impeded their abilities to ever trust others again.

CHAPTER 4

THE BIG "D"

IT IS TRUTH, not legend, that:

John Neely Bryan stood on the bluff above the river. The sun was low and red, and the November wind was cool on his face. To the west the two streams became one, and the plains beyond were dotted with trees. No living thing moved within his sight. Only the water flowed slowly to the east, and it ran smooth and clear.

"Mi a ka—wash tay," he said, and turned to the Cherokee chief called Indian Ned. "Here is the place we heard speak of, old friend. The Land of the Three Forks—"

"Yes, I remember."

"It is a good place. We will return here to settle."

Bryan's gray pony, Neshoba, breathed noisily behind them. The Indian's sorrel raised her head and whinnied, and the brown-and-white bear dog yawned.

Bryan shouldered his rifle, a faint smile playing on his lips.

Behind them a twig cracked. Bryan turned.

> *Six Cherokee stood not thirty feet away. At their*
> *head was the half-breed chief, Jesse Chisolm . . .*
> —Jim Donovan,
> *Dallas: Shining Star of Texas*
> *Reprinted by permission of publisher*

In fact, the first white men to travel through the gently rolling prairies and lush woodlands that would one day be the site of Dallas, Texas were a ragtag band of survivors of Hernando de Soto's failed Spanish expedition. In 1542 the disoriented conquistadors crossed the lands of the various subtribes of the Native American Caddos tribe, passing through the Three Forks area of the Trinity River in search of a suitable site upon which to establish New Spain in the new world. Native Americans had hunted bison, deer and bear in the forests and on the prairies, had fished the sparkling rivers and camped on the banks of a pristine lake for at least forty thousand years before the first Europeans appeared. Most of the early inhabitants of present day Dallas were Caddo Indians who traversed the triangle formed by what is now Oklahoma, Arkansas and Texas. Perhaps coincidentally, perhaps prophetically, the Caddos were described in 1828 by a French biologist, Jean Louis Berlindier, as a people fascinated by shiny ornaments and paints with which they decorated their bodies and faces, a vanity that twentieth-century residents of the land would come to emulate.

Both French and Spanish explorers and traders criss-crossed the territory over the years, never establishing a permanent colony or even a lasting impression. Around 1819, tribal war broke out when a branch of the Cherokee tribe settled on the land, having abandoned their Arkansas homeland. Even after the colonized portion of Texas won its independence from Mexico in 1836, the Three Forks area of the Trinity River remained strictly Indian country, with not one white settler living there.

John Neely Bryan, born and bred in Tennessee, an attorney who lived for four years with the Cherokee and other tribes in the Arkansas wilderness and a visionary who developed the town of Van Buren, Arkansas into a bustling center of trade, turned his ambitious, adventuring eyes toward the fertile lands of the Three Forks. He had heard tales of the hospitable geography and the potential that flowed with the waters of the Trinity River.

With a Cherokee pal named Indian Ned, Tubby his dog and Neshoba his horse, Bryan reached the Three Forks region in November, 1841. He stood on a bluff overlooking the river and declared this was a fine site for a new town, which he named Dallas, most likely after Commodore Alexander James Dallas, a famous naval hero of the war of 1812. The location was on the route of the proposed national highway, the soil was fertile and the river—that fine river—would ensure success for the fledgling town. Bryan was convinced that the proximity and navigability of the river would turn Dallas into a major port city of trade and, ultimately, wealth.

By 1843 about twenty-five families had joined Bryan in his makeshift town of Dallas, living in shacks built of poles, boards and mud. Eschewing Bryan's grand dreams and schemes, the settlers were mostly concerned with surviving the rough frontier environment they had chosen. Along with the hardships, they endured several incidents of attacks and killings at the hands of the Native American tribes, who were not pleased with having their lands invaded.

Only after Sam Houston, the president of the Republic of Texas, with John Neely Bryan assisting, called on the chiefs of the nine area tribes to talk peace with him, did the violence come to an end with the signing of a peace treaty in 1843. Even without the constant threat of attack, however, life in Dallas was harsh and deprived for the settlers. It was only the dream of a bright future, the black, rich soil, the herds of buffalo and wild mustangs and the life-giving force of the Trinity River that continued to beguile and attract new settlers. Many of them were recent European emigrants, especially well-educated Swiss, French and Belgians who attempted to form a utopian cooperative colony, La Réunion, near Dallas. Victor Consideran, a disciple of the French Socialist Marie Charles Fournier, believed human beings' acquisitive nature could be regulated through communal living. Eventually, three hundred fifty highly educated professionals, scientists, artists, writers and musicians joined the colony. When the colony floundered after three years, the leaders returned to Europe but most others stayed. These people came to Dallas, enriching the city with their cultural histories and over the years they, their children and their grandchildren helped establish many of the city's significant cultural institutions.

However, Dallas was also a violent place, home to Buffalo trappers, day laborers and the heroes and infamous figures of the West including John "Doc" Holliday, who among his other pursuits, practiced dentistry; Belle Starr; who sang in one of the dance halls and fenced stolen horses; as well as Frank James, Jesse's brother who added to the family's outlaw saga.

Eventually, the settlers discovered there was simply not enough fertile soil to support large-scale farming; the river proved to be unpredictable and without a viable outlet to the sea; mineral resources were never found. Nevertheless, the new citizens of Dallas soon put Bryan's dream of a great port city behind them and worked determinedly to make Dallas an important city. In 1850 Dallas won two close elections, making it the county seat; in the 1870s the city managed to bring not one but two railroads chugging their way through Dallas, making it a primary distribution center for the region; in 1912 the city became home to a Federal Reserve Bank, validating Dallas as a stable financial center; in 1936 the citizens fought for and won the right to hold the Texas Centennial Exposition in their backyard, constructing the finest collection of art deco buildings in the world and attracting thirteen million visitors and their money, virtually pulling Dallas out of the Depression that gripped the country. In less than a hundred years, Dallas had established itself as the most important, most vibrant city in the state.

Over the years, Dallas has been home to talented, far-sighted individuals who know how to make things happen—the movers, shakers and seers of the modern world. Among them: John Howard Griffin, author of *Black Like Me*, an extraordinary look at Griffin's travels through the

South disguised as a black man; Lyndon Baines Johnson, the first Texan president of the United States; Lamar Hunt, founder of the American Football League and the Super Bowl; H. L. Hunt, the oilman who once was considered to be the world's richest man; Bette Graham, the inventor of Liquid Paper; Robert Crandall, the American Airlines chief honcho; Mary Kay Ash, the *doyenne* of direct-sales cosmetics and pink Cadillacs; the Marcus family, retailers *extraordinaire*; Kenneth Cooper, the aerobics innovator; Ebby Halliday, the super-successful realtor; J. M. Hagger, the largest men's dress trouser manufacturer in the world; H. Ross Perot, self-made multi-millionaire and one-time presidential candidate; Roger Horchow, the mail-order magnate; George W. Bush, former governor of Texas and the president of the United States—all of them have seen their dreams and schemes come to fruition in Dallas.

Today, Dallas is one of the country's premier centers of banking and finance, the headquarters of myriad Fortune 500 companies and sustains a diverse economy based on petroleum-based products and oil production, aeronautics, meat packing, electronics, fashion, printing and publishing, cotton goods and advertising. In 1948, the *Wall Street Journal* recognized Dallas as a financial center by establishing there a southwest edition. Success seems to breed success in the Big "D" and the city sings a siren song to the ambitious, the driven and all those folks with big dreams and bigger appetites.

While the Dallas Cowboys contributed to the manly image of their heritage by winning constantly and being dubbed America's team, the Dallas Cowboy cheerleaders pranced in short shorts on the football field of a stadium that was a cantilevered superstructure and a miracle of engineering. The Dallas Cowboy cheerleaders were considered by some to be highbrow entertainment compared with what a few old timers laughingly called their predecessors at the strip clubs that used to be near the Adolphus Hotel. This was the area that had given the nation such superstars as Candy Barr, arguably the finest naked dancer to work the clubs and certainly the most beautiful in and out of her gown. In typical Big D myth-making fashion, Candy had formerly been Juanita Dale Slusher, forced into white slavery, enjoyed by the most prominent men in Dallas, then sentenced to fifteen years in prison for possession of two marijuana cigarettes. Her real crime wasn't smoking. It was maintaining a little black book with the names of civic leaders who had paid the man who "owned" her to use her body in any way they chose.

Entertainment is expansive in Dallas. The 1570-seat Majestic Theater, designed in 1921 and donated to the city in 1979, today hosts dance, theater and music companies. The Dallas Theater Center, which opened in 1957, was designed by Frank Lloyd Wright and is located in a wooded area alongside Turtle Creek. Paul Baber, who was trained at Yale School of Drama and director of Baylor University's drama department, headed the Center. Preston Jones, a company member, won national acclaim with his Texas Trilogy, which eventually moved to the Kennedy Center in Washington, D.C. Two other playwrights with prominent Dallas ties won Pulitzer Prizes: Don Coburn (*The Gin Game*) and Beth Henley (*Crimes of the Heart*).

This is Dallas history and by the time Carol Bryan moved there, Dallas, Texas had become a city so big, so bold and so brazen that it embraced both the ideals and the excesses of America. Here was a city of myth and magic, a haven for schemers and dreamers, hustlers and empire-builders. It had the charisma of the old west, where men were men and women were women, and the savagery, where guns and riches were the ultimate authority.

In New York Harbor, the Statue of Liberty has served as a beacon of hope for immigrants, both young and old, seeking freedom from fear, from want and from a future with no hope for a better tomorrow. In Big D, newly rich business executives and their wives delighted in—some said worshipped—the flagship Neiman Marcus store where they could experience the tantalizing sensuality of $250 an ounce perfume, a plebeian item sold many times a day by sales clerks wielding atomizers like six-shooters, and where they could find small custom jet planes advertised in the Christmas catalog. And for everyday transportation, that same Christmas catalog offered such items as matching his-and-her, top-of-the-line Jaguars.

In the Midwest, a career minded businessperson could be considered to be doing well when bringing home an annual income equal to his or her age multiplied by $1,000. By that reasoning, a twenty-five-year-old college graduate was quite happy to be earning $25,000 a year and numerous men and women were delighted with salaries that had reached between $65,000 and $70,000 when they retired.

Big D had its own measure of business success—"points"—with each point representing one hundred million dollars. One business leader might be known as a "two point man." Another would have investments and real estate qualifying him as a "three point man." Anything under one point might assure a comfortable lifestyle, but was not something mentioned to anyone but your closest friends.

Church attendance was also a necessity in the Big D, the home to some of the largest churches in the United States. Congregations of 5,000 were considered baby churches by some of the pastors who filled massive buildings just long enough to raise the money to create even larger structures for their flocks. Many offered activities seven days a week, from day care and schools to recreation, theatrical groups, Scouts and support groups for youth, young adults, young marrieds, the widowed, the divorced, single parents. . . . The list was endless. Whatever would keep the faithful, from exercise classes to Bible studies, someone would be hired to teach, to preach and/or to lead. And because in Big D size matters, being right with God frequently meant having to give the church far more than the traditional tithe.

And crime was bigger, better and more outrageous in Big D. Two stories were still in people's thoughts and conversation—Danny Faulkner and prison overcrowding. The former was a classic white collar crime; a scam so big the ripple effect cost both the public and the United States government more than three hundred billion dollars. The latter was a situation in which felons served just one day for every thirty and major felons served one month for every year of their sentence. This had been court mandated to end prison overcrowding. Texas, unlike almost every other state in the nation, could only build prisons by using money from the general revenue. It was 1995 before bonds could legally be issued to pay for desperately needed facilities. The general revenue was inadequate for other critical needs—from road repairs to education—so there was no choice but to let the prisons be a rapidly revolving door, a place where men who committed dastardly deeds could rest for a short time before returning to the streets.

The prison situation helped Dallas become the felony capital of the nation, leading the country in rapes and murders, statistics rarely disclosed to or in the media. By contrast, the white-collar criminal Danny Faulkner was a celebrated local hero.

David Lamar "Danny" Faulkner was born in Kosciusko, Mississippi on Christmas Day, 1932. His father was a sharecropper and sometime house painter. Danny was dyslexic, a genius at math who never learned to read or write because of his learning disability. He became a grade school dropout, then moved to Dallas where his need to earn a living took him to the union hall so he could become a $3 an hour painter. It was 1962 and he was proud to be making double the minimum wage. However, he was also ambitious, gradually starting his own painting business, hiring crews and eventually employing 250 men. With the profits from the painting venture, he began a series of business investments designed to make himself as rich as J.R. Ewing, though his financial vehicle of choice was banking and land development, not oil. By 1979, having bought controlling interest in the Town East Savings Association of Mesquite, Texas and changing its name to Empire Savings & Loan, he managed to raise its assets from $40 million per year to $320 million through what would later be found to be a series of interrelated frauds. He also started a complex investment/development scam, buying near worthless land, then selling it, "flipping" it several times in the same day. One parcel was purchased for one dollar per square foot, then sold and resold in a series of phony deals until, at the end of the day, the "value" was fifteen dollars per square foot. Appraisers were bribed. Bank officers were given a piece of the action. Investors were scammed but held responsible for some of the financial deals and in four years Faulkner was Big D rich. His personal helicopter flew him to his private landing pad at Texas Stadium where he had a million-dollar Circle Suite from which to enjoy the games. He owned a Lear Jet, several Rolls Royces, a ranch, a newspaper, expensive jewelry and every other item he desired.

Danny was also generous, giving $500,000 to endow the W.A. Criswell Chair of Preaching at Dallas Baptist University. Friends routinely received $8,000 Rolex watches as gifts. All those strangers who ate breakfast at his favorite coffee shop were treated to their meals whenever Danny walked in the door. A million dollars was donated to Jupiter Road Baptist Church to build a new sanctuary. And when he saw a poor woman and her son collecting aluminum cans from the side of the road to earn a little extra money, he handed her all the $100 bills in his pocket—well in excess of $1,000.

Eventually the empire unraveled, the frauds revealed, Empire Savings and several subsidiaries bankrupted. Danny was sentenced to twenty years in jail (only a small fraction of the sentence would be served, like all felons at that time) and ordered to pay forty million dollars in fines. The thousands of condominiums he was in the process of building along Interstate 30 just outside Dallas were found to be so poorly made that most of them had to be destroyed.

THE PEOPLE OF Dallas were rich, the city was not. Growth had come too fast and the constitution of the state was an antiquated document that needed amending by the state legislature. But the state legislature was truly a citizen government where the elected state representatives journeyed to Austin for only six months of work every two years. That brief period of time was when all new laws were proposed, reviewed and either enacted or defeated, a fact that greatly limited legislative productivity. Something so controversial as a constitutional amendment took three sessions of the legislature (six years) to achieve, on average. If the Stetson hat and cowboy boots were the symbols of Texas growth, then the moribund slug trapped in a pan of water after a rainstorm should have been the symbol of the legislature in that era.

The biggest problem for law enforcement, beyond serious under-staffing in Dallas and other Texas cities, was that there was no place to send the bad guys. Texas had prisons, of course, but not enough. Huntsville, the site of the men's penitentiary, had long been the center of both positive and negative notoriety and controversy. Overcrowded and with living conditions that bordered on unhealthy for inmates and guards alike, the prison also was nationally known for its rodeo. In the 1950s, for example, some of the biggest name talent in the nation vied to perform at the prison rodeo. It was a great moneymaker and focused on one positive side of prison life. But by the late 1980s, statistics were grim. The state penitentiary could only take in 38,000 new inmates a year and Dallas County alone had 20,000 felons who needed to be housed there. With no money to build more prisons and a federal judge demanding an immediate end to overcrowding, the prison soon had a virtual revolving door. Commit a crime that required time in your local jail and you would probably be released with a stern lecture and the order to make regularly scheduled visits to an assigned probation officer. Commit a felony and you would be given the same Texas Department of Corrections number as if you were sent to Huntsville, but you would often do your time in a county jail instead. (Because time served could be as limited as one day for every thirty days of a sentence, someone sentenced to three years in Huntsville might do as little as a month or two in the county jail before being released on parole.) Serious felons, including those whose cases were "aggravated" as a result of the use of a weapon, would go to Huntsville. However, their time served would be one month for every year of the sentence. A rapist sentenced to ten years in jail was frequently released in ten months.

Some of the inmates delighted in the realities of the system. Their time in prison was like a vacation. There were no responsibilities outside of jail regulations. There was relatively little prison violence compared with institutions where men were locked up for many years. Inmates took control of the cellblocks, using extortion and intimidation to dominate. And those who had been drug addicts often appreciated the free detox time, because it meant that they would get a stronger "high" when they returned to drugs.

Rehabilitation programs were often meaningless. Officially sanctioned education programs were futile, because the men would be released before they could finish any training. Only the unofficial "seminars" conducted by inmates in the form of clandestine, continuing criminal education were successful. Thus a man who was caught by a home alarm system would learn how to disconnect the power source coming into the home. He might learn how to enter through a window without showing obvious signs of tampering. He might learn how to rig an office or apartment outer entrance door so it would remain unlocked while closed and appear to be securely locked.

Inmates taught one another the ins and outs of larceny, about the use of gloves and how to keep from leaving trace evidence behind. Sometimes the courses were taught one-on-one. Sometimes the classes were conducted in small groups just outside the hearing of the guards. No one noticed that the "teachers" were as much losers in their own right as the inmate "students." Why else would they keep returning to prison? But even though an objective observer would see that despite better training most of the inmates who returned to crime would get caught, the inmates did not seem to care. Their crime sprees might last longer. Their take from other people's property might increase. And even if they did return to jail, the time served was neither a meaningful deterrent nor a serious protection for society. The punishment of a prison sentence ultimately did almost nothing to change behavior or prepare a released inmate for a life that did not involve crime. The situation was so conducive to future criminal achievements that some convicted felons revolted when they did not have to serve time in Huntsville. An entire class of felons, some of whom had committed murder, were ordered PIA—Paroled

In Absentia. They were tried, convicted, sentenced to several years in Huntsville and fully processed, including being given a TDC number as though they were actually housed in the state prison. Then they were paroled, never having gone to Huntsville, never having spent time outside a county jail.

It would have seemed that to be Paroled In Absentia would have been ideal for a felon. He could commit a major crime, be convicted and never serve a day very far from home. He would still have a "rap sheet" (arrest record) that notes a conviction. He would still have certain restrictions within society at large, such as periodically reporting to a parole officer. But the person would be in the free world.

Ironically, in the convoluted world of Texas criminal justice, some of the men who were granted PIA status were outraged. Men who went to Huntsville, served at least some time and then were released received $200 to help them return to society. Men who were declared PIA had the same record sheets and parole restrictions of someone who served time in the state penitentiary, but they did not receive the $200. The fact that the prison inmates often returned to a world without a job or a home and many in the PIA program retained both, was lost to them. $200 would buy cigarettes or drugs, booze or women, or just let them purchase something nice for a spouse, girlfriend or mother. They committed the same types of crimes. They felt they should be compensated accordingly.

A few of the PIA men brought a lawsuit against the state, demanding their $200, ostensibly as a reward for never being denied their freedom. Fortunately, not even Texas was foolish enough to honor such a demand.

The newspapers rarely investigated the financial problems that were behind the rise in crime in Dallas. Even the mention of crime was a delicate matter. Dallas was working toward becoming a world class city in every way. The city wanted a diversified economy and the state itself had already begun to be considered as a possible new location for television and motion picture production. Some of the Hollywood studios were considering expanding or even relocating there. Texas had the weather, the non-union work-force and the varied scenery that would allow easy location shooting for the film companies.

More and more, corporate headquarters were also moving to Dallas and the surrounding communities. Where once New York, Chicago and Boston had dominated as headquarters for many corporations, along with such support services as top echelon advertising and law firms, many corporations were seeking better weather and tax concessions for relocation. They were making their way south and west and Dallas was reaping the benefits.

Some crimes did make the news, of course, but many people saw them as aberrations. They happened to other people—barrio residents perhaps or in the case of sexual assault, women who somehow asked for it.

Sex crimes were only beginning to be viewed as offenses requiring careful attention. Some of the officers were intensely sympathetic towards the victims and outraged by the violence. They treated the women with care and dignity, recognizing them as victims who had lost all sense of security after being violated in their homes or offices, locations where most of us feel we are safe from danger. These were officers who had helped form a sexual assault unit in the late 1980s. These were also the officers who became involved with an organization to help all crime victims called Victims Outreach. This organization was the result of the work of Patsy Day, a woman whose daughter had been kidnapped and murdered. Overwhelming grief had stimulated her inherent compassion for others. She could not stand to see the suffering of victims of violent crimes or families who had suffered the loss of a loved one to crime. She turned her own heartbreak into a program that would eventually nurture and help restore thousands of peoples' lives. And all of this was taking place during the worst outbreak of violent crimes against its citizens that Dallas had ever encountered.

Unfortunately, little of this was known to Carol Bryan when she began to search for a place to live. Dallas was, as her real estate rental agent assured Carol, a place where anyone with ambition could succeed. It was a fact that would be borne out by the men and women she soon would meet. Some owed their diamonds, their expensive cars and their luxury condos to intensely hard work. Carol had ambitions to prosper by the same ethic. She had come to Dallas to be near her daughters. She wanted to start another business or invest in one, to work hard and to become financially secure through her skills as an artist and the success of whatever type of business she eventually acquired.

Even if all the city's problems had been acknowledged, Big D was still about searching for mega success, success on a grand scale. Thus those who flocked to the city often had stars in their eyes. They believed hard work, luck and good looks could lead to success beyond one's wildest dreams. Big D was about tall, sun-bronzed men and women and, to Carol and others who came from nameless towns, a future that seemed limitless with opportunity.

CHAPTER 5

DISPARATE LIVES

TWO MEN HAD come to the police department ride-along program with equal enthusiasm but radically different results. Both were Baptists. Both made the Bible central to their lives.

One man, Dennis Henderson, lived scripture as best he could. He was a pastor who had moved to Dallas to lead the congregation of Marsh Lane Baptist Church. He was also a man beset by doubts concerning how best to minister to others. He felt there was a special calling awaiting him, one that he had yet to recognize, but to which he would one day have to respond.

The second man, Gilbert Escobedo, was a successful businessman. Gilbert's father had run an upholstery shop in a neighborhood where most people buy used cars. The few who could buy new did not trade them in every two or three years as was typical in upscale communities. Instead, they carefully maintained them or customized them.

Some of the youths enjoyed the low riders so popular in Southern California, Southern Arizona and other regions where such cars were in demand among Mexican and other Hispanic youth. Some decorated their vehicles with elaborate paintings of the Virgin Mary. In parts of Mexico, it was considered an act of veneration to enhance a car in such manner. The work was done carefully, lovingly, by artists who were proud to let a visual symbol of their faith travel the city streets. A religious lowrider was a car that was like a traveling billboard for the Blessed Virgin.

Others just liked the altering of the hydraulics so that the cars rode only an inch or two above the street, the reason they were called "low riders." Often they were designed so that a switch inside the car could make it bounce up and down. And always there would be a time to parade the vehicles down a bustling main street, often on a Friday or Saturday night.

Whatever the car, Gilbert's father was in demand to handle customizing and repair of the upholstery. The money was excellent and the work was steady. Even in bad economic times, the cars would be maintained because Dallas did not yet have the quality public transportation that the city would eventually install.

Gilbert said his father offered other services as well, including what some people outside the barrio considered loan-sharking. He would take some of his profits and make loans to customers and neighbors he knew. They would then be expected to pay back double what they borrowed. The interest was steep, but the people who needed the loans had no other choice. The banks and savings-and-loan companies weren't interested in them. They didn't make enough money to qualify or they were street hustlers who could usually scrounge up whatever they needed, but they could never point to a regular payday.

After a troubled period in his youth, Gilbert started a service business, the type of enterprise his father had taught him to respect, but in the kind of upscale neighborhood where Gilbert could charge sky-high prices. His "white glove" service and attention to his customers earned him a good reputation. The business not only prospered until Gilbert was considered a self-made success story, but many of his customers became friends.

Gilbert was devout, but at the same time, he also saw the church as a social enterprise. He recognized that within the Baptist community a man who could quote some of the more obscure Bible passages was widely respected. He listened carefully to his church pastor's readings each Sunday. He talked with people who ardently read the Bible. He had a hunger for information that would make him part of the Dallas "in crowd," most of whom were regular churchgoers.

He studied hard. As Gilbert identified verses he wanted to learn, he had a friend coach him. He practiced over and over, the friend reading a verse as Gilbert memorized all the words. Then Gilbert repeated it with different inflections, different emphasis, until he felt he had the perfect reading.

Gilbert carried his Bible with him almost everywhere. He left a copy in his car, because he so regularly attended Bible study that he needed it handy. He kept a Bible at his business and he frequently carried one with him when he visited friends. It was as much a part of his appearance as his increasingly expensive suits, shirts, neckties and shoes.

DENNIS HENDERSON'S CHURCH deacon was a police officer who suggested the pastor might like to ride along in a patrol car one night. The Dallas force was constantly trying to improve its community relations. The men were so poorly paid compared with other cities in the state that there was a high turnover of officers who trained there, gained some experience on Dallas streets, then moved to Houston, Austin and elsewhere within the state for better salaries. A ride-along program, in which citizens accompanied police officers on their shifts of duty, might make the public sensitive to the officers, aware of the quality of the men and women and help the department gain support for whatever ballot issues were necessary to provide better salaries. The public would also become more sensitive to its civic responsibility to work with the police as partners in fighting crime. Citizens would be more willing to report suspicious activities if they saw themselves helping the friends they made during the rides.

The helicopter division also allowed civilians to ride along, a situation not found in many other cities because of liability issues. But most of the police pilots were military veterans and all were well experienced. The helicopter was probably safer than the police car, because there were no civilian vehicles to get dangerously in the way during a high-speed chase.

Dennis Henderson never rode in the helicopters. Instead, he went out in a police cruiser on a Friday night, one of the two busiest nights of the week for law enforcement.

Some cities try to make the ride-along program as safe as possible. The officer driving the car is encouraged not to respond to emergencies if there are other, equally close police vehicles to take such calls. The idea is to protect both the life and the emotions of the civilian passenger.

This was not the case in Dallas. Too few officers meant that Pastor Henderson was thrown into the usual Friday night mix of violence and alcohol-related incidents. First came a call about domestic violence. The neighbors had heard angry words, shouting and a gun being fired. By the time Pastor Henderson stepped through the door with the two officers showing him their world, a man was dead, blood from a head wound covering his face, his girlfriend holding a gun with an expression of both shock and satisfaction.

The officers returned to the road, responding to a serious car crash at 2:00 A.M. A drunk thought he could drive home from a bar. He never expected to encounter a telephone pole that somehow leaped out in front of him, destroying the front of his car and sending him into the windshield.

At 4:00 A.M. there was another body, this time alone and in an alley. It may have been a drug deal gone bad. It may have been a robbery. It may have been the result of two more lovers settling their differences with bullets. There was no way of knowing at that moment. The crime scene was secured, the detectives arrived, the scientific unit began looking for trace evidence and an ambulance removed the corpse from the scene. Then the responding officers returned to the station to fill out their reports and Pastor Henderson went home, feeling surprisingly satisfied about helping the lawmen. Later, his deacon told him that, although the average citizen is limited to going on one ride-along per year, the limitation is not placed on members of the clergy. If he wanted to go with other officers the following weekend, he would be allowed to do so.

THE SOCIABLE, CHURCHGOING gentleman met the Dallas Police officers through his business. As customers, they found they enjoyed the compact, gregarious man who was so devout. He became particularly close to one officer. The policemen invited him to ride along in both the police car and the helicopter. A ride-along in the latter, though not routine, was permitted at the discretion of the pilots.

Soon Gilbert was a regular rider in one officer's cruiser and in the helicopter. He was good company and though one individual repeatedly riding in the police car was not the way the program was supposed to work, no one complained. The officers enjoyed having an extra pair of eyes and ears. As to the helicopter, since no one had ever asked to be allowed to ride on a frequent basis, there was no precedent. Gilbert showed up, Bible in hand and a smile on his face, and no one objected. He was given a police department baseball cap as a gift from the patrol officer and the helicopter pilot gave him a shoulder patch. Civilians were not supposed to have such items, but officers were permitted to give out such souvenirs as goodwill gestures providing they could trust the recipient to not wear it where he or she might be mistaken for an officer. The man accepted the cap and shoulder patch as badges of honor.

ONE NIGHT WHEN Gilbert was accompanying him, the helicopter pilot flew slowly over the North Dallas area, crisscrossing a territory bounded by the LBJ freeway, the Central Expressway and the tollway. The searchlight used for hot pursuit chases and to expose hiding miscreants was turned off. The officer/pilot and his companion wore binoculars slung around their necks and listened intently to the voices coming over the police radio, helping them find the cunning criminal they were seeking.

Their prey that night was a man who loved the night. He

was a stalker, a thief and a violator. The police had given him the name "Ski Mask Rapist." As his attacks continued, the man had refined his actions. The ski mask was only worn at times when no one could spot him entering or leaving someone's home. He wore gloves and carried a handgun. He relied upon pillowcases and other bedding to keep his victims from seeing him. His voice was gentle at the beginning of the attack, though he advanced to the edge of rage if the victim did not cooperate. If the victim was reasonably passive, then he would treat her as though she was willingly having sex with him—as though he was her boyfriend—so long as she didn't fight him. If she did fight back, he pistol-whipped her or pressed the handgun against her temple and told her he would kill her—and if she didn't obey him, he meant it.

He used a washcloth or towel to clean away anything that might link him to the rape. He wanted no bodily fluids available to the scientific investigation unit. He left no fingerprints and no other trace evidence that could scientifically identify him as the perpetrator.

Studying the Ski Mask Rapist's past assaults resulted in little information other than identifying his "rape kit"—gloves, ski mask and a handgun.

He was the most dangerous criminal the Dallas police had experienced in years—a serial rapist and perhaps even a murderer whose victims would eventually be estimated at somewhere between one and two hundred.

His attacks, if too widely publicized in the news media, could hurt the economic growth plans of the community at large. That was a further reason many of the officers in the department were concerned about the growing problem that was shattering the lives of an increasing number of bright, attractive and successful women in the area. That was why there was political pressure to find the perpetrator coming from real estate industry professionals and community leaders concerned with attracting new residents and new businesses to the area. That was why the man in the passenger seat of the police helicopter was focused intently on the ground below, searching for the Ski Mask Rapist and gaining new insights into the frustrations, the limitations and the ongoing resolve of the Dallas Police Department. That was why his police officer friends appreciated his kind assistance with their seemingly impossible task.

PERHAPS IT WAS only in Big D that these seemingly totally disparate people could come together in ways that would forever change all of their lives and create a case unique in law enforcement. There was the attractive blonde woman, Carol Bryan—an artist and art consultant for major corporations, divorced, with college-age daughters and a zest for life. There was the preacher who found his calling as much in the midst of prostitutes and drug abusers, burglars, robbers, rapists and killers, as he did in the sanctuary of his church. There was the social, churchgoing businessman who found policework so exhilarating. And there was the criminal whose larcenous desire not only for the objects, but their women, grew more and more ravenous as he added victim after victim to the notches on his belt.

When they arrived in Big D none imagined that their lives would intertwine. Yet they did come together in a way both unexpected and explosive, very much like the violent boom, bust and renewed frenetic tension that was Dallas itself.

CHAPTER 6

MAJOR AND MINOR INDISCRETIONS

IT WAS CALLED the Minor Indiscretion Act when it ruled Dallas, Texas courtrooms through the early 1950s. The premise behind the law was that women should be by nature strictly monogamous—and were psychologically and physiologically sick if they strayed from committed relationships. Thus, if a man caught his wife in bed with another man, killing one or both of the illicit lovers in the heat of his anguish, the law did not consider the killings a major crime. It was rare that the man would go to jail, rarer still that he would serve more than a few weeks or months if he were sent behind bars.

By contrast, men were considered physiologically wired for minor indiscretions. They were simply incapable of having sexual relationships with only one woman during their lives. They were expected to commit to marriage and expected to not have mistresses, for ongoing, long-term relationships with other women were blatant affronts to their sacred marriage vows. But men were also expected, due to their natures, to occasionally engage in "minor indiscretions" with co-workers, prostitutes or other willing women. The indiscretions were usually one-time experiences. They were strictly sexual in nature and did not alter the fact that the men loved their wives. As a result, if a wife found her husband in bed with another woman and *she* killed one or both of the lovers, she faced serious felony murder charges.

Such thinking carried into the home. Domestic violence in Dallas was as prevalent in post-World War II times as it would be on the threshold of the twenty-first century. But into the early 1980s, domestic violence was a civil matter. A parent had the right to discipline a child with a "rod" or other implement. The father was head of the household and whatever he felt was necessary to maintain order and discipline within the family environment was deemed acceptable.

Certainly there were times when a parent went too far, causing physical harm to the child being disciplined. And there were times when a man asserted his authority over his wife with his fists. While most people would say he went too far, among others there was also a question of his motivation (i.e. What actions of the wife or child led to the violence?) and other issues. How much was too much was deemed a matter both for the church and for the civil courts to decide. As a result, domestic violence calls were not handled by the police. Instead, the couple was referred to the civil agencies that would deal with such matters.

This attitude toward women created other problems. There was an occasional police officer who thought that it was all right to use the implied authority of his position to coerce women into having sex. Sometimes this was a consensual exchange, the equivalent of a bribe, with sex being the currency of choice. At other times it was closer to rape, the unwilling woman fearing violence or other consequence that the officer insisted he never threatened. In either case, when a scandal was revealed, the officer involved was severely disciplined and often fired.

Times had changed in Dallas by the time Carol Bryan was relocating. There was a growing awareness that men as well as some women could engage in abusive behavior, comforted by the knowledge that they would probably not be held accountable. There was also a growing sensitivity to the emotional and physical tolls such abuse takes on victims. Women's shelters were built. The media began noting that there was nothing positive about a family where one or more members lived in fear of physical or emotional violence.

Soon there were groups lobbying the Texas State legislature and new laws began to make their way through the ponderously slow system. Police officers received new training. What had been ignored because of the old regulations became a crime under the new. Uniformed men and women who once walked away from domestic violence began responding differently, separating the family where necessary, making arrests when warranted and helping to put some violent family members in jail.

The educational level of men and women seeking to become police officers also increased during this period. "Dallas has always been a city based on finance, banking and insurance," said Sgt. Bob Rommel, a young Dallas police officer during this period. "The police department has always been largely blue collar. It has also historically been extremely strict. You could be fired in a heartbeat for failing to meet the smallest standard. That has changed a little, but you still have to tell the truth. If you make a mistake, the department will work with you. But if you lie about the mistake, you're out.

"There were a lot of reasons men and women were drawn to the department. Unemployment was fairly high and there were quite a few college graduates looking for work when the department was hiring. There has always been a requirement that an officer have some college education, but we were getting a lot of applicants with degrees.

"There were a lot of reasons, though certainly the low pay wasn't one of them. It was a career, not just a job. You could retire after twenty years and for someone in his mid-to-late twenties, that looked pretty good.

"Of course, you had to be service oriented. Otherwise you would not last. You had to care about people to a certain extent, though some did more than others.

"But it was a challenging job where you had to do everything right or you would fail. When you're on the street, no two days are alike. There are always new calls, new challenges. There is an excitement to it. You look forward to going to work, solving problems, putting bad people in jail."

There was also great respect for the law enforcement officers in Dallas. The poor people living in areas where everyone was just striving to feed and clothe their families and keep a roof over their heads respected the hard working officers. In North Dallas, the area where the greatest wealth was concentrated, there was intense fear of violent crime. The wealthy understood that their possessions were targets for the criminals and they saw the police as the thin blue line that was there to protect them. Many of the wealthy, like high school teenagers, sought status in what they owned, how they dressed and with whom they associated. They viewed the police officers as protecting father figures, perhaps not quite "with it" and never going to achieve much status in life, yet still loving, kind and determined to keep them safe. It was a comfortable relationship for everyone involved.

Despite all this, however, the citizens of Dallas often felt some frustration with the police. There was a sense that the department was failing to protect the citizenry when there were rashes of burglaries and rapes, as there were when Carol made her way to Big D. The newspapers at the time often failed to adequately explain that the police could only investigate and arrest, the prosecutors could only present the facts and the juries could only decide guilt or innocence. The overcrowded prison system was the real problem, as were the legal mandates that enforced the revolving door policy that quickly returned career criminals to the streets. The police were doing their job to the best of their abilities, but where extremely violent and/or career criminals in other states might be locked away until they were too old to resume their nefarious ways, Dallas criminals could count on only brief respites from their pursuits. Men and some women who would likely have been in prison for extended stays in other states were living free and well in Dallas.

HER NAME WAS Marion. On the surface she was what Carol would come to see as the Dallas ideal. Her hair was blonde, her bosom perky and when she entered a room she looked as though she stepped off the screen from a movie in which she played Pamela Anderson's older sister. She also had the gregarious personality, expensive jewelry, luxury car and salty language that usually marked the successful, suddenly single women of North Dallas.

Marion was in real estate, but more important to many of her clients, she was a master of the unspoken caste system that marked Big D residential neighborhoods. First came old money and established power in the premier areas. The males were CEOs of some of the most successful businesses in the city, on the boards of the right organizations and with salaries, stock options and bonus plans that enabled them to earn more in a year than some lesser executives would take home in a lifetime. The women shopped at not only the right department stores, but also the right branch of the right department store. Neiman Marcus was one of the "right" stores, but it was an equal opportunity provider of needful things for the city's elite. All the branches offered the same merchandise, but some branches were located in shopping districts catering to the privileged few and some could be found where the middle class went to spend their money.

Next came the neighborhoods where the residents were on the rise. They lived well. They drove cars by makers like Mercedes, BMW, Cadillac and similar luxury models. They frequently ate dinner in expensive restaurants. They attended the "right" social events. But they had no history, no family money. Some were in blue-collar professions, albeit at the top or at a level rarely achieved by others. For instance, the cosmetics salesperson who was making $150,000 a year fit this category. Carol, because of her past business success, her striking good looks and a rosy future that seemed certain, was also seen as a part of this group. In addition, there were young stockbrokers, middle management business executives being fast tracked to the top, investment advisers and the like. Occasionally there was also the attractive, older man—wise in the ways of investments and pension funds, carefully affixed to his golden parachute and temporarily between marriages. Not that he was as prized as someone who had remained in his proper place, but still he was white, possibly came from old money and had a face that drew the camera whenever society functions were covered by the newspapers.

Marion also knew the "undesirable" sides of Dallas such as Little Mexico. These were neighborhoods filled with people who could not afford to miss a day's work, who cared more about price and quality than the location of a store in which they had to shop, who struggled with often menial jobs so their children could attend college. These were the people who, a century earlier, would have been encouraged by writer Horatio Alger's stories of young men who used "pluck and luck" to carry them from poverty backgrounds to triumph in school, on the athletic field and in the business world. In the superficial status-conscious environment Marion felt was the "right" Dallas, a modern writer creating Alger-like inspirational messages for the poor would quite possibly be stoned.

There was also an area somewhere between the untouchables and the people on the rise. In these communities, people had families, decent jobs, modest cars and the optimism to think of themselves as being happy. To these folks, there was nothing wrong with shopping or working at K-Mart, Wal-Mart, Family Dollar Stores and numerous other similar retail locations. Many could afford a few luxury items and they helped fill the less desirable, less costly seats at sporting events and live stage shows. But this was a level of society Marion could not comprehend anyone willingly sharing.

What went unstated, probably unnoticed, about Marion was a condition experienced by many of the divorcees who had managed to remain sans husbands within the small social circle that was considered the elite of Big D. She was intensely lonely. That was why she invited Carol Bryan, her newest client, to share her home while Carol searched for a suitable and permanent place to live. Carol was spending her first week in the city with her middle daughter, but her daughter's apartment was small. Since Marion seemed to be as vivacious and outgoing as she was and was closer in age, which seemed to give them much in common, Carol agreed.

The relationship between the two women seemed, if not ideal, at least workable. There was much that was troubling about Marion—the harsh, demanding tone of her voice, the slightly devilish look of her blue eyes, the "I'll do anything for you," phoniness of her salesperson's persona. At the same time there was something caring and real about the woman, as though she knew she was playing dress-up and that her less desirable traits could be shed as easily as her designer suits. Besides, Carol reasoned, an offbeat, hyper-aggressive friend in a strange, big city was better than no friend at all.

At first the friendship was easy for Carol. Marion seemed to radiate constant happiness, always laughing, always appearing to give undivided attention to the person with whom she was speaking. Her enthusiasm appeared to be as genuine as that of a freelance cheerleader, moving from team to team, seeming to give 100 percent support even as she went from one rival to another.

Marion also represented a transition for Carol. They had made contact through the real estate agency before Carol came to Dallas. There had been telephone calls, the exchange of letters and a bombardment of brochures about living in Dallas with the help of the realty company for which Marion worked.

Opportunism and compassion, though, forged the greatest bond between the two women. The salesperson in Marion wanted her commission when she helped Carol locate a place to live and a business in which to invest.

At this point in her life, Carol understood what many Dallas women did not. Marriage needed to be taken more seriously than living the "good life." She had made mistakes, she knew, and while her bad experiences were not all of her doing, she had matured and knew that marriage had to be approached with cool, rational analysis as much as with feelings of attraction and sexual desire. She had no intention of applying the Dallas standard for men—money, power and social position. Carol wanted to understand why she had failures in her past relationships, where she could change things and where she could not. She wanted to approach her next relationship with understanding and maturity so there would be no crisis great enough to destroy it. As much as possible, she wanted to be psychologically ready to weather any marital storm with a new husband an equal partner in the bad and the good. She would commit to a new relationship only when she was certain she had made as much effort as possible to assure such a result. Dallas, near her daughters, seemed the ideal location to begin this process.

Marion was convincing enough that Carol spent a week with her daughter, then moved in with the real estate agent for two more weeks. Unlike Marion, Carol was comfortable being alone. A military wife spends more time on her own than with her husband. Carol craved the love and companionship of a man, but unlike Marion, she did not need another person to help her combat loneliness.

Part of Marion's problem was her personal history. She had deeply loved her husband of twenty years, never suspecting his infidelity. His request for a divorce was unexpected and far more painful than if the deterioration in their relationship had been evident prior to his moving out. Worse, Marion had never been truly alone and the lack of another person in her home was extremely upsetting. Marion feared the city as much as she embraced it. She feared the crime she read about in the papers and heard about from the neighbors. She feared the unknown and, even more, she feared facing it alone.

Marion intensified her efforts to find her new friend the right home for her. She wanted Carol in a safe, upscale area. It took thirty tries, but she eventually found not only the perfect location, but also a landlord who would give a lease for just six months to a year, allowing Carol to leave fairly quickly if she decided she wasn't happy there.

Marion knew what she was doing. She was sure there were no problems with the location and Carol would be happy there. Most of the homes in the complex were condominiums, some owner occupied and some rented as investments. Adding to the image of quality and safety was the fact that a member of the family that owned the development, among many others, had chosen to buy one of the condominiums for his own home.

There was a sense of peace and quiet to the complex that bordered the Prestonwood Country Club. Several of the condominium patios were just five feet from a small creek that divided the lush wooded area of the complex and the golf course greens. Three sides of the complex were separated from the streets by a twelve-foot brick privacy wall that was lined with trees and tall bushes. The wall provided both security and a buffer against the street sounds from the nearby Lyndon Baines Johnson Freeway.

Across the street, also surrounded by a twelve-foot privacy wall, was an enclave with exclusive homes starting at $400,000. And on the other side of the golf course, five blocks away, was the most exclusive area in North Dallas. The houses were mansions cared for by both live-in and part-time staff members. The vast majority had swimming pools and tennis courts. A "starter" mansion ran $1.5 million. Selling prices as high as $8 million were common.

Marion knew this particular community was the right place for Carol. Here she could pursue her dream of starting her own business, for this was a terrific location for networking with the people who mattered. And if she developed the appropriate Dallas mentality, this was also the right location for seeking a man of influence and means to be her next husband. After all, Carol was blonde, pretty and vibrant. Marion knew Carol would be noticed jogging through the neighborhood every morning or exercising on the tennis court or in the swimming pool. She would be seen as the ideal trophy wife. Marion smiled—she enjoyed being a matchmaker.

THERE ARE MANY ways people develop a comfort level for themselves. Some achieve it by living in the same community all their lives. They are born in one town, go to school there, marry a local man or woman, settle in a familiar neighborhood, get a job and/or raise a family and ultimately retire in the same home or one close-by. They are the pillars of whatever religious institution they attend. They are enthusiastic supporters of local schools and local merchants. And they patronize local recreation and entertainment facilities on weekends and when going out for a night on the town.

Military wives seldom establish roots the way other people do. Instead, they must find their own means of making themselves comfortable. For Carol, comfort came from surrounding herself with her possessions in each new home. She could walk through new rooms in a new house in a new city and see familiar family photographs, artwork, figurines and the like. The outside structure might be unfamiliar, but inside would be her treasured crystal, china and silver, all collected over the course of thirty years. Even clothing was retained, her figure changing little over the years. She treasured the new and the stylish, but she also kept a link to the past for its familiarity. And when styles returned, she often found she could wear the "latest trend" once more.

The first few days in her new Dallas condominium were miserable ones. She had more furniture than fit the rooms and it had not been properly arranged. The possessions that gave her comfort remained in boxes. Her deepest friendships, ones she had left behind in California, North Carolina and Tennessee, could now be conducted only through letters and long distance telephone calls. And the children were all busy with their own lives.

"I started crying as I looked at the stark, still bare walls and rooms. I moved to Dallas to be there for my girls and to find out what I wanted to do in life. I realized that for the first seventeen years of my life I had lived with my parents and siblings. For over twenty years I had been married. It was only now, with all the children grown, that I was truly alone. I had to remind myself that this was another adventure. I planned to paint, wallpaper and change the colors that surrounded me. I used decoration to fight what I later came to think of as homesickness for places I had never considered my home."

The sadness lasted only a few weeks. Then Carol plunged into turning the sterile-looking condo into a place that was once again home. She called no one. She went out only for supplies. Finally she sat down and rested, content with her decorating efforts. Soon there was an insistent

knock at the door. Marion had been so worried about Carol
that she had demanded that the complex manager let her
inside to be certain Carol was safe.

"I have been worried sick about you," Marion said. "You
haven't answered the phone. I thought you were dead.
Why haven't you called?" And then she saw what Carol
had done and smiled. She understood.

"I'll get some housewarming wine and we'll go out to
dinner!" Marion said excitedly. "Let's have a party to celebrate."

> He noticed the woman, as did so many other peo-
> ple in the area. She lived in the kind of neighborhood
> that he coveted and she had the perfect blonde hair
> and figure that made women's heads turn with jeal-
> ousy and men's with desire. He watched her run
> from her front door to the golf course, legs taut and
> shapely, arms pumping, chest breathing deeply, her
> eyes blue and saucer-like. The woman was Dallas at
> its best.
>   He followed her when he could, his appearance so
> familiar in the neighborhood that no one thought
> twice when they saw him. He found an opportunity to
> peek in her window. Even though the blinds were
> closed, the cord holes formed tiny openings through
> which he could see. He had used that trick many
> times and now he used it with her.
>   He saw the paintings, the fine crystal and the
> prized possessions so artistically displayed. They
> were the type of tasteful accessories he knew he
> would have if he had the money and opportunity to
> acquire them. Certainly he had learned to recognize
> such quality when he was burglarizing a home. But
> he did not want to burglarize this woman's place.
> Not any more than he had to. She was a treasure of
> her own, the type of woman who every man would
> consider his prized possession. That she did not
> seem to have a man in her life when he followed her
> or looked inside her home reassured him that he had
> a chance for a relationship with her. His history,

however, reminded him that in order to love her, he would have to possess her. And in order to possess her, he would have to crush the very spirit that made her so desirable, so deserving of the best, so. . . .

Soon it would be time to meet her. Soon it would be time to enter the home in which he so furtively looked whenever possible. Soon he would need to put on his ski mask, pocket his handgun and show the bitch what a real man was like.

Marion had changed her attitude about Carol's life the moment she saw the finished interior of the condominium. On her second visit she walked from shelf to shelf, cabinet to closet, opening drawers, lifting various objects, touching everything and talking endlessly. "I can't believe this is the same place. This is beautiful. I guess you *are* going to stay. I mean, how could you live anywhere but Dallas? I knew you had taste when I first laid eyes on you."

"I have to launch a business in a couple of months," Carol told Marion when she could finally remind her of the next step she needed to take. "I've got to open that boutique."

Marion laughed. "Girl, this is the first of October! You're dreaming. Try to be more realistic."

But Carol had her plan. With Marion's help, she interviewed business brokers and searched for retail space. Unfortunately, the brokers were either more familiar with Dallas than she was or they could not think in terms of a small business. The first three with whom she spoke explained that between their fees and the cost of start-up, she would need to spend nearly $100,000, which meant there would be little money remaining for operating expenses.

Carol was convinced the brokers were speaking nonsense. She also knew that using them had been an expensive lesson about starting a small business. She sent each a polite letter thanking him for his help, explaining that his service would not be needed further at this time. She was determined to work alone, even if it took a little longer to become established.

The plan to open by December, a plan both Marion and an attorney Carol located and trusted, was unrealistic. Texas was not especially hospitable to new business. There was no rush in the handling of permits, licenses and contracts as might have been expected in other communities. It seemed as though if a business did not already exist in Dallas, there was no urgent need to open it. The bureaucrats would do the work as they got around to it, no matter how long that took. The only high spot was when Carol entered a shop in Highland Park where Sophie, an older Russian immigrant, was working. Carol was impressed with the woman and asked if she would consider coming to work for her. Sophie, with a delightful accent, great charm and a gentle yet aggressive sales approach, took to Carol immediately. "I would enjoy helping you with your new business provided I don't have to start work until after the January sales."

By November, Carol accepted the fact that though she would eventually open a boutique, she might have to find secretarial or other temp work for a few months while the legal and business issues were resolved. She did not want to deplete her savings and it appeared that it would take more time than she had anticipated before she could open a shop. Still, she daydreamed about her future business success.

She made a few more acquaintances, including Norwood Dixon, a businessman who provided her with sound advice concerning the location of galleries and their relative success rate. He was quiet, respectful, extremely gentle and devoted to his religion. Though Carol didn't find herself attracted to him, she liked him and was glad to have someone with whom she could discuss art at social gatherings.

CHAPTER 7

SEXUAL FANTASIES AND SAVAGE REALITIES

He rarely spoke about his fantasies. There was no one to tell except the police and he wasn't about to do that. But the fantasies encouraged him, made him feel comfortable and confident moving from spotting a woman on the street, to following her, to "window peeping" and, finally, to entering her home.

In Carol's case, the fantasy was about her sexuality. Carol was a beautiful woman who thoroughly enjoyed sex with the right man. But she did not need sex, as some people do, like a chain smoker or an alcoholic. She did not feel the need to relieve sexual tension when she was not involved in a committed relationship. It was her love for a man that aroused her. And she did not own what are commonly called "sex toys" either when apart from her husband or now, divorced. But in the man's fantasy, the woman he desired would pleasure herself in front of his prying eyes. It wasn't true, of course.

He was a stalker. He had been watching as Carol moved in and then saw her running. He had followed her as he followed other women who lived in the same condominium complex. He knew her car, where

*she went and some of her friends. He was aware that
her friend Marion came by with some frequency and
had even planned a burglary of Marion's home in
order to gain the valuable jewelry—multi-carat diamond rings she inherited from her mother, expensive
earrings and the like—she flashed when she went
out. However, his primary attention was focused
upon Carol and he used whatever fantasies he
needed to further arouse himself to action.*

*"I came back on November seventh and, as far as
the time, oh, it was probably three in the morning I
believe. About two or three in the morning when I
entered Carol's residence. I watched her enter her
bedroom and get ready for bed. I left and came back
about an hour later assuming she was sound asleep
by then. That's when I took the screen off quietly and
I pried the window up. I entered the residence and
basically did the same thing [I did to the other vic-
tims]. I covered her mouth and told her, you know, if
she made any kind of noise or sound that I would,
you know, that I would . . . that I had a pistol at
Carol's head, which I can't remember if I had one or
not. Cause sometimes I would say I had one and then
didn't have one. I just used my finger up to, you
know, an individual's head and they could feel the
solidness and they would think it was a pistol. But I
can't recall if I had the pistol with me or not at that
time. But, anyway I must have told her I had a pistol
and she believed that I had one, and so she cooperated." The confession went on to to describe in detail
how the rapist "seduced" his victim, Carol Bryan.*

Carol's frightening thoughts were quite different.

"There was the weight, the heavy feeling. My first
thought was trying to figure out why my head hurt, why
there was pressure and pain. Then I heard a man's voice."

"Wake up. Can you hear me? Wake up."

Something or someone was shaking Carol, but she
couldn't see. Everything was black.

"Wake up. Wake up." The voice again. So close. She was awake, yet everything was dark. The weight on her torso felt heavier. Something was pressing into her temple. She felt her temple pulsating.

"Wake up!"

Her eyes were open. "I was sure of that, but I couldn't see. I realized that the weight on me was a body. I felt something cold against my temple, the side of my face . . . There was a towel over my face. I was suddenly very awake and intensely nauseated."

There was the voice again. "Don't make a sound or I'll blow your head off."

Silence. The hard, cold object pressing against her temple was a gun. She knew that instinctively. She had been around too many over the years.

Then the voice again, demanding, "Can you hear me?"

Carol didn't speak. She just nodded her head, yes. She didn't want to upset whoever it was, but this time the voice was intensely angry. His words hissed at her through clenched teeth. It was as though he wanted to explode, to tear at her flesh, and was desperately trying to restrain himself from the almost overwhelming urge.

"Don't move or I'll kill you!" he said.

His face, covered by a dark ski mask was no more than an inch or two from her face. Hot, acidic liquid rushed up her throat. She fought for control, fought to swallow the foulness she nearly regurgitated. Anything might make him pull the trigger and kill her. No matter what might happen, she was certain she did not want to die. Her children needed her. She had too much yet to do in life to let this monster destroy her.

For a moment Carol remembered flypaper, the ultra sticky traps her grandmother had hung from the porch. Carol had been a small child then, watching fascinated as flies would buzz about the hanging paper, land, then frantically beat their wings in a desperate effort to escape the sticky trap. The more the fly fought, the more it became enmeshed. Once Carol had touched the paper, then found removing it from her finger a near impossibility. She understood how deadly the flypaper must be for something so tiny as the winged insects it was meant to trap. And now this man was the trap and she the fly.

What happened next would never be clearly remembered in its entirety. Carol's face was covered, adding to the terror.

"Can you hear me? Don't make a sound or I'll blow your head off. Do you understand me?"

Carol nodded her head yes.

"Don't move or I will kill you," he said. The gun remained against her head, but he shifted, pulling the sheet from her body. He put his hand on her breast, then began talking.

He moved the cloth from her face. Because her eyes were now accustomed to darkness, she saw the outline of his head, a bristle of moustache protruding through the knit-fabric, dark-colored ski mask. He put his mouth on hers. There was a terrible odor about him as he attempted to kiss her. An odor like a dead animal—something rotted and left in the sun. He kept rubbing his hand on her breasts and stomach, trying to kiss her, but not concentrating on kissing as he looked at her body. "Do you work out at a gym?" he asked. Not waiting for a response, he said, "You have a beautiful body. Your skin is so smooth. You are pretty, aren't you?"

The conversation was strange, as though he could make her feel good about what was happening by complimenting her. "Can you hear me?" he asked again when she didn't respond. She nodded yes and he said, "Can't you talk?"

Her throat was sore, hoarse. "Why are you doing this?"

"I've been watching you for a long time. You are beautiful. I wanted to be near you so I watched you."

Sometime in the course of his talking while still holding the gun to her head, he took Carol's hand and put it on his penis, saying, "Isn't that what you want?"

She shook her head no.

He said, "Once you have it, you will always want it."

Carol began to tremble, then shake all over.

He pulled away from her and said, "I'm sorry." Still

holding the gun, he pulled her back to him and went on, "I don't want to hurt you. Don't cry." Yet it was as he spoke that he began to rape her.

"You would never look at me if you saw me in the daytime," he said during one of the times when he stopped hurting her.

"What's your name?" she asked. "Please take the mask off."

He chuckled and said, "I can't do that."

Carol asked him why he was doing this. That was when he showed his anger, pulled her to him and forced himself into her again, never answering, all the while holding the gun. When he finished, he rolled over on his back and put the gun on the night table. He must have felt her starting to move toward it, because he quickly said, "Don't move. Don't make a sound. And don't try anything or I'll kill you." Then he picked the gun up.

Carol lay very still, collecting her thoughts. "Why would you want to kill me?"

"I'll only do that if you try to get away from me or scream or do anything."

"I won't do anything. Just don't kill me, because I'm the mother of three girls."

Then he began talking as if they were old friends holding an ordinary conversation. "I've watched you through your window. I've been in your house. I see the people who come to visit you. I follow you in your car and I think you are beautiful. I want to be your friend."

"If you wanted to be my friend, why didn't you just walk up to me and introduce yourself or have someone introduce you? If you wanted me to be a friend, you would never have harmed or threatened me."

Her words angered him. He grabbed her and raped her again.

She felt nothing. When he was finished, he pulled away from her and she began to shake. Carol shook so much, her teeth began to chatter, even though it was a warm morning with the temperature in the bedroom near seventy degrees.

He spun the memories his own insidious way.

"And so I lay there afterwards with Carol and talked to her for a while. And we were just lying there talking and she just said, 'I can't believe that you are doing something like this. You seem like a nice guy and you sound like a nice guy, and you're just so nonviolent. . . . ' "

He took her hand in his and again said, "I'm sorry." He stood over her, his frame outlined by light coming through the doorway, weak sunlight from the breaking dawn. More light came from the streetlight that was about fifty feet from the patio outside her bedroom.

He spoke sternly. "Be still. Don't move." He pulled the top sheet over Carol, covering her from head to toe like a body in the morgue. It was an image that would return again and again, horrifying her. Then he backed away.

Carol feared she would soon be dead. She felt certain he was going to kill her. She could not see that he was moving away from the bed. She whispered, "Please, don't hurt me."

She heard him chuckle. She wanted to see the creature that was going to kill her before she died so she slowly raised her left hand under the sheet and pulled the edge from her eyes. She could only see, framed in the doorway, the dark outline of a man-thing with wide shoulders.

With the gun still in his hand, he called out, "Do not move. Do not make a sound. I'll be watching you and if you call the police, I'll kill you."

In a whispering voice she pleaded, "Please don't kill me. You will hurt my children more than me. I won't do anything." He backed out the door, making not a sound as he disappeared.

"When I left Carol's residence I was on my way to get my vehicle, which was parked about three blocks away and I noticed a resident of Carol's complex coming out of his front door. At that time it was about five or five-thirty in the morning when I noticed the resident. He came out of his residence and went jogging. I had been to that certain residence before and

I knew that there was a lady there. She was around my age 'cause I window-peeked that window before. But anyway, I was assuming that he was going to be jogging for a little while so I believed that he left the front door open, which he did. I entered his residence and basically did the same thing, sexually assaulting her in the same pattern as previous with Carol Bryan. But I just spent about five minutes max with this resident, because I knew her husband was out jogging."

Carol lay in her bed, dazed, uncomprehending. She drifted in and out of a conscious state, then awakened to silence. For a few moments she lay still, unfeeling. Carol wasn't sure how long she lay there before she got up. Then, as though touched by fire, she jolted upright in bed and began screaming. Her battered flesh felt alive with flames, the raw bruises burning. She screamed louder and louder, pleading with God to put out the fire.

The screams became sobs as she curled into a fetal position, then realized she had to move, to slide down the nearby hill onto the soft, cool grass that would cool her skin.

Not a hill. A carpet. Soft, though. Cool in its own right. Like clouds.

Floating. She felt herself floating. Not grass or carpet, but clouds. She began to move through them, then felt the bile rise in her throat, again trying to stop the vomit, but this time because she knew she would pass out and drown in the liquid.

On the floor, on her hands and knees, she tried to stand, her body limp, her legs seemingly devoid of bones capable of supporting her.

Slowly, inch by inch, Carol moved across the carpeted floor to the bathroom with its smooth, cold tile. She lay her cheek against it, finding comfort in the coolness just before rising up and trying to reach the toilet before the vomiting began. Too slow, too weak, she drenched the floor and the walls in the waste that rose from her stomach.

Dry heaves came next, a relief after several minutes

when she thought her body would explode. When she could, she lay her head against a dry section of tile, drifting almost to sleep, the cold easing the flames inside her head.

Finally Carol reached the shower, crawled in and turned on the water, letting it beat against her numbed flesh. She took soap and lathered herself. When it washed down the drain, she used more soap, then more still. Over and over she scrubbed her flesh, cleaning every inch. The smell of the intruder clogged her nostrils and she wondered if she would ever smell anything else.

The fragrance of the soap was as strong as the most aromatic flower, yet it did little to free her from the sensory memory of the foul flesh that had overwhelmed her. Later she would learn that she should not have showered. Later she would learn that the police like to have all possible evidence, including that which could be removed from her skin and from inside her vagina. Later she would learn that she should have called the police and let their experts deal with the concerns of her body. But even if she had known the "right" thing to do, even if she had posted a list of procedures for just such an emergency, nothing would have changed. She was desperate to rid herself of the rapist's stench.

Finally, when her body was red from scrubbing, Carol dried herself and put on clothes. Then she walked around the apartment, checking doors and windows. They were locked, as if what she had experienced was a nightmare. No one had come or gone from the door. None of the windows were open. Nothing seemed to be missing. "I later learned he had gone through the contents of my purse and wallet before he woke me for the attack." Finally, certain her apartment was safe again, Carol called Norwood Dixon.

"I don't know why I called him and not the police." Somehow she knew that if she called Norwood, he would come to help her, asking no questions until she was ready to volunteer information about what had happened.

Carol called him around 6:00 A.M. He arrived at her condo a few minutes later. He stared at her. "What's happened, Carol? Your face is white as a sheet and you're shaking."

She was staring back at him without really seeing. She seemed like a lost waif he could barely recognize. She kept swaying as she struggled to stand, needing him to help her to the car. She talked in mumbled, incoherent sentences, trying to tell him what had happened. He drove her to the hospital and took her inside the emergency room.

Everything about that day was a blur to Carol.

THE PROCEDURES WERE routine, clinical and essential. To some observers, a rape victim is nothing more than the sum of her violated parts. Was she struck? Check for bruises. Was she bound? Check for rope burn or other signs that either she was tightly secured or struggled for freedom. Was she scratched? Did she bleed? Was there a struggle? What remains? Pubic hairs? Saliva? Semer? Sperm? Was the man a secretor or non-secretor of his blood type in his saliva? Are there stains on clothing, bedding or elsewhere? Had the woman been sexually active in the time shortly before the rape? Can the boyfriend or husband be eliminated as a possible rapist? What is the alleged victim's demeanor?

Carol was treated at Parkland Memorial Hospital, Dallas' primary center for emergency care and the place where President John F. Kennedy was taken when shot many years earlier. Hospital rape protocols were still evolving when Carol Bryan was raped.

The police were also just beginning to be sensitive to the victims of rape. Some of the old timers thought that there could be no crime of sexual violence unless the woman was battered or murdered. The less outward violence in evidence, the less they wanted to believe she had been a victim. Adding to the lack of compassion was the impersonal nature of the police report, officially titled Dallas Police Department Offense Incident Report.

The officer responding was identified by name—"Runnels, Gerald 5309"—and other pertinent data: "Beat: 612 Watch: 1." Then came the victim's name—"Bryan, Carol, Lee" and her address on Arapaho. Her unit was identified, as was her telephone number.

Offense/Incident: Agg[ravated] Sexual Assault UCR Code 1:02111 2:02111

"M/O: Masked susp[ect] entered unlocked window, pulled gun, sexually assaulted comp[lainant]

There was more listed, including that a private individual took the victim to Parkland. Then, in an understatement ignoring the psychological, the report states:

"Injuries: Sexually Assaulted   Cond[ition]:Good

-NARRATIVE-

"Officer was advised by complainant that at approximately 0300 hours 11-7 she was alone in her apartment asleep when the above described suspect entered into her apartment through the unlocked rear bedroom window. [The report was mistaken. The window was locked and pried open.] Suspect laid on top of complainant and put a small caliber automatic weapon to the left side of her head. Suspect then began sexually assaulting complainant.

"Complainant stated that suspect did inject his penis into her vagina but according to complainant she is unsure if suspect ejaculated or not. Complainant stated that the sex act lasted for approximately two hours. Complainant stated that during the entire time the suspect covered her face with a towel to prevent her from seeing him. Complainant stated that she believed the suspect had been in her apartment for some time based on what suspect advised her.

"Complainant stated suspect advised her that he had been watching her for some time and was very attracted to her. Complainant stated that suspect was very apologetic to her. Suspect and complainant talked casually for approximately thirty minutes after she was assaulted. Complainant stated the suspect left out the rear door. [Another report mistake. The man left out the front door.] Complainant was examined at PMH by Dr. Cunningham."

There was nothing in the report that would indicate Carol Bryan's nightmare was just beginning.

CHAPTER 8

MIXED MESSAGES

CAROL BRYAN WOULD be designated "Victim 23" on the Dallas Police Department's records but, of course, that number was uncertain. Many thought the diabolical rapist who had so nimbly eluded detection had preyed on many more women and they knew his violence was escalating. Some women would say they were not only raped but also pistol-whipped and brutalized by the man wearing a ski mask, carrying a handgun and covering the faces of his victims. And some would not or could not speak about the brutal attacks they endured.

Calling Carol Bryan "Victim 23" was probably meant to be a kindness of sorts. Sexual assault is the only crime in which many people feel that the victim would not want to be identified, since she would experience greater shame than the perpetrator. Some people fantasize that rape is an "impossible" crime unless the victim is found physically battered or restrained and helpless. There have been police academy instructors who started their talks about the legal definition of rape with a personal aside: "I believe in the theory of the Coke bottle and the soda straw. So long as the Coke bottle is moving, you can't insert the soda straw." The growing number of women attending the academies reduced the expression of this blatant bias, but the attitude frequently remained. Even when police departments began specially training officers to handle the early stages of a rape investigation, choosing young men and women of sensitivity and caring, these young officers often remained the exceptions.

Dallas was no anomaly to the skeptical attitudes toward rape victims. That was why victim advocates such as Patsy Day, founder of Victims Outreach, began teaching at the police academy. She wanted the young soon-to-be officers sensitive to the needs of the victim. The men and women with whom she spoke prior to their going on the streets rarely perpetuated old stereotypes and myths. They were mostly sensitive, caring and truly helpful. But they were not yet the people in charge. They were still finding their own way, often with an older partner whose insensitive attitude was a not uncommon response when a woman called for help after experiencing sexual violence.

Ironically, the real beneficiary of the anonymity of the victims was the Dallas Chamber of Commerce, which continued its efforts to attract tourism and new corporate headquarters. Statistically, Dallas had become the violent crime capital of the nation. However, so long as victims were either seen as anonymous numbers or had addresses from the low income sections of the city, the negative publicity had limited impact.

JOURNALISM PROFESSORS DELIGHT in noting a particular truism to their students every semester. The best thing about newspapers is that they are filled with bad news. People like to read about what is unfamiliar, what is different from their experiences. Most people lead lives that are not shattered by unexpected violence. Gunshots do not send bullets exploding through their windows or striking their sleeping children. Kidnappers do not lay in prey in the parking lots of their shopping malls. They are not stripped of valuables on their jobs or in the restaurants where they dine. And their homes are not invaded by masked men with guns. The newspapers are filled with bad news, because bad news is what is different.

Until you become a victim.

Carol Bryan became a victim, the exception to the majority of residents of the city of Dallas. The city led the nation in violent crimes. Yet given the number of people who lived in town homes, apartments and single family dwellings, the people who commuted into Dallas to work each day and play each night, the tourists and the business travelers, very few ever directly experienced violence. More important from a law enforcement perspective, the minority of citizens who committed crimes were repeat offenders, men and some women who went through the revolving door of justice, attacking over and over again.

None of these realities mattered for Carol Bryan, other than that she was a victim of an assault by a man neither she nor the police could as yet identify. Almost as difficult emotionally was Carol's status as an outsider in Dallas. Her friends, the people on whom she needed to rely in the immediate aftermath of one of the most terrifying crimes anyone can endure, were all somewhere else. Several of them would likely have left their homes and families to rush to her side had they known she had been attacked, but she chose not to tell them. In her horror and confusion, she went back to the psychological modus operandi of the career military wife. You handle your own problems within your own community. The trouble was that, even with the kindness of Norwood Dixon, Carol Bryan had become a community of one.

There were resources of sorts, but in the initial time immediately after the trauma, all was a blur. The drive to Parkland Memorial Hospital probably took thirty minutes. Carol remembered none of it.

There was a nurse, a doctor and police officers who talked with her. She saw them. She answered their questions. But in the immediate aftermath of the experience, she could remember none of their faces and too few of their words to put together a coherent thought.

Carol was suffering from traumatic amnesia, a condition

familiar to physicians and psychologists who have treated combat hardened military veterans. There was "shell shock" in World Wars I and II. There was Post-Traumatic Stress Syndrome for soldiers in Vietnam. They were the same manifestation. The mind temporarily erased what had been an intolerable experience, then allowed it to return in brief flashbacks in the days, weeks, months and years that would follow.

Carol would come to have those flashbacks. She would gradually remember bits and pieces of her living nightmare—the physical size of her assailant, his body structure when silhouetted in the night-light, a touch here, a word there, a scream . . . Most of the images would come at night. For some creatures, darkness is a friend, a time of safety when predators are far. Humans living in cities like Dallas tend to embrace the darkness, believing that when they are tucked away in their beds, they have nothing to fear. Night is a respite from the cares and stresses of the day . . . for some.

For centuries the guardians of the night—the lamplighters, the constables, the patrolling police officers—knew better. They would tell anyone who would listen that there are things a person will do in the darkness that he or she will never do in the daylight. Now Carol Bryan understood that concept in ways many others could not. Where once she had been open and trusting, much like a puppy that assumes all humans are good until shown to be otherwise, now she trusted no one. She could remember that she had been in Norwood's company, that he had represented safety, but she could not always remember the reason, nor would she call him to ask. Every face she saw during the day was a potential enemy, someone to be feared, to be considered unworthy of trust. Time made no sense to her, though she tried to handle all her personal business while the sun was bright in the sky. She just could not always remember the reason for such urgency, such anxiety.

Nights were impossible to handle. Sleep, when it came, lasted thirty minutes. She would awaken with the memory of the black mask, her body soaked with perspiration, her face and pillow wet with tears. Yet when she tried to put her nightmares into perspective, she could not. Everything disoriented her. She was frequently confused.

She had been a military wife. She told herself she could fend for herself. She had friends. She had daughters. She had . . . frightening visions that seemed to strike her again and again. The black mask. The figure in the doorway. The man she feared with all her being.

Her doctor felt Carol needed rest. He gave her tranquilizers and sleeping pills. Days and nights would pass as they always did. Except the hours moved slowly, especially at night, and the sedatives were worthless. Fear had a way of blocking all chemicals, of rendering useless whatever comfort drugs were supposed to bring.

Perhaps Carol could have called someone, reached out, returned to living. Spent time with her daughters. But she did not want to alarm them; even that was something more to hide from. She did not want to make more new friends and she really had no old ones in Dallas. Marion's aggression, abrasiveness and opinions that had once been so amusingly quirky—mildly endearing at best and tolerable at worst—were suddenly grating and annoying. Carol found reasons to keep herself aloof, becoming increasingly isolated and gradually removing herself from everyone and everything until most of her time was spent in the home that had been despoiled.

Carol told herself she would start seeing her daughters again as soon as she was calmer. She didn't want to frighten or worry them. She would stay in Dallas until her lease was up, she decided, then flee the city. Big D now stood for death, not only an emotional death, but the death of her dreams.

Reading helped. She found the largest, most interesting books she could locate, then immersed herself in the text. The outside world disappeared. The need for sleep vanished. She read page after page, book after book, letting exhaustion slowly overwhelm her until she fell asleep with the book in her hands. And if she was lucky, it was the story from the book that remained in her mind, temporarily shoving out the memories of the horror she had endured.

Sometimes she would remember happier days and the hope and optimism with which she had come to Dallas, searching for a better tomorrow. But then she would remember the terror and the emptiness in her heart and her life and she would begin to sob with such depth of emotion she could barely breathe.

Business plans were forgotten. She knew her life could not continue as it was, yet the upbeat expectations she held before the invasion of her home and violation of her body had disappeared. She had to earn money, if nothing else. Winter was coming and her lease would not be up until spring. She needed to begin looking ahead.

The first step towards moving forward occurred on a Saturday. Carol went to a travel agency, gathering books and brochures on every location that seemed interesting. She told herself that when her lease was up she would put everything she owned into storage and travel for a while. She would visit her mother in Ohio, friends in Tennessee and North Carolina and after that, perhaps go to New England and then on to Idaho and Montana. She had driven through many states over the years when she was a military wife, usually with the children and a limited time schedule. Now she would reward herself with the gift of time, staying in interesting places for as short or as long a period as she wanted.

At first nothing seemed to attract her, but she told herself to persevere. She looked at the books and brochures over and over. Finally, she decided. Montana appealed to her. She remembered driving through the state on her way to or from one of the many relocations she and her children had experienced. She recalled traveling a hundred miles without seeing so much as a bird. The occasional car that went by almost seemed out of place. But there were electric lines, telephone poles and other indications that people did, indeed, live in the sparsely populated, beautiful countryside. And the occasional town she encountered along the stretches of isolated road seemed almost magical.

She told herself Montana was a good place to go. She told herself she would be safe in Montana in the spring.

* * *

THERE WERE OTHER shocks motivating Carol's return to some semblance of normal life, not the least of which was her reflection in the mirror. There were days when she looked to herself like a drunk whose body had been so ravaged from malnutrition that she seemed near death. Her face was haggard, tired, pale and almost lifeless. There were stress lines around her mouth that seemed to appear only when she remembered the rape, then disappeared during those rare moments when she was distracted.

Carol wondered if what was happening to her was normal for someone who had been raped. She didn't know anyone who had been sexually assaulted. She was unaware that every day or two when she dragged herself outside, she passed an equally hurting neighbor, the second victim from that night of horrors.

Even the word "rape" was filled with mixed messages. Her attack had come at a time when rape was the most controversial of all crimes of violence.

Some people felt that rape was impossible if the woman struggled. For it to be termed rape, they needed to see battering. They needed to see black eyes, perhaps missing teeth. They wanted the woman to look like she had fought for her life in the middle of a combat zone. Bruises, contusions, discolored flesh, disheveled hair, dried blood around the nose and mouth—this was the acceptable aftermath of a claimed sexual assault. Anything less and they assumed that the sex was consensual or the woman invited the man to hurt her, that perhaps she secretly wanted it or even enjoyed it.

The psychological aspects of the crime were ignored by such ignorant skeptics. First the private domain of the victim was penetrated by the attacker's entry. Then came his surprise presence during the time of greatest helplessness—in bed asleep, in the shower preparing for the day or relaxing at the end of it or some other location where attack is not anticipated. Finally there was the assault, the deliberate penetration of an area that is considered so private that rituals for cleansing and lovemaking are a part of

many cultures. The rapist claims what he has no right to
consider viewing, much less touching. And the terror of the
victim who is being violated so many different ways in the
course of the attack is often overlooked.

The media often added to the problems of rape victims.
Rape is the only crime where the victim is sometimes
placed on a par with the victimizer. Her name is usually
withheld in the newspapers, though the man she accuses
will be identified. Her name is usually withheld from court
proceedings, even after the attacker is convicted by a jury
of his peers or admits to his crime(s) in open court. She
must be protected from being revealed. She must be protected from being disgraced, embarrassed, humiliated. And
though the victim may seek such privacy, the truth is that
all the restrictions add to the idea that the rape victim has
been stigmatized. She is not allowed to publicly express
her outrage, to damn her attacker, to join with others in ap-
plauding the fact that he is going behind bars. Yet such
public display of grief, anger and triumph would be encouraged if she had "only" been shot, stabbed, kidnapped,
battered or otherwise brutalized. Society's ambiguity towards a crime where the violence has a sexual component
only hurts the woman more.

Rape is sometimes used as a psychological weapon in
wartime when soldiers rape the enemies' civilian mothers,
wives, daughters and girlfriends as a way of challenging
the men they are fighting and demoralizing the population
as a whole. Worse, instead of loved ones and the community coming to the support of those who are so victimized,
the women and the children born of wartime rapes, they often shun them. The younger victims rarely marry and receive little or no counseling. In the eyes of others and often
in their own minds, they are despoiled.

Carol Bryan, not unlike these other women, convinced
herself that she had to try and recover almost entirely
silently and alone. There would be others she would eventually tell, especially within her immediate family, but not
yet, not now. In these present, trying moments, she was
alone.

* * *

WEEKS LATER, DESPITE her fears, both necessity and desire finally caused Carol to finish coming out of her cocoon. Her funds were dwindling. She needed to work so she took a job as an administrative assistant to an executive at Love Field, a Dallas airport. He hired a competent professional who performed flawlessly, like a robot. He never got to know the vivacious woman now hidden inside a protective shell. But that lack of knowledge did not matter. Carol found herself confronting the office politics of a less accomplished secretary who felt she should have been given the job. Normally Carol would have handled the office politics as a matter of course. Now so petty a battle seemed meaningless. She had no interest in being in the middle of such nonsense. Carol left after ninety days.

Equally difficult to cope with was her constant exhaustion. Carol was a high-energy individual who now dragged herself around as though she was experiencing the onset of flu. She knew she now had reason to fear AIDS and asked a doctor to give her a blood test. It was negative. Still terrified, she would continue to have blood tests every three to five months for the next five years.

SHE TRIED TO renew her religious faith, but Carol, like most, had never worshipped in what are often called the mega-churches that seemed to proliferate in the Dallas area. Carol's idea of a large congregation was one that could support several clergy, each with specially assigned tasks such as education, youth ministry, music and the like. She expected to have her choice among three, four or five Sunday services, with weekday activities ranging from Bible study to groups for singles, widows, the elderly and others. Carol had found in the past that despite the size and diversity of such congregations, the clergy and the parishioners made a point of being familiar with one another, like a large high school where the students might not know each other's names, but would recognize one another in shopping malls, at sporting events and other locations.

Attending a mega-church, she found, was like attending a sporting event where the spectators are nameless, faceless fillers of seats. They share an experience. They are swept up in the spiritual excitement of the moment. But just as fans rarely know any of the athletes, so the members of a mega-church rarely have a close personal relationship with the clergy. Instead, those who wish to get involved gravitate toward one or another group. They may join one of several choirs—gospel, traditional, youth, etc. They may participate in one of several Bible study programs. They may join with other members in going to area prisons or to help with food programs for the hungry.

Technically the clergy provide the leadership and guidance for the various programs. The reality of the mega-church is that it runs with both a paid and a volunteer lay staff. It is not unusual for a member to participate in several groups, including some as high profile as one of the choirs and never have the senior clergy know his or her name.

PEOPLE WHO ATTEND the mega-churches do so for as many reasons as people who attend storefront churches where congregations of twenty-five people are considered a good turnout. Some are drawn to what they feel is a spirit-filled ministry where they can be uplifted by the prayers of thousands. Others like the anonymity of so large a congregation. They want to be lost in the crowd, not having others know their problems, because most of the parishioners will have little more than a nodding acquaintance with them.

The isolation of the individual member can sometimes work to his or her advantage. A shy person in a smaller church is likely to stay in the background, attending worship, attending coffee hour, but not feeling comfortable with the more aggressive members who dominate committees and special events. A mega-church has enough members so that shy individuals can recognize kindred spirits and get together in a manner that is comfortable for them. They may shun the coffee hour and spend an hour or two with one another at a nearby inexpensive restaurant. They may avoid the regular Bible study and choose to meet in one another's homes. Whatever the case, it is the impersonal nature of the mega-church that gives them the opportunity to reach out to others.

Where a mega-church frequently fails is in a time of private crisis. The clergy will respond to a need when called. The clergy are available for all traditional rites of passage—birth, baptism, marriage, death and the like. But they rarely know when a member has an unspoken need caused by financial problems, family difficulties, drug and/or alcohol abuse or being the low-profile victim of a violent crime.

Carol Bryan had always been active in her religion. She had attended various churches over the years and continued to explore different Sunday services in Dallas. But Big D was the center of the world of mega-churches. There were churches that boasted 10,000 members, 15,000 members and more. They reached out through television. They broadcasted services on the radio. They had status based on their location and the wealth of their congregations and, in Big D, belonging to the right church was almost as important as shopping at the right branch of Neiman Marcus. What they did not have, at least for a woman trying to recover from a nightmare, was warmth. There was no special attention given to her as a newcomer. The ushers did not recognize that she was present for the first time. There was no chance to talk with the clergy. You could call the church office during the week to gain brochures. What you could not do was walk up to someone, tell the person you were hurting and expect them to do more than ask you to put your name on a prayer list. Then the members of the congregation who maintained a prayer circle could offer your name up to God throughout the week.

A true cry for help to a pastor undoubtedly would have gained a response. It was the love for others that often brought clergymen to their calling in the first place. But

Carol, like other strangers going to the mega-churches, was not encouraged to call the pastor. She, like other strangers, was even uncertain as to which clergy member would be the most sensitive to the problem. Thus, even when isolation after a trauma is not deliberate, it may be created and reinforced by the system nonetheless.

CHAPTER 9

ISOLATION

CAROL BRYAN FELT her isolation even more acutely as days passed. Her attempts to reconnect with her faith were failing and she still did not want to burden her daughters. She tried to call on her inner strength and independent nature, things that she had always valued and tried to pass on to her girls. Nevertheless, she moved about her daily tasks almost in a dazed state.

It was a Saturday morning in late December when Carol had washed a load of clothing as usual, put the wet clothes in the dryer and turned it on. After years of good service, going to Dallas was one trip too many for the appliances. The washer and dryer had both suffered an unusual amount of damage, but while the washer continued to work, Carol discovered to her frustration that the heating element of the dryer died one load too soon. Calls to three different repair services revealed that dryers all over Dallas seemed to be losing their heating elements, as though there was an epidemic rather than a single mechanical failure here and there. It would be two weeks before the earliest in-home appointment could be scheduled. Hanging up the phone after the third call, she burst into tears.

Even such a small frustration made her overreact these

days, she realized sadly. Fortunately, she remembered, the complex had its own laundry room for those residents who did not own their own equipment. Although she felt uncomfortable leaving her apartment, woodenly she placed all the wet clothes in a basket and carried them downstairs. In the laundry room, there was only one other resident, a woman Carol vaguely knew as Lorna. Feeling awkward, Carol forced herself to make small talk for a few moments.

The dryer had just started when a clean-cut, well-dressed man in a designer jogging suit entered the laundry room by the door near a soft drink machine.

"I hate to bother you," he added, "but do either of you have change for a dollar? I'm terribly thirsty and want to buy a Coke."

Lorna smiled at the man and said she lacked change. Then she said, "Carol, this is Gilbert."

Carol tried to smile, and while she lacked sufficient change, she had enough for a can of soda pop. She handed the man the money and said, "Here, have a Coke on me."

"I really appreciate this," he said, thanking her. He got his drink and left. Lorna said nothing further, but her introduction indicated they were probably friends.

SEVERAL DAYS LATER Carol was driving home from a job interview on the tollway south toward Mockingbird. As she checked the lane next to her before moving over to the exit, she noticed a white Lincoln. The male driver smiled and waved. She hesitated and then realizing it was a perfectly normal gesture, she smiled back, changed lanes and exited, stopping at a traffic light. A moment later there was a tapping at her car window. Startled, she began to tremble. Then she looked and there was Gilbert, the man she'd given money to in the laundry room, holding out his business card, smiling at her.

She let the window down enough to hear him. She felt safe enough, because there were cars all around her in rush hour traffic.

He smiled genially. "Hello, Carol. I'm the man you gave

Coke money to. I wanted to repay you," he said. "Take my card and come in for a free car wash."

The light changed. He got back in his car and she continued through the intersection, leaving the card on the seat next to her. By the time she returned home, she had forgotten all about it.

Carol loved the look of sleek cars and their design. She loved to watch them race. Her Cadillac was the best car she could afford, and she cared for it as though it was a showpiece. It was washed every weekend, waxed with far greater frequency than the polish makers recommended and she cleaned the interior every Saturday.

That Saturday, she cleaned out the Cadillac and found Gilbert's card. The business was a detailing company, an auto repair and cleaning service for cars, and the address was in the heart of downtown, near expensive office complexes. His name—Gilbert Escobedo—was printed as owner. On the back he had written "One free car wash" and he had signed his name. After a quick trip to the grocery store, health food store and pharmacy, Carol called the number on the card to schedule a car wash for the following Saturday. "I was told that I would have a ten A.M. appointment and that the car wash would arrange to pick up my car, leaving me with a loaner.

"I was intrigued by the offer. I had never heard of a car wash business giving customers a loaner car," Carol later recalled. "But this was Dallas, where an excess of service was often the only possible competitive edge."

A WEEK LATER, promptly at 10:00 A.M., there was a knock on Carol's door. "I looked through the peephole and could see the smiling face of the man I had met in the laundry room, the man who had given me his business card on the street. When I opened the door, he removed the blue baseball-style cap he was wearing, smiled a wide, friendly grin and said, 'Good morning. I hope I haven't disturbed you; I'm picking up your car for a full service wash.'"

He was so polite, so professional, it was almost humorous to Carol. She had come to hate Dallas and the people, but here was a guileless businessman, well dressed, thanking her for buying him a soft drink. Gilbert went on, "I've brought you a loaner car in case you have to do some errands. I'll have your car for a couple of hours. I parked near your car if you want to move it into your space when I leave."

Carol's heart began to pound as she nervously wondered how he knew where her car was parked. Then she remembered that he had seen her in the Cadillac when she was out driving and she had mentioned the Cadillac when she set the appointment. She breathed a sigh of relief.

"Do you live in the complex?" she asked Gil.

"Oh, no, ma'am." He shook his head and smiled shyly. "I have lots of friends and customers who live here, though. I live a few blocks away. Is it alright if I call you Carol?"

The polite formality in his attitude and tone were a welcome change from the usual Texas male. She had been introduced to him as Carol and even if he had forgotten her name after she gave him the Coke money, she had used her name when she made the appointment.

Gilbert appeared to be a true gentleman and given the neighborhood Carol lived in, perhaps such white-glove service for a potential long-term customer was appropriate. Certainly she appreciated it.

Carol walked with Gilbert to her white and blue Cadillac. He ran his hands across the surface with the gentleness and appreciation of someone admiring a finely tailored fabric. He obviously appreciated well made, well maintained cars. It was another plus in Carol's eyes.

"Real nice car, ma'am. You must take good care of it."

"Carol," she said and genuinely smiled for what felt like the first time in weeks. "And, yes, I do take good care of it. But I miss having a garage to keep it in."

Gilbert took out the keys to the loaner car, which he explained was his own vehicle. Carol expected to see something that was older but well maintained. Instead, it was a beautiful dark green Jaguar, a better car than she was giving him. He opened the door to reveal an immaculately clean interior of saddle leather and polished wood. Gilbert seemed delighted to show Carol how to turn on the radio, the air conditioning, the heat and the alarm. He showed her the controls for the window buttons and the turn signals.

For a moment, when he turned that happy, wide smile towards her, Carol expected Gilbert to suddenly explain that she could keep the car for just $2,000 down and payments of $500 per month. He was as enthusiastic as a car dealer with a pre-approved credit customer, but he wasn't selling anything. She realized that he was as proud of his car as Carol was of hers. He was giving her a loaner car that he wanted to make certain she could fully appreciate as well as drive properly.

"Here's the keys. Enjoy her. She's a nice car. I'll bring yours back at about four o'clock," he said.

For a moment, as Carol watched her Cadillac being carefully maneuvered out of the parking lot and onto the street, she relaxed and smiled. This man was being genuinely nice to her. He didn't have to leave her a loaner car. Paying for his soda hadn't been a big deal and his response seemed a little like overkill. At the same time, she had enough business insight to realize what he was doing. In a city where the quality of service was often less important to people than the specific stores in which they shopped and the cost of the merchandise carried within, attention to service was a way to win customer loyalty beyond the snob appeal. If she liked what he did when he returned her car, she would probably become a paying customer. If she liked the work. If he returned the car. . . .

Carol was suddenly terrified. The Jaguar was obviously stolen. Why else would it be left with her? This man, this stranger with a business card, had taken her precious Cadillac. He was a scam artist who stole cars!

She slumped onto the front seat of the Jaguar, certain she had lost her Cadillac, certain she would never see this man again. Then Carol realized that she was being foolish. She had never been so distrustful before the rape, had never feared someone based on the number of acts of kindness they performed.

Glancing at the passenger seat Carol noticed a well-worn

Bible. She picked it up and flipped it open. Book markers had been placed about the text and notes scribbled in the margins. The name on the front was "Gilbert H. Escobedo."

She sighed. He said his name was Gil, and the name on the Bible was the same as the name on the business card. The book was obviously well used. Maybe he . . .

"I forced myself to think rationally. I had made no friends since I was attacked. I assumed that everyone I met had my worst interests at heart. I realized that I had to start trusting people again. This was a legitimate businessman and instinctively I felt there was no risk. He wouldn't be driving a Jaguar, I told myself, if he wasn't legitimate."

Making the decision to trust was as far as Carol could go at that moment. She could not bring herself to take advantage of Gil's generosity, much as she once would have delighted in driving the expensive, high performance car. Instead, she placed the Bible back on the seat, climbed out and locked the car. Then she went back inside her apartment to pass the hours reading.

IT WAS 4:00 P.M. when Gilbert knocked on Carol's apartment door. He obviously valued promptness, a trait Carol also appreciated.

When she opened the door, he smiled in that warm, friendly manner of his. "Your car is ready. Please come see it." He reminded Carol of her daughters when they were little girls and would make a Mother's Day surprise in their elementary school art class. He was obviously proud of the work he did for others. However, when he spotted his car, he seemed slightly saddened. "Didn't you use the Jag?" he asked. "It's parked in the same space."

"No. I decided I would do my errands after you brought my car back. I wasn't comfortable driving your car, but I certainly appreciate your policy of providing for your clients. You must have happy customers."

Gil's face lit up, obviously pleased with her comments. Again she was reminded of a child eager to please. Not that she thought of him as a child, but it was an unsophisticated enthusiasm that was endearing and not something she had seen in the Dallas business community to which she had been exposed.

"Oh, yes, I have lots of satisfied customers. I personally inspect every car before it leaves the shop. I've got the best detailing service in town," he told her.

"Where is your shop?" Carol asked, momentarily forgetting.

"Downtown. I've got a great location. I get all the business people who work around there. There's even a bank vice president with whom I've become friendly who has me service all their repossessions. They number about sixty right now." He looked down at his shoes, blushing. "I guess I'm pretty successful."

Carol was embarrassed by his words. Of course, he had a good business. Of course, he was respectable. He drove an expensive car. He knew people in her complex. He knew important business people downtown. She told herself she should have been more trusting. She'd always known that most people were nice. She hated the fearful, hostile cynic she had become since the attack.

"Come feel this. It's like silk," he said, gently rubbing the palm of his hand over the finish of the car.

"It gleams," Carol told him, impressed. "The chrome looks like new. The glass is spotless. The interior leather glows."

"We waxed it," he said, beaming.

"But I thought it was just going for a car wash."

"Well, I wanted to repay you for your kindness to me. Don't find many people in the big city who care about other people. I just liked what you did and wanted to do something to say thank you and welcome you to Dallas."

For a moment she wondered how Gil knew she was new here. Her Cadillac had Texas plates and was registered in Dallas County. She'd taken care of that right after she moved to Dallas. Then she remembered the woman who introduced them in the laundry room. Lorna knew Carol was new to the city. Obviously she had mentioned to Gilbert the little of Carol's background Carol had shared with her. Embarrassed once again by her distrustful attitude, Carol quietly thanked him.

"It's been nice to meet you, Gil, but I've got to go. I have to do some errands before it gets dark." They exchanged keys, but as she started to walk away, he called, "Carol, where do you go to church?"

Again she was surprised until she remembered the Bible in the car. It was well used, not the type of Bible some people keep for show in their homes or dutifully take to church for reading one or two passages. Church was probably important to him. It was as natural for him to ask as it would be for her ex-husband to ask some youth walking around San Diego with an obvious military haircut and shoes which branch of the service he was in.

"I haven't found one I like yet," she told Gil. "I've gone to several but haven't decided which one I want to attend."

"Would you like to go to church with me and some of my friends?" he asked.

"Not right now, but I'll think about it." It was getting late. Carol didn't want to be out after dusk, but she couldn't tell this man that. She couldn't tell him that even though she had been raped in her home, it was as close to an island of safety as she was going to find. She wasn't ready to be out and about after dark. That was when she wanted to be in her protective box with the lights on and the doors and windows locked.

"It's big, but it's a real friendly church. Just down the street. I could come pick you up. I pick up several friends almost every Sunday."

Carol almost laughed at what she was hearing. Here was the first man who seemed to almost fit Marion's description of the type she should date—successful businessman living in the neighborhood and going to a mega-church with an extremely wealthy congregation. She'd be disappointed to hear Carol tell him no. "Not this Sunday, but thank you for asking. Perhaps another time."

GIL LOOKED DISAPPOINTED too, but Carol hurried him along by walking away. She got in her car and hurried to the nearest drug store. She had to get there and back home before dark. All she could think was that Gil had stayed too long. It wasn't his fault. It wasn't anyone's fault. The rest of the world functioned as Carol had functioned in the lifetime before the rape. But Carol had lost the ability to think clearly much of the time, especially when darkness was coming. She had learned that darkness was the enemy. She had learned that darkness held only evil.

At the store, she rushed down the aisles grabbing the things she needed. As she searched for the last item she needed in the store, a bath product, everything changed. Glancing out the large, plate glass window, Carol saw the sky change color as the sun began its slow descent and she felt a wave of panic. Suddenly, she was so overwhelmed by the selection of products she didn't know what to purchase. She'd bought such things dozens of times, perhaps hundreds of times in the past, but this time she only saw a sea of bottles in a multitude of sizes, aromas and prices. Some bottles that were all the same size had prices varying from five to ten dollars. Confused, Carol tried to read the labels, to see what the difference might be, but nothing made sense any more. Her adrenaline rushed, her heart rate increased. She began to sweat, looking about for possible escape routes. Finally, she grabbed a mid-size bottle and bolted for the cash register.

"My hands began to shake as I took out my purse and tried to figure out the money I needed to pay. Then I looked at the several bags of items and realized I was beginning to shake so hard I could not carry anything. I asked if someone in the store could help me."

The cashier asked a teenager who worked there to carry out her bags. "I must have looked ridiculous needing help, but I didn't care." The youth did as he was asked and Carol was so grateful, she tipped him five dollars. From the look on his face, it was the largest tip he had ever received for so simple a task.

Carol got in the car, locked the doors and windows, started the motor and then fled from the lot. By the time she turned into the condominium complex, shadows had formed from the setting sun and she wasn't certain that she'd be able to make it to her front door.

She parked the car and sat motionless for a moment.

Everything seemed quiet. Everything seemed safe. Finally, she got out of the car and, balancing the shopping bags in one arm, looked at her front door. She stared at the door's lock and aimed her key. Then she stepped away from the car, slammed the door closed and started to run. It was no more than fifty feet from the car door to the house door and she covered the distance like an Olympic athlete testing herself against world class competition.

Finally she reached the front door, shaking. She held the key in her hand, pointing it forward like a dagger. Carol inserted the key in the lock then paused to look into the shadows. She watched for movement, watched for something out of the ordinary. "I was certain the rapist was watching me. I was certain he was waiting for . . . I don't know what. The police told me about other rapes. He did his violence and moved on. It was over. I was history. But I couldn't accept that. He had said he'd still be watching me and would kill me if I talked to the police. I never thought such violence could touch my life and when it did, I was equally certain that I would never again be safe."

In seconds Carol was inside. "I locked the doors, checked the windows, walked through the house and made certain I was alone. Then I set down the bag and went into the bathroom, glancing in the mirror and saw again a stranger so upsetting, I almost forgot it was me. My face, which had looked fine when I put on make-up that morning, was again drawn, haggard. The stress was destroying my appearance as it had destroyed my sense of personal safety." Horrified by how much the assailant had taken from her, how lingering his grip, she backed against the wall, slid to the floor and began to sob.

CHAPTER 10

POLICE WORK

THERE IS AN image of big city police work that is fostered by television and the movies. A major crime occurs and the police mount an aggressive, concerted action to resolve the matter, help the victims and stop the bad guys. Beat patrol officers and experienced detectives begin talking with informants in bars, during secret telephone conversations and in the late night shadows of shuttered downtowns or low cost apartment projects. Other detectives use computer skills, court-ordered wiretaps, round-the-clock surveillance with multiple cars whenever someone has to be followed. Helicopters take to the sky, slowly cruising over neighborhoods, as silent and deadly as Batman poised on the roof of a building in Gotham City. Newspapers print information and hot lines for the public to call. Area business leaders post rewards. And within a few days or weeks at the most, the bad guys are caught.

In real life, whatever evidence and eyewitness accounts are gathered in the first ten minutes after investigators arrive at the scene of a major crime often determine whether or not the case is going to be solved. Eyewitnesses, others who remember the sounds of voices, church bells, trash haulers and the like, trace evidence and numerous other items all help reconstruct what took place and help to identify the perpetrator. Not that the criminal will be caught so easily. It might be days, weeks, months or more before the perpetrator is brought to justice. But when the prosecutor walks into the courtroom, it is the evidence gathered in those early minutes that greatly determines success or failure before a jury.

A task force—a group of officers and technical experts assembled to devote most or all of their working time to a single criminal or type of crime—also helps bring lawbreakers to justice. The task force constantly reviews information gained by talking with neighbors where the crime was committed, answering hot line calls, listening to informants and reading documents prepared by scientific investigators studying trace evidence connected with the crime. Fingerprint analysis, semen analysis, blood analysis, hair and fiber analysis, tire tread analysis, DNA analysis and similar forensic concerns all are thrown into the mix, gradually narrowing the investigation until a likely suspect has been identified.

At least that seems to be the approach often shown on television. Certainly it is an ideal occasionally found in the largest of police departments, though never on every case. But none of this happened in Dallas. There were too few officers, too little equipment and too many crimes to put together the kind of investigation the public has been misled by television to believe always occurs when a large American city has a problem like a serial rapist.

The closest the Dallas Police Department could come to a task force was a group of men and women who were responding to some of the major crimes, then regularly trying to review what they knew with each other. The Ski Mask Rapist, as Carol Bryan's attacker was nicknamed, was among the individuals being studied. But nothing in his method of operation indicated a pattern that would allow police to anticipate his next assault or uncover the identity of the predator. There was no way to saturate North Dallas with plainclothes officers and unmarked patrol cars, all looking for a man with a ski mask, a gun and a lust for raping attractive, well-to-do blondes. There was no way to determine when an attack would occur, because there was no one particular time he seemed to function. He preferred the dark, because most criminals prefer the dark. They had come to believe that he pinpointed his victims in the daylight and that he was so familiar a face in the areas where he was striking that no one ever saw anything out of the ordinary. This prevented the creation of the type of special unit used successfully and highly publicized in journals for law enforcement officers.

For example, more than a decade earlier, Detroit, Michigan, was one of the cities that created a much-imitated unit called STRESS. There had been a series of inner-city liquor store robberies the police needed to end. Clerks and customers had been threatened and frequently hurt. The STRESS unit's job was to determine when the robberies were taking place, where they were taking place and put armed officers in hidden sections of the businesses to stop the hold-ups.

The effort was simple. The robberies were all taking place when the cash registers were ringing up the most sales. This meant pay day Friday nights just after people flush with cash stopped off for anything from a six pack of beer to drink while watching television or barbecuing in the backyard, to quality wine for a party, to hard liquor to be enjoyed alone or with friends. It was also found that the liquor stores being robbed were all in blue-collar areas where the casually dressed robbers blended in with the customers.

Detroit was basically a one-industry town. No matter what jobs residents held in manufacturing, the majority of the products they produced were related to the automobile industry. And the nature of housing development in Detroit was such that workers often moved from area to area as they gained seniority and higher paychecks, allowing them to move to bigger houses. It was easy to determine when payday affected most people and where the robbers were likely to strike. As a result, each liquor store in the area would have two plainclothes officers hiding near the clerk, watching for the moment when the bad guys would arrive.

The public relations impact of STRESS was enormous

and everyone who read the newspapers knew that the Detroit Police were determined to "Stop the Robberies. Enjoy Safe Streets." The police had a different take on the highly successful undercover operation. Among themselves and in law enforcement journals they called the unit "Shoot the Robbers. Enjoy Social Security." And shoot the bad guys they did, in one of the most successful sting operations involving gunfire that wounded or killed the armed robbers who made the mistake of trying to violently resist arrest.

The difference between cities like Detroit in earlier times and Dallas at this point was that Detroit was an established city with a stable population and sizable budget for quality police work and the support equipment they needed. Dallas's population growth was exploding. There was a small budget for the police officers, an even smaller budget for equipment and an influx of new residents that made it one of the fastest growing cities in the country. Procedures that the public had been led to think of as routine, especially if they watched a lot of cops and robbers programs on television, were impossible in Dallas.

The Dallas police did their best. They assigned a group of officers to try and stop the crimes, but not as a full time unit exclusively committed to a single series of cases. This was a luxury the public expected, but the department could not afford. Every day brought new cases for the uniformed patrol, for the detectives and for the forensic personnel. Given their limitations, the criticism they often received in the media was unjustified. It was actually amazing how much they did accomplish.

Carol Bryan and most other victims also based their expectations of police work on television programs, not the realities of the Dallas department. They thought they would receive more personal attention and, when the violence was epidemic, they thought extra officers would be working night and day to end the nightmare. Not only was this impossible, but no police officer, no matter how honest, would dare explain that someone like the serial rapist who was now ravaging women in Dallas might not be caught . . . ever. Such honesty would alarm women and the men who loved them even more than they already were.

Victim 23 certainly fell into this category. Just as Carol had once gained a sense of safety from closing her doors and enjoying the quality collectibles she had accumulated over the years, so the idea of a task force quickly isolating the bad guys brought a sense that security was again at hand. She told herself the man who had violated her so horribly was himself about to be cornered. An arrest was imminent. The police were taking the assailant from the streets. This was Big D after all.

Among the police officers, the frustrations of the combination of too high public expectations, a desire to do quality work and the various limitations on the actions they could take were extremely painful. One officer explained, "Everyone knew we were rich with oil money. Everyone knew we were a city where the wealthy dominated. Even the locals, who should have known better, were certain that essential services like law enforcement were the best equipped, best trained and highest paid in the nation. Yet they read the papers. They knew the efforts to provide funds for more city services often failed. They knew that they didn't vote for the changes we needed. They were living in some fairy tale world where they didn't relate their own inaction in helping to improve the department with our problems."

"I can't tell you how many hours of unpaid overtime I have put in patrolling some of the streets in my own car," said another officer who was assigned to the Ski Mask Rapist, along with many other cases. "I knew he went into expensive areas and blended with those who lived there. I had a sense that his victims were somewhat similar in appearance. I also knew that there were miles of streets from which he could choose and the blondes he seemed to favor were a Dallas stereotype. There was really no chance of my spotting anyone, but I had to try. I couldn't live with myself otherwise. So I drove an hour or two a night when I could. Just cruising. Just imagining what it might be like for a woman to wake up with a stranger in her room. And each time a new rape was reported by anyone, anywhere in the city, I wanted to scream, to cry, to bang my head against a wall in frustration and shame." He looked out the

window to see a sky that had suddenly darkened. A storm
was coming and soon.

"We were just so limited. . . . So damned limited . . . ,"
he lamented.

IT WAS AT the start of a similar rainstorm that Carol
Bryan made a decision about the future. She was offered
the job for which she had recently interviewed and decided
to accept it. She didn't relish going back to join the outside
world every day and she worried that she might have a
similar experience to the one she'd had on the first job, but
she badly needed the income.

As she slid into the front seat of her car and closed the
door, she looked up through the windshield. The sky had
darkened quickly and though rain was expected that afternoon, the storm that struck so viciously was not something
she had anticipated. Sheets of rain plastered the windows
of her Cadillac in waves. The rapidly moving wipers afforded only seconds of uninterrupted visibility. She had to
move slowly in order to keep a safe stopping distance, yet
several near misses were proof that no one could safely be
on the streets. It was only four o'clock in the afternoon, yet
the weather was so dark that the streetlights had gone on.

Carol relaxed slightly as she steered the car into her
complex parking lot. Then, as she stopped in her assigned
space, she realized she could barely see the cars parked immediately adjacent to her own. Someone could be standing
on the passenger side of her car and would be virtually invisible until she was out of her car, defenseless.

Other cities had parking garages. The Sunbelt had out-
door parking even in the more expensive areas. There was
no reason for better shelter for the cars. There was no rock
salt or sand used on the streets in winter. There was nothing corrosive to attack the paint and steel. There was no
need for anything more than an overhang at most. Until a
day like today, when the rain created the illusion of being
in a box with translucent windows and the memory of the
rapist made Carol terrified of whatever lurked just outside
her area of visibility.

The wind grew stronger. The rain struck the windshield as though an old-fashioned fire bucket brigade was lined up in front of the hood of her car, rhythmically tossing massive quantities of water against the glass. Her hands were chilled as she felt the door lock, hesitating to open it, yet knowing she needed to get inside the house. Even after the rape, even with the early darkness from the storm, there was still greater safety inside her condominium than there was within the confines of her car.

"He's watching me," she murmured, remembering his vow before leaving her apartment the night he raped her. She knew it was irrational; even evil does not want to get drenched in a Dallas rainstorm. But being raped in your own home in your own bed was also irrational and that had been her fate. "He's watching me, laughing at me, like a cat that has taken one swipe at a mouse, then backed off to watch its struggle to continue to its hole. He's playing with me. He knows that all I can do is put myself in a corner where he can strike again." Yet just as the mouse is compelled to return to the safety of his hole, so Carol knew she had to get into her house.

Carol grabbed the car door, opened it and stepped into the driving rain. The drops were cold and sharp. Her face felt as though it was being pelted with tiny razor blades. She started running, felt the keys slip from her hand onto the rain soaked ground, returned to pick them up, then ran faster towards her front door. Fumbling with the key, she managed to open the door, slam it shut behind her, then secure both locks and place a bar across the threshold. The windows had been nailed shut after the rape. They remained sealed.

Dripping wet, shaking from fear and cold, she turned around. With her back to the front door, she scanned the room, making certain everything she owned was in its proper place. "I'm not home," she whispered miserably. "I'm just in the same place as my furniture and the possessions I cherish." Everything was neat, orderly, beautifully decorated, flawlessly arranged and sterile. She had become the outsider. The precautions meant to keep violence from her inner sanctum had actually created a jail. She lacked a garage for her car. The air wasn't clean because of all the car exhaust. The. . . .

She leaned back against the front door and quietly prayed, "Please, God, take me home, wherever that is."

CHAPTER 11

SEARCHING FOR EVIL

GILBERT INCREASED HIS time riding along in patrol cars or in the police helicopter with friends on the police force. They were still searching for the Ski Mask Rapist. All the citizens of greater Dallas who read the newspapers or saw brief crime reports on television were aware of the man terrorizing the city's women. Carol had not told Gil of the assault she endured, nor had any of the other women with whom he was friendly, if, indeed, any of them had been victims. Gilbert, as the other professionals were doing, was trying to help spot trouble in the making. That was why he joined in the hunt for suspicious men who might be breaking into homes within his line of sight from the road or from the air.

The real trouble was that no one knew for whom to watch. Rape is a monstrous crime of violence against women frequently committed by men whose rage and twisted perversions are sometimes hidden within the body of the helpful store clerk, the caring clergy member, the beloved schoolteacher or the hard working laborer. The overwhelming compulsion to hurt another person through sexual violence creates no identifying marks on the surface of the skin. There are no outer deformities that can be instantly spotted by passersby. Rapists are neither mutants nor ogres; neither awful smelling, razor toothed behemoths nor no-necked, broad shouldered Neanderthals with knuckles that drag along the ground and breath foul enough to fell a tree.

Still, the police and the civilian ride-alongs spent hour after hour searching. . . .

No one had a description of the man that was entirely reliable. Privately many of the officers felt there was no way they would catch him prowling the city, not through routine patrols, task forces or anything else. They knew that the rapist undoubtedly looked like any respectable citizen. They knew that he would probably do nothing to call attention to himself just before he broke into a home. They felt that the rapist eventually would be caught by chance. Perhaps a resident of the complex might spot him prowling at a time of night that seemed suspicious. Or, a passerby might stumble upon the rapist in the act of breaking into a home. Yet even this was uncertain, for most serial criminals have learned to act like everyone else, to be strangers who are perceived as belonging wherever they happen to be.

The only consistent pattern among serial rapists and similar repeat violent offenders is that they usually commit their first crime by the age of twenty-one and never start a crime spree after the age of forty. No one knows why such a pattern exists, but most detectives building a serial rape or serial murder case against someone in his mid-to-late twenties will check where he was living and working from the time he left high school. There is a quest to see if there are unsolved crimes with which he might be connected.

The Dallas police had learned their lessons about serial rapists years before Carol Bryan's arrival in the city. In July of 1974, a rapist became known to the officers when he targeted the apartment complexes north of the city's downtown, attacking women there. This burgeoning community was an ideal location for a man who wanted to remain anonymous. Most of the residents were young, often in their first apartments and working their first real jobs. Everyone was a newcomer in these areas. Everyone was open and accepting of someone new walking about. And because many of the residents were single, diverse, unfamiliar men coming and going at odd hours of the night seemed perfectly normal. So long as no one looked threatening, none of the residents felt threatened.

The earlier serial rapist moving about the apartment complex north of the city carried a simple rape kit that did not call attention to himself. He carried a woman's stocking he could pull over his head just as he entered an unlocked window or door to an apartment. He carried gloves and he carried a knife. Everything was easily concealed as he moved about. The mask and the gloves could be donned in seconds. In the dark he would not be noticed when standing by a patio door and he would be disguised the moment he slid it open and passed through to the inside.

The rapist had three concerns he always shared with his victims. The first was the mention of his pick-up truck. He made certain that each victim knew he drove such a vehicle, an extremely common one even among upscale residents of Dallas. The police immediately discounted this comment, because they felt he was trying to mislead them.

The second concern was that the victim be comfortable. He would hold his knife to the throat of a victim so she could not struggle without accidentally causing a fatal injury. Yet he did not want her to be scared. He wanted her to understand he was in control, but other than that, he wanted a friend. He was calm, gentle and apologetic for any physical or emotional discomfort he may have caused during the rape.

Finally, the attacker wanted each victim to understand that he was a burglar. He was apparently concerned that someone might think he was a rapist, an idea that troubled him. He ignored the fact that he always forced the women to have sex.

The distinction upon which the assailant insisted—that he was a burglar not a rapist—might have meant a number of possibilities. Rapists are not respected within the prison system of any state. Had he been jailed before, he would not want to be known as a rapist. Burglarizing an occupied dwelling was seen as taking skill and courage. His insistence that he was just a burglar may have been the result of his having been in a prison.

The other likely possibility was that the man was uncomfortable with the crimes he was committing. He may have been a loving husband and father, doting on his family, yet regularly overwhelmed with anger against women. He may have been trying to reassure himself that he was not evil, that he was not trying to hurt someone, that the sex had occurred for whatever reasons sex occurs other than rape.

The theories expressed were based on knowledge gained from previous convictions of rapists, both in Dallas and in other parts of the country. However, such conjecture meant little if the man could not be found.

There were facts that seemed consistent between the current investigation and the one that occurred in the 1970s that let the police know they were again dealing with a serial rapist. The Ski Mask Rapist liked to enter homes and look around before the rape. No one knew whether he would enter, explore and rape or if he would enter, explore and leave, then return for the rape. The latter would mean escalating violations of the victims and the police were beginning to see this alarming pattern.

In the case of the earlier rapist with the stocking and the knife, he also explored his victims' homes, but this took place after the rape. He would frequently use whatever was available to bind his victims following the assaults. Then, while they were helpless, he would go to the refrigerators and get either juice or milk. He would look at the magazines to which they subscribed. He would look at the items on the shelf and the walls, then go through their purses. He wanted to see the personal items they used every day or the items they treasured, such as photographs. He checked their driver's licenses, frequently reading aloud their names and addresses, then calling them by name.

Again the meaning of all this was unclear. What was certain was that one man wanted to know his victims before possessing them; the other wanted to know them after his attack. The Ski Mask Rapist wanted the sex to be as intimate as possible and personalized the attacks by calling each woman by name, traumatizing his victims even more.

Neither distinction, however, brought the police any closer to resolving the crime.

The Dallas Police Department called the earlier offender the Friendly Rapist because of his casual conversations and concerns for his victims. They also began looking for ways to identify him as being different from other rapists. After all, as with the Ski Mask Rapist who would make his appearance later, there had to be a distinctive pattern to his crimes.

The person responsible for the capture of the Friendly Rapist was actually someone no one in the department originally wanted anywhere near a badge and a gun. This was Detective Corporal Evelyn Crowder, one of ten women who joined the Dallas Police Department in the nineteen-seventies. She had courage, tenacity, intelligence and aggression, but she also had one fatal flaw as viewed by the all-male force over the years. She had the misfortune to be a woman in a field where they believed only a man could handle the work.

SOME OF THE thinking about using large, well-muscled male patrol officers made sense in the early days of modern police work. There were no two-way radios. Streets had call boxes the officers would use, and when radios were put into patrol cars, they were one-way radios. There was no such thing as being able to call for a backup while in hot pursuit. A pay telephone was needed to get support if a perpetrator ran into a building and was hiding from the officers, perhaps armed and determined to not be taken out alive. Many of the men who joined the force had been in the military, were trained to fight and were deemed physically more effective than small, slight men or women.

Affirmative action programs changed height, sex and other requirements. Better training and weapons provided an edge for all police officer candidates. And officers of both sexes were shown to be heroic, compassionate and capable or, in some cases involving both men and women, not qualified to wear the blue uniform.

Dallas was again lagging behind many other cities. The

first class of uniformed female officers was in 1970, as much as twenty years after departments of equal size had hired policewomen. Among the members of that first class was Evelyn Crowder who worked as a dispatcher for the department, a civilian job that gave her an intimate understanding of what police work can mean. She understood that the first women officers were not expected to go on street patrol. Instead, they were likely to be assigned to the juvenile unit or work in the Personnel Department. She wanted none of that, though she knew she would have to prove herself.

Officer Crowder's first assignment was the worst one she could have imagined—Personnel. She wore the uniform, carried the gun and kept the city of Dallas safe from too much paperwork. She did not see action. She was not really a participant in the helping profession of which she had long dreamed. After more than a year on the job, doing the work, never complaining, she managed to get assigned to Crimes Against Persons, the most dangerous and arguably the most rewarding division of the department.

Crimes Against Persons was exactly what the name implied. The perpetrators were the most violent in the city. The victims were often the most traumatized. Officer Crowder argued that a woman would have an easier time getting information from a rape victim than would a man, an argument Captain Jack Davis agreed had validity. He decided to give her the promotion, though the old boys network of the police department was such that assignments did not go with the promotion. For six months Officer Crowder was a detective without a case of her own. In a department where each detective is expected to be responsible for individual cases, as well as working with other detectives during investigations, the bias was blatant and obvious. Finally Crowder returned to the captain and demanded that she be given a chance to prove what she could do in the field. As a result, the case she was given was meant to help her recognize she would never be wanted in the department.

A homicide in West Dallas had resulted in a John Doe corpse—no name, no address other than the housing project where he was found. Detective Crowder was told to solve the matter by the assigning sergeant, a man who delighted in what he felt was a joke.

It took Detective Crowder just five hours to handle the matter. She worked the old fashioned way, knocking on door after door. First came a street name for the corpse. Then came his real name and the fact that he was involved in a love triangle with a man who lived two doors away. When she knocked on his door, the man had a handgun in plain sight. Detective Crowder, still alone, was able to get the gun, arrest the man and call for backup. While she continued to work the project, looking for the woman both men loved, a hurried ballistics analysis of the weapon owned by the man she arrested proved the bullet matched the one shot into the victim's head.

It was one o'clock in the afternoon of the same day Detective Crowder had been given her first assignment. The surprised sergeant had a closed case and a woman he now knew to at least be his equal. Her comment to the sergeant became legendary and has been quoted in the media: "I apologize. I know you wanted this wrapped up by noon, but traffic was a bitch."

By the time the Friendly Rapist was working the Dallas streets, Detective Crowder had developed methods of pursuing men committing serial violence. She had learned that there were patterns each followed. Some crimes were so well planned that the perpetrator's capture would seem miraculous. Others were so blatant, you felt as though the criminal wanted to go to jail. Unfortunately, her gradual realization of crime patterns had, for a period of time following the apprehension of that first murder suspect, also created intense enemies within the department.

The only thing worse than being a woman trying to advance in the Dallas Police Department at that point was being a woman who felt a fellow officer was a criminal. In this case, the man was Officer Felix Florio, one of those people everyone liked. He was also a cop's cop, a man who was sensitive to the realities of the street, who was not averse to going outside department policy to build a case and make an arrest.

Florio was a handsome, single man who enjoyed spending his time off in the clubs that were near Dallas' airport. He knew that flight attendants for the airlines that used Love Field often dropped in after work. He enjoyed carousing until he fell in love with Braniff flight attendant Karen De Phillips. Tragically, one night, when she was sleeping with him and he had placed a .45-automatic, loaded and cocked, under his pillow, she accidentally bumped him as he was reaching for the pistol. The weapon discharged, striking her.

Florio put his wounded lover in his car and raced to Parkland Memorial Hospital. There she was pronounced dead and he fled the area. He was missing for most of the day before he showed up, explaining to investigating officers that he was so distraught, he thought he would kill himself. Ultimately the case went before the Dallas County Grand Jury where the jurors believed the story. Florio did not return to the streets, however. Instead, he was temporarily assigned to Central Headquarters, where he wore the uniform, carried the gun, but did not patrol the streets.

Detective Crowder knew as much about Officer Florio as police gossip and newspaper stories provided. She thought nothing of him beyond that. She was more concerned with the case she and her partner were working on—a rapist pretending to be a police officer. The man had entered at least two apartments of two different women. Each time he displayed a police badge. Each time he identified himself as an officer. Each time he explained that he needed to search their apartments.

The rapist was counting on the naiveté of the victims. A police badge is not adequate identification. Every officer and detective carries identification that looks a little like a driver's license, fully identifying the officer by name, photo (usually) and other pertinent information. A request to search is not the same as a search warrant and even when such a request is valid, officers do not do this alone. There is too great a chance that they will encounter unexpected dangers they should not be handling alone.

The first reported victim was raped and her money taken. The second rape victim was so badly beaten that she lost her left eye. Both described, among other identifying marks, a large scar on the attacker's left thigh. It was the kind of scar that might have been caused by a severe injury ripping open part of his leg or perhaps by a burn that had required surgery. Whatever it was, it was dramatic enough to catch their attention.

Detective Crowder handled the questioning of the victims. The second victim was able to help a police artist create a composite sketch. When she saw it, she was adamant that it was a perfect likeness.

The sketch that was produced shook Detective Crowder. It also was likely wrong, she reminded herself. Many trauma victims focus on the wrong person when describing an assailant. Sometimes they remember the last few people they see before working with the identification specialist. The artist ends up drawing an image of the President of the United States, the Mayor, the Safety Director or an officer they saw briefly while in the station. The latter was apparently what happened to this victim, for the likeness she had described and which was drawn was of Dallas Police Officer Felix Florio.

Detective Crowder knew she needed something more if a mistake had not been made. She arranged for the victim to come to police headquarters, then set her where she could see both police and civilian employees coming for work the next morning. The victim was given a cup of coffee and encouraged to watch until everyone was in place. The moment she saw Officer Florio, though, she identified him as the rapist. She even noticed that he had grown a mustache, something he did not have at the time of the rape.

Officer Florio was arrested, as required by law. He had been identified and, though few members of the department wanted to think that an officer could commit rape, Detective Crowder and her partner had to build a case if there was one to be found. They obtained a search warrant for his apartment and found a secret area in his closet that contained theatrical makeup. There were makeup pencils, including a white one that could easily produce the witnessed scar, along with various other items with which he could disguise himself.

It took nine months for the case to come to trial, nine months during which Detective Crowder investigated numerous other crimes all the while living with threats. Police officers protected one another. They did not build cases against each other. The guilt or innocence of Officer Florio was not a consideration. Even if he was guilty, he was one of them and to some of the officers that meant he could not have been as bad as he was portrayed. Crowder should have left things alone, a sentiment she almost shared except for the violence of the crimes and the betrayal of the community they were all sworn to serve. Officer Florio got fifty years in prison, a harsh sentence that proved the case was well founded. However, the revolving door was such that even that sentence could put the ex-cop back on the streets in a relatively short period of time.

Detective Crowder did not concern herself with Florio's eventual return, though. She was back to trying to catch the Friendly Rapist.

Working without the future computer systems that would have made comparisons easier, Detective Crowder reasoned that information could be assembled from rape to rape. Every detail of every rape would be placed on a sheet of paper. Who was the victim? Where did she live? What did the rapist say? What did the rapist wear?

There were many rapes and more than one rapist. Detective Crowder put down everything, then began separating the characteristics she felt were unique to the Friendly Rapist. The pattern, if there was one, meant nothing. Sometimes it would go almost eight months between reported rapes that could be linked to him, three or four weeks in other instances. There was no way of knowing who he was, for even when a fingerprint was found, it turned out that the perpetrator had never been fingerprinted. They had solid evidence for court, but no one to take to jail.

Detective Crowder began interviewing the victims for information that went beyond the reporting being done by the responding officers following yet another rape. She wanted to know as much about the victims, their neighborhoods and their activities as possible. She even went so far as to ask three of the victims to meet with her, a fellow officer who was trained in psychology and the department's psychologist. There they would talk about what they knew, trying to gain some sense of the man. This was an early version of the type of criminal profiling that would be refined by experts in the computer age, then used intensely by the FBI and others.

Hour after hour, Detective Crowder made crime comparison lists by hand and studied them. She was looking for similarities and differences, always seeking the pattern that might lead to an arrest.

The profile that evolved, as so many of them proved to be in those days, was a fascinating look at the perpetrator that would only be of value when he was off the streets. It was like being handed a horoscope, the accuracy of which can only be checked when you look back on the course of the day.

Among other details, the profile revealed that the man was a somewhat introverted professional whose intelligence fit the definition of bright normal. He was probably middle class, though his parents came from a more sophisticated background than he did. He was considered a repressed homosexual who identified with his victims. By raping he made himself feel he was masculine and virile.

The only problem was that immediately after the profile had been formed, the rapist began working a different area. Detective Crowder arranged to be called any time a rape occurred that might be connected to the Friendly Rapist. Since she was the single mother of two girls and since the calls invariably were late at night, this created serious problems at home. But there was nothing else to be done. In the first four years that Detective Crowder, the other members of the Crimes Against Persons unit and the patrol officers all had been pursuing the Friendly Rapist, forty-nine women were confirmed victims. Other women were believed to have not reported what happened to them. Yet even that theory, based on the fact that many victims of rape do not contact the police, was also wrong.

The Friendly Rapist was also keeping count. The first victim he attacked after the police tallied forty-nine assaults was a woman to whom he proudly bragged that she was his fiftieth victim. To celebrate this milestone, he raped her twice.

Still not knowing how many days would elapse between rapes, the Dallas Police Department took a second look at the profiling and analysis Detective Crowder had worked so hard to develop. It was noted that the criminal usually raped between nine P.M. and three A.M. on Sundays, Tuesdays and Thursdays. He was working an apartment complex area that covered six square miles. It was too large an area to saturate, but not too much to cover loosely. Three groups of three plainclothes officers each, all part of the experienced and well trained tactical division, spent two weeks being deployed on the northern and southern fringes of the identified location, as well as in the center. They were looking for anything that might help them.

The end came swiftly and, as expected, it was almost an accident. Guy Williams Marble, Jr., twenty-nine years old, was walking by an apartment complex at ten minutes after one in the morning on a Tuesday. It was not so late as to be unusual. He was wearing casual clothes—faded jeans, hooded sweatshirt and athletic shoes. He could have been a young businessman with a problem he was trying to work through by taking a late walk. He might have worked in a restaurant and been returning home. He might have been visiting a girlfriend. Whatever the case, the only reason he caught the attention of Officer Barry Whitfield of the Tactical unit was that he kept looking up at an apartment's windows. He did not seem to be looking for anyone in particular, such as a lover to whom he would blow a kiss before getting into his car and driving home. He was just looking.

Officer Whitfield approached the man, who promptly ran. It was then that the officer felt Detective Crowder's work had paid off. The officer, in plain clothes, identified himself and ordered the man to stop. Before a chase could ensue, Marble tripped on the sidewalk and the officer quickly handcuffed him. It was then that the officer found nylon panty hose and a pair of golf gloves on the man. He was read his rights and placed under arrest for suspicion of rape.

Much of the profile proved accurate after the arrest. Guy Marble was vice-president of a highly respected public relations firm that had, among other clients, the Baptist General Convention. He was married and the father of a seven-year-old child.

Marble never denied his actions. He plea-bargained a sentence of sixty years after stating that he had committed seven counts of burglary with the intent of committing rape. He never admitted any of the rape charges and there was no evidence available to link him to the inside of any of the apartments he had entered.

The case was a sobering learning experience for the Crimes Against Persons unit and Detective Crowder. If Marble was the rapist, he committed more than fifty such crimes by his own admission to victim number 50. However, the crime of rape is not on his record. He only confessed to the plan to commit rape following the burglaries. Assuming he was, indeed, the rapist and assuming that a serial rapist will continue his violent actions so long as the opportunity exists, the quiet, polite, respected public relations expert would return to society with the same urges and still be young enough to act on them.

Ultimately the members of the unit recognized that there was nothing they could do about the administration of criminal justice in the courts, the way the legislature slowly moves itself forward and other factors. All they could do was stop the bad guys, if only for a short while.

By the time the Ski Mask Rapist was working the Dallas area, none of the officers assigned to Crimes Against Person were naïve. They had learned in their experience with Officer Florio that even a police officer could be a rapist, something not mentioned to Carol Bryan or the other victims of the current crime spree. The question became how to pinpoint the Ski Mask Rapist when seemingly any man in Dallas could be a suspect.

CHAPTER 12

FEARFUL STRANGERS, WELCOME FRIENDS

CAROL ASSUMED AS she tried to return to some sense of what had been normal that she grasped what had happened to her and could cope with it. She understood that the rapist had shattered her sense of security, of order, of the idea that there could be one special place in each person's existence that was inviolable. She understood why she was fearful of strangers she once would have trusted enough to give them a chance to prove what they were like as individuals. She accepted the sleep deprivation and nightmares that replaced the peace with which she once greeted the end of a productive day. And she understood that her sudden paranoia about people, places and types of activities was suddenly critical for her physical survival. Like one out of four women, a statistic of which she was then unaware, Carol now knew there were bad people in the world intent on hurting women. Instead of being irrationally afraid, she was a realist in ways she previously could never have imagined.

However, there were other changes in her personality and actions she didn't understand. They could be attributed to the post-traumatic response to rape but, of course, she didn't know that. One change was her attitude towards her coworkers on the job.

Carol had always been an outgoing person, enjoying the good in whatever she did, ignoring the unpleasant and taking pleasure from the people around her even when their attitudes were quite different from her own. She had always been sensitive to the problems of others. She had sympathized with the shy and inexperienced. Of course, there had always been complainers. There had always been individuals who felt that somehow they were being wronged, because they were overlooked for a promotion or expected to do more work than they felt should be required of them. Carol always knew they were wrong, their whining unpleasant, but she had never previously become angry with them. She had tried to understand that some people have very little insight into their own feelings or the consequences of their actions on others.

Not any more. Such tolerance had vanished with the rape, as had her outgoing, friendly manner. She was somber, robotic and unfriendly to those she didn't know or who did less than their best, especially Elsbeth, one clerk who was directly under Carol in the office hierarchy.

The graying, heavyset woman insisted upon constantly focusing on her misery and she was able to find something negative in every aspect of her day. Her chair squeaked or someone had borrowed it briefly, leaving the seat set too high or too low for her comfort. She complained that the light was so bright that the glare made it difficult to read the computer screen or it was so dim that she had to strain to read the papers on her desk. The woman said her work area was too small or positioned so she was forever straining to reach this object or that. She complained of being too near the copy machine and that the noise was a constant disturbance, except when she had to make copies and found herself walking endlessly to get to it because it was placed so inconveniently. She whined that she was the only person who ever made coffee, but always complained about how terrible the coffee tasted when anyone else made it.

There was no way the complaints could be resolved and

no way Elsbeth would lapse into much desired silence except when putting small morsels of food in her mouth at lunchtime. The constant whine had become torture, each sniveling word pounding on Carol's head like drops of water slowly eroding a mountainside. Finally she could take it no more. One day, Carol stared at the woman and said, "Is there anything you *like* around here? You make everyone in this office miserable. You complain about everything. If you are so unhappy and miserable, why don't you just leave?"

The words were loud and harsh. They were words everyone in the room had wanted to say, but no one had ever done so. And when Carol was finished, there was shocked silence.

Suddenly Elsbeth burst into tears. "You bitch!" she screamed and ran to the boss' office.

Carol was amazed that she had acted so out of character, yet when the clerk left, the other employees came up and congratulated her. They all felt that it was "about time somebody told her off." Some became more vicious, referring to Elsbeth as "menopause mama" and announcing that if they were all as fortunate as they hoped to be, she would be fired.

For fifteen minutes the office seemed to hum with the activities of happy employees. Then the boss' door opened, Elsbeth came out and breezed past Carol, a smirk on her face and one more "bitch" on her lips, though this time said softly enough so that the boss, standing in his doorway, would not hear the word. When she passed, Carol was asked into his office.

There the boss chewed her out. Carol explained that she could not handle Elsbeth's constant barrage of complaints. And when the boss called in the other employees who had long been working with the clerk, they all backed-up what Carol had said. They were all glad she had done it.

It was to no avail. Carol received a reprimand.

Carol worked until closing time, speaking only when she had to, doing her work as best she could while seething over the new injustice, which reminded her once again of all that had unfairly happened to her. As she left the building, got in her car and started on the road home, she cried out, "I hate this job. I hate this town. I hate being in this life." Over and over as she spoke the words, the present faded and the past filled her mind. By the time she was inside her own house, the vision of the masked man who had ruined the oasis of security filled her thoughts until her head ached. She knew she had to do something or depression would overcome any chance she had of returning to normal. Collapsing in a chair, she vowed that the next day, Saturday, she would have to do something to change her life. She could not continue the way she felt.

He never said why he continued to watch her, to follow her, to note the people in her life following the rape. He used different cars when she was driving so she would not recognize that the same vehicle was always behind her.

Sometimes he stayed in the distance. Sometimes he was close enough for her to be aware of his presence. Never did she recognize him. Never did she connect him with the night he "seduced" her. There was a risk in doing what he was doing, but he had been so careful, he apparently did not worry about it.

Carol Bryan was someone who haunted him. He was obsessed with her. And since he had not been arrested, he was free to continue watching her.

The only question was what he should do next. He did not have the answer to that. Neither did the police. All that was certain was that when the urge struck, he would take his gun, his ski mask and the other paraphernalia he needed to avoid having his victims resist too hard or be able to identify him. He would enter someone's home after watching her for days, weeks or longer. And then he would do to that woman what he had done to Carol and so many others.

It was a pattern, though untraceable. It was a pattern he could not stop even if he wanted to.

"Hi!" said a voice greeting Carol as she prepared to do her usual Saturday morning errands. Startled, she looked around, then relaxed when she saw it was Gilbert Escobedo. "I was here to pick up a car and then I saw you. I thought I'd walk over to ask again if you would like to come to church with my friends and me tomorrow. I can pick you up after I pick up Josie."

There was something about the friendliness of the man in contrast to all she had been through that made her gratefully accept his offer. She would not be alone. Not only would there be other people, she would not be the first to be picked up. She didn't expect to get some dramatic change from attending the services. She wasn't certain what she thought about God after being raped. However, she knew she wanted to reconnect with a life that did not involve hating. "All right," she said. "What time?"

"I'll be here at 9:30. See you tomorrow." And then he was gone, heading down the walkway around the building, handling the business that had brought him to the complex.

The car was the same as before—Gil's Jaguar Sedan. One woman was inside when he arrived precisely at 9:30. Another man was picked up immediately afterwards. Then another woman. Everyone was friendly, talking constantly on the way to Prestonwood Baptist Church. Only Carol was silent, but no one minded. If she didn't want to talk, that was just fine with them.

What Carol did not say was how frightened she felt as they entered the building. She had gone to other churches in the time since the rape. She had entered each sanctuary desperate to reach God. She could not understand why He hadn't saved her first from the rape itself and now from this horrible despair. Perhaps in this church there could be a reconciliation, a new discovery, a . . .

Suddenly, the choir broke out in song. Carol listened to the hymns, all familiar ones, yet could not find her voice to sing along. She tried to pray, but couldn't stop wondering why He had allowed her to suffer, why she had been stripped of her dignity, her soul taken, then the very essence of her being burned beyond recognition.

For weeks she had been searching for an answer to at least a part of the puzzle. She had visited different churches, praying and meditating, but no answers had come and she always left in tears before the service was complete.

Prestonwood Baptist Church seemed different. Though it was another mega-church, it was by far the largest Carol had been to since moving to Texas. The seating reminded her of a professional sports arena, not in its appearance but in the number of people it held. It was like being present in a massive television studio which, in effect, it was since services were broadcast to the community.

Gil later confided that he often sang in the choir, especially during holiday celebrations. The choir was also accompanied by an orchestra. There were skilled soloists. There was also impressive preaching. And according to the bulletin a church member handed her, there were all manner of activities taking place regularly, from Bible study groups, to which Gil and some of the others belonged, to outreach ministries to the prisons. The sick were visited. Singles had special activities. Whatever someone might desire for socialization was likely to be found in some form in the church.

This time Carol was able to get through the service without leaving. She did not cry. She did not flee from the building. She still felt out of place, though lately she felt that way everywhere she went. Nevertheless, it was a change and any change felt positive right then.

The experience was comforting. It was normal, rational, the way many people lived their lives. She could sit quietly if she chose, talk when she desired, laugh when the conversation called for it and let her mind drift when she felt overwhelmed by thoughts of her recent past. It was the closest to experiencing real friends she had felt since moving to Dallas.

Carol discovered there was a ritual to attending church with Gil and his friends. That is, church worship was followed with breaking bread at Luby's, a popular restaurant chain in Dallas. The food was varied, the prices reasonable and the customer base came from all walks of life. It was a regular destination after the service and Carol was taken there for lunch as though her presence was a foregone conclusion.

Gil and the others entered the cafeteria, getting their

food, then finding a large table where a half dozen other people who had been to Prestonwood were already seated. Many of them greeted Gil. They were all well dressed and all of them wore expensive jewelry. Carol noticed Gil had on a Rolex watch, two diamond rings, and a heavy gold bracelet. The women and other man who rode to church in Gil's car were equally expensively adorned.

For Carol, the jewelry and expensive clothes seemed out of place. She had been raised to view church services as a time of humility, prayer and sharing. These people seemed to want to show that God had blessed them in material ways. Not that anyone said anything to make her feel uncomfortable. They accepted her as though she had been going to Prestonwood Baptist her entire life. They talked about the sermon, the weather, the church activities that they were interested in attending in the near future and their personal lives. All seemed pleased that Carol had joined them. All seemed to be looking forward to seeing her again.

Lunch was Gil's treat, a situation that made Carol feel slightly uncomfortable. She didn't say anything about going Dutch and it was obvious the man had money and that no one else objected to his paying. Then she realized that just as the group routinely met to eat following church, so Gil routinely paid the bill.

The ritual would prove to be the same each time. Gil would take a roll of money from his pocket and peel off whatever was necessary plus a large tip.

The action was a mix of flash and substance. Carol was used to military men who did not believe in showing off. They acted discreetly, paying quietly, not wanting to call attention to themselves.

In Dallas, Carol had noticed the flash as well, the men who had a "Texas bankroll" consisting of a $100 bill wrapped around a quantity of singles, fives, and tens. The wad looked large, but often was just enough to pay for food and drinks.

Gil was different. He routinely carried $2,000 or $3,000 in cash in his pocket.

Carol felt the money was the action of an insecure man,

self-made in a city where everyone was always trying to prove himself. Nevertheless, Gil didn't seem to be a phony. He obviously was devoted to his church, devoted to his friends and had given her the first break from her self-imposed exile.

After lunch, Carol was the first person to be dropped off. As Gil pulled his car into her apartment complex, everyone made it clear they assumed she would be a regular for church, commenting that they would see her the next Sunday. Carol was noncommittal, though she knew she would probably return. This was as normal as life had been since she had come to Dallas. Finally, the car stopped in front of her apartment and Carol climbed out. She thanked Gil and hurried inside.

The message light on Carol's answering machine was blinking when she walked in the door. Carol flipped on the switch. Marion had called. "Where have you been? Why haven't you telephoned? Why haven't we been doing anything together? I really want to see you. Let's get together."

Somewhat reluctantly, Carol returned the call, inviting Marion to her apartment to spend the afternoon.

Marion seemed fascinated by the stories Carol told about her job and the stress with Elsbeth. However, when Carol described her morning at church, Marion became upset.

"Carol, the man sounds like a Mexican. His name and all. He is a Mexican, isn't he? You should know by now that you can't be keeping company with a Mexican. You don't want to be seen with someone like him in Texas."

There it was again, Carol thought, one of the reasons she had avoided Marion as much as possible. Wherever she had lived, there was always someone to dislike. One city might be embarrassed by residents whose ancestors came from Korea, Japan, China or other parts of Southeast Asia. Another city might focus their disdain on people of the Jewish faith. Other cities had people who looked down upon Italians, Germans, French, African-Americans, Native Americans or some other group. Rarely was she expected to avoid the same people in two different cities, but always she was expected to know the social hierarchy so she would not embarrass herself by being seen with the wrong people.

Big D was no different. Here she had gone with a group of individuals to an extremely wealthy, socially elite megachurch and all Marion could focus on was the fact that the man who had driven her group there was of Mexican descent. He had the money Marion so admired. He drove the right type of car, probably lived in the right area and certainly went to the "correct" stores to make his purchases. *Besides*, Carol thought with annoyance, *the morning activities were not social.*

"It wasn't a date, Marion!" Carol told the woman, exasperated. "It was going to church with him and three others." *Get a grip, Marion*, Carol thought to herself.

"Well, I don't want you being around the wrong kind of people!" Marion exclaimed.

"Marion, these aren't *wrong* people. They all are professionals. They dress nicely and live near me so they must live in good neighborhoods. They regularly go to church. And they treat people they meet with kindness and respect instead of making negative assumptions."

The latter comment was a subtle dig at Marion. Another reason, Carol realized, why she hadn't spent much time of late with the person who had been her first friend in Dallas was that Marion criticized everything and everyone. She was a woman of definite opinions with little basis in reality. The occasional instance when her pre-formed conclusions happened to be correct only served to reinforce her misguided beliefs. Marion ignored the fact that most of the time she was one hundred percent wrong.

"You look thinner," said Marion, changing the subject to one that would cause less conflict—criticizing Carol's appearance. "You must not be eating right. You don't look well. Your eyes aren't sparkling like they did when I first met you. You don't like it here, do you?" She shook her head. "You aren't fun like you were when you first got here. What's really wrong, Carol?"

Avoiding the subject of the rape, Carol sighed, "Well,

you just said it. I don't like it here. As soon as my lease is up, I'm leaving."

MARION'S HARSHNESS WAS countered by the kindness of Gil and his friends. During that week, he called Carol to confirm that she would be part of the group he was driving to church the next Sunday. She told him she would be joining them and even offered to drive. But he flatly refused her kind offer. It was Texas, after all, and a man was not a gentleman unless he took care of a lady, including handling the driving. She found this way of thinking somewhat amusing. Gilbert was a product of the macho Big D culture, as were so many of the men and women she met in the city. But Carol didn't mind. Besides, she saw going to church, with the ritual lunch at Luby's or a coffee house, as a way to begin making the changes in her cloistered existence she'd been promising herself.

She soon learned that Prestonwood Baptist Church may have been overwhelmingly large and impersonal as an institution, but the diversity of groups that utilized the space provided a genuine social life for many of the members. Tuesday and Wednesday were Bible study nights, several groups meeting both in the church and in private homes. Saturdays had a range of social activities. When Gil and the others found out that Carol had been working, doing chores and staying in her home alone on weeknights and all weekend, Sunday mornings being her only diversion, they encouraged her to join them for other activities.

Gil seemed especially determined to get Carol involved in a variety of church activities. He was nice, caring and though he was quite unlike the polished, sophisticated military officers she had known for so many years, she was enjoying her time with him as a friend, not looking at him as a prospective date.

The friendship grew, as Gil and Carol's paths kept crossing. Every Saturday he was at the condominium complex, either visiting friends or picking up a car to clean and detail. He always spotted her going to or coming from her errands. He always waved. He always smiled. And he always went on about his business, never intruding in her world. His devotion to his customers was obvious and she could understand how he had become so successful and could afford so many expensive possessions. He worked hard and he gave quality service.

Carol watched others respond to him and she could see he was well respected. She learned that a number of people in the Sunday social circle that had developed after church services asked Gil to watch their houses or apartments when they were away. He would take in the mail, water the plants and do whatever else needed to be done so the owners would not have to worry about what might happen.

Gil was not an educated man, but he had a good heart. She liked the fact that he did what he felt was right by his friends, never thinking of himself as trying to buy their friendship when he treated them to lunch. The others understood this as well, sometimes joking that they wondered what Gilbert knew about their personal lives, about the dirty little secrets everyone harbors. They said they wondered if they would one day have to pay for their pasts, including all the free lunches they had enjoyed over the years. When Gil became embarrassed, they suggested that perhaps it was he who was paying penance and they should just go on being treated. It was the joking of intimates who enjoy each other's company. Carol still felt she needed to leave Big D, but at least one day of her week was filled with laughter and an absence of fear, anger and remorse.

By the end of January, Carol felt she had both a social circle and a real friend. She still attended church with the group, though there were times a handful of them would go someplace other than Prestonwood in order to hear a special sermon. She also began going alone to some Bible study groups, as well as going with Gil to restaurants and a couple of movies.

Soon Gil was dropping by Carol's apartment unannounced. Sometimes he would bring flowers. At other times they would talk business—both Carol's now delayed plans and Gil's concerns with his own enterprises. The two of them slipped into a camaraderie of shared interests, shared needs and mutual respect. Gil learned about the men who had been in Carol's life and she learned about his various girlfriends.

Then, in February, Gil made an offer that surprised Carol. "I want you to become my business partner." Given his obvious success and her dislike of her present job, the idea seemed worth exploring. Perhaps, Carol reasoned, with her business acumen and the money she still had available for investing, they could expand his business and open new locations. She arranged to go to his office, where he showed her around, even opening his books for her to study. Soon thereafter, the two had papers drawn up and happily shook hands as they embarked upon what they hoped would be a successful and satisfying business partnership.

CHAPTER 13

THE SKI MASK RAPIST

"It happened on a Friday morning," the burglar later explained. "I'd been in the residence previously and I've window peeked there before," the man said. He had been following his intended victim, the pretty blonde with the tall, good looking husband. He had seen her jewelry, seen where she lived. He had followed her, looked in the window. Then, when she was gone from her home, he had found an unlocked window through which he gained entrance while she was away. He was increasingly realizing that simple theft provided no excitement unless the victim was also in the home.

The first time the man had gained entry to the woman's home, he had looked carefully at her possessions. He had worn gloves to assure he would leave no trace of his presence. He just looked at what she owned, opening and closing drawers while being careful to not disturb anything inside. He wanted to know her by the things she treasured, whether that was a photograph, a souvenir dish, the books she read or the movies stacked atop her VCR. He also found and pocketed one of her husband's business cards, as though the simple theft would assure a certain amount of power over the man he did not know and would never meet. Then he left. It was later, when he told himself that he needed the money his fence would provide for the jewelry she owned, that he decided to return more boldly than before.

"I was after a diamond ring that she had on. It was about four carats, a single round diamond that caught my eye. I wasn't after her as a victim as far as sexually assaulting her, but I called that morning and I asked for her husband, because I knew that he was an M.D. from the business card that I picked up when I was in their residence. The wife indicated that her husband wasn't in, so then and there I knew that she was home alone. I went over there. I had a Dallas Police Department baseball cap. I left the baseball cap in a wastebasket there, in a trashcan. Or I could have dropped it on the driveway there, because I didn't want to go into the residence with it on.

"Entering the garage door to the house, I heard a vacuum cleaner, which was the maid, so I figured she wouldn't hear or see me, so I went inside. I entered the lady's bedroom and then I noticed she was taking a shower so I waited till she finished taking her shower. I had a small pistol with me at the time. It was a silver Derringer and I pointed it at her. I told her that if she made any noise that I would take action. So she didn't make any noise. She was just drying herself and then she dropped the towel. I told her to lie down and she did and then that's when I seduced her. Then I asked her for her diamond ring and she gave it to me. So that's when I left. The maid didn't see me leave. No one saw me leave so I went back to the wastebasket to see if the . . . to pick up the Dallas Police Department cap and it wasn't there so I assumed that something was wrong, somebody had seen me. So I kinda panicked then. . . ."

As his attacks continued, the man refined what he did and he became more calculating, more cunning. The ski mask was only worn when no one could spot him entering or leaving someone's home. At this point, he wore gloves. He carried a handgun. He was gentle at the beginning, but he could easily become enraged if the victim did not cooperate. Then he might press the pistol hard against her temple or beat her with it. When he told his victim he would kill her, she had every reason to believe he meant it. And he did.

He was both wary and cunning. He was careful to clean away anything—bodily fluids, fingerprints—that might link him to the rape. He made sure he left no trace evidence that could identify him.

The police knew, as did the Ski Mask Rapist, that time was of the essence. Texas has a five-year statute of limitations for the prosecution of rape. Psychologically destroy a woman by violating her home and forcibly entering her body, wait five years and one day you'll be home free. After that period of time, cases are essentially closed and though records are kept, they are not routinely examined.

No one knew when the Ski Mask Rapist's crimes had started. No one knew when he developed the pattern of escalating violence he seemed to be following. In one of the earliest cases police were aware, he had used some sort of white head covering, perhaps a shirt pulled over his head, while he covered the eyes of his victim with a pillow case. In other assaults during the same period, he wore the ski mask that eventually became his signature disguise. In the beginning he seemed to have no gun, though he threatened the women with a non-existent weapon before physically overpowering his victims. As time went on, he was definitely armed.

Usually he entered dwellings with only one woman present, though in his early rapes there was one case where he entered a condominium shared by three women. His victim slept downstairs. The other two women had bedrooms on the second floor. The area was Woodbend Lane, a moderate income area near Richland College. Young couples in their first jobs, older couples living on modest pensions and singles often sharing space were common in the area.

He knew all this. He had been in the condominium before the attack just as he had with other residences. He stayed with his victim, using terror and the threat of his revolver to keep her silent through two hours of repeated assaults, seemingly taunting fate. He was familiar with the condo, with the fact that three women were there, that two of them could, at any time, come down the stairs and find him in their roommate's bedroom.

There were a few slips during this same period. Once he left the ski mask on his face following a rape and was noticed by a woman when he left the apartment. He chased the witness while waving his gun. She escaped, as did he. Yet there would have been no problem had he removed the mask before leaving the victim's home. The witness would never have thought anything about the good-looking, well-dressed man had the mask not made clear he was up to no good.

He was becoming both more daring and more confident of his own prowess. He no longer always sought the cover of night. At least two rapes were committed in the afternoon, adding to the chance of being caught. The more daring involved walking up to an apartment door and ringing the bell, claiming to be selling candy. When the teenager who was home alone answered, the attacker forced his way inside. He moved her about the apartment to a spot where he could assault her, obviously familiar with the layout. He either lived in the building, a situation the police eventually ruled out, or he had entered the place when it was empty, familiarizing himself with the different rooms and escape routes.

The attack was swift and brutal, his rage so great that the girl's struggles proved futile. He told the teenager he had a gun, but she never saw one. His greater strength led her to be subdued. Yet, though she had kicked, scratched, bitten and hit, when it was over, he insisted she kiss him. It was the final insult, as though he had taken her out on a date and wanted a chaste good-bye kiss before leaving.

Another afternoon assault with a similar ending involved an attack on a baby-sitter while her three-year-old charge was at home. The child was not hurt nor was she a witness to what the rapist did in the bedroom.

With that rape, the time spent was minimal. He first seemed to think that his presence should be enjoyable and he became angry when there was no pleasure response from his victim after he forced himself inside her. Then, when he was done, he scolded her for leaving the sliding glass door in the bedroom unlocked, a fact that allowed him to sneak inside. Finally, he insisted she kiss him.

He had by this time abandoned locations such as the one near the college. His victims were now wealthier and also more mature.

Finally, the victims were all of a particular type—taller than average, blonde, intelligent and successful. There was style to them, a look. Maybe the next victim could not be predicted, but after the rape, when she was interviewed, it was always obvious to police that she had been attacked by the Ski Mask criminal.

Though the police now knew more, the discovery that the Ski Mask Rapist's victims had similarities of appearance made the possibility of solving the rapes more difficult. The implication was that the Ski Mask Rapist was a stalker. He would find his victim and follow her. He would enter her life when and where he could without being recognized as out of the ordinary. He would often enter her home when no one was there, caressing her possessions with his eyes and his hands. He was a careful planner, either familiar in the neighborhoods where he committed his crimes or so nondescript that he seemed to belong wherever he might be traveling.

For the criminal to be both a stalker of the women he raped and someone who must have lived or spent time in the victims' neighborhoods without drawing attention to himself over a period of several years were chilling revelations to the police. No matter how careless or inappropriately daring the man might have been in the early attacks, now he had matured into a smooth but savage criminal sophisticate. With each passing day, with each new rape, the likelihood of the Ski Mask Rapist being caught seemed to fade, not increase. He had an uncanny ability to be invisible to the police who had never even caught a glimpse of him.

The Dallas police had their hands tied. They assigned a

group of officers to try and stop the crimes, but there was neither the money nor the manpower to have a full time unit exclusively committed to a single series of cases. Even with a serial criminal stalking women, there were other new cases every day that took the time and attention of the uniformed patrol, detectives and forensic personnel. They couldn't stop policing the city to work on one case. Yet they were pounded with intense criticism for not succeeding in catching the Ski Mask Rapist.

Carol Bryan and most of the other victims did not know of the limitations facing the Dallas police. They assumed the big city police department would assign extra officers to major cases, perhaps even create a specially trained task force. Not only was this impossible, no police officer, no matter how honest, would dare reveal to the public that someone like the Ski Mask Rapist might never be caught. Such brutal honesty would terrify the law-abiding citizens of Big D.

Carol Bryan didn't know the truth for some time. All she could do was hope and pray that the police would quickly catch the savage criminal and bring him to justice. She would only begin to feel safe again when she knew the man who had committed such horrible crimes would be locked up in prison. She and other victims hoped an arrest was imminent and the police would take the rapist off the streets. This was Big D after all. But as newspaper reports of attacks continued, with no new information indicating police were coming closer to solving the case, Carol began to realize her hopes were more illusion than reality.

That he was a stalker made a kind of crazy sense in Big D. The city itself was physically cosmopolitan—soaring skyscrapers, so many restaurants that a resident could eat in a different one every night of the week for an entire year and not come close to sampling the variety of locations available, freeway traffic jams and Happy Hour conversations about 401(k) plans, stock options and "golden parachutes." At the same time, parked among the Mercedes and Cadillacs in shopping mall lots were pick-up trucks with gun racks and bumper stickers reading, "If you love some-

thing, let it go. If it loves you, it will return. If it doesn't return, hunt it down and kill it."

Texas is an agri-business state with some of the largest
ranches in the nation located on its vast acreage. Men and
women frequently are hunters, some delighting in the sport
and others using official hunting seasons to provide their
families with adequate meat for the year. The latter often
have low income jobs and/or large families. They own a
freezer and avidly vie for hunting permits, sometimes using two different types of weapons to assure two different
permits (e.g. bow hunting and rifle hunting). The animals
they shoot are dressed, butchered and frozen, saving the
hunters hundreds of dollars a year.

Not that the rapist thought of himself as a hunter of
women. Not yet. He was still playing a liar's game with
himself and his victims, never realizing how, over the
years, the anger propelling his actions had become violent
rage.

The stalking always came first. He spotted the woman,
recognized the type as one he desired and began to follow
her. He watched how she walked, what she wore, where
she shopped. He saw the car she drove and followed her to
her home. He learned the pattern of her life, her friends,
her spouse or lover.

Slowly, over days or weeks he insinuated himself into
the rhythm of the woman's existence. He saw her and of-
tentimes he became a familiar sight. She did not recognize
he was a danger. He just became a part of the neighborhood where she lived or worked. He was a familiar but unknown face in the supermarket and the shopping mall. And
in the familiarity, he attained anonymity in the same manner as store clerks, post office employees, police officers
and others.

Then, when she wasn't there, he entered the woman's
home. He looked at her possessions. He memorized the
layout of the rooms, even counting the number of steps
from the door or the window to the bed. He learned it as
someone who wanted to be able to maneuver to and from
the bed in the dark.

What the man did not realize was that in the growing

psychological intimacy he was creating, he was also building the anger he needed to justify the violent action he still did not think he would take. In his mind, he was a lover, a seducer of women, a man who already felt himself a part of the woman's life and thus a welcome guest whose arrival was anticipated.

For years the man could not admit to himself that he was a rapist. He insisted upon a kiss from his victims before leaving, a quiet good night ritual that in his mind diminished the horrors he had inflicted. When he was finally able to admit that he did rape, indeed, assault and sometimes pistol-whip unwilling women, he had gone a step farther and was looking to justify trying even greater violence.

And so his attacks continued:

It happened on a Thursday evening about 12:00 midnight. I was window peeking and I saw the individual. I wasn't looking at her diamond at the time. I was looking at her. She was physically in good shape, with a heavy top. Anyway, she fell asleep and everything. She had a little dog with her so that kind of alarmed me a little bit, but anyway she fell asleep and I noticed there was a front window of her residence. The front window was unlocked; it wasn't open, it was unlocked, so I didn't know if she had an alarm or not. Anyway, I opened the window, got in, but I was still concerned about the little dog that she had. I knew she was home alone, but she was married after, you know, I had a conversation with her and found out she was married. But anyway, basically I went in there and covered her mouth and told her that I had a pistol and I would use it if she didn't cooperate. And she gave me some problems. She kind of fought with me and we struggled around the bed and then we ended up on the floor and I was still struggling, because she was fighting. She was fighting with me and I told her, "Cooperate and everything will work out. I won't harm you." I finally got her calmed down. But I guess you could say I sexually assaulted her. I more or less had physical con-

tact so I can consider this sexual assault. Anyway, she had a big diamond ring on and I noticed that when I first grabbed her by the mouth and told her to keep quiet. Later, I noticed the diamond ring was gone so I asked her for it and she said she swallowed it. What really happened was she laid it by the foot of a table in the bedroom. I told her, "Hey, well, it's not worth your life, not a ring." So she went to get it and she gave me the ring. Then I exited from the residence from the same window that I came in.

Battling to catch such a cunning serial criminal became just another source of great frustration for the police. The citizens of Dallas expected a great deal of their public servants. After all, Big D was rich with oil money and populated by the wealthy. *Therefore, our city's law enforcement must be the best in the nation*, the citizens thought. Yet the very people who made such assumptions—the residents of Dallas—read the newspapers, watched the local televised news and should have known the truth: efforts to provide funds for more city services had failed. The citizens had not voted for the referendums that would have produced desperately needed changes in the city's budget. The police were frustrated with trying to do their best to protect the very people who didn't seem to appreciate the dire circumstances the department faced. But still, many officers were very dedicated to their jobs, especially those working long, hard hours on the Ski Mask Rapist case.

CHAPTER 14

LEARNING CRIME'S INS AND OUTS

PASTOR DENNIS HENDERSON had been riding along with the Dallas Police Department every Friday night for almost a year when one of the sergeants suggested he might like to become a part of the Dallas Police reserves. A reservist would be sent through a portion of the Dallas Police Academy training. When he finished, he would have skills that would allow him to work more effectively with regular officers. He would be able to make arrests and be available for traffic problems, crime scene protection, minor disputes among neighbors and other non-violent assignments. Henderson accepted.

The classes ran for six months. Henderson attended the academy from 6:00 to 10:00 P.M. on Tuesday and Thursday nights. "There was training all day Saturday and also some Friday nights. We had to learn the law, patrol operations, go to the morgue, come-along holds, basic restraints. We didn't have all the physical training of a regular officer, but we did have agility tests and had to run an eight-minute mile. There were regular exams and the total course ran 280 hours over several months' time," Pastor Henderson stated.

Dallas had different levels of police training for the re-

serve officers and they were licensed after each segment
was completed. All the men and women had the same thor-
ough background checks as regular police officers. All the
men and women reserve officers were certified for handling small arms, shotguns and giving first aid. And all the
reserve officers were provided full uniforms.

After the schooling, Pastor Henderson began patrolling
in a manner he felt was more meaningful. He no longer
was a civilian ride-along who was not a direct part of the
department. Now he shared the color of blue, with all the
respect and all the hatred the uniform inspired in others.
He also found that he was more effective as a counselor.
The officers knew he was a minister. Some attended his
church each Sunday. But now he was also one of them,
sharing their risks, understanding their heartbreaks, their
stresses and their dreams.

Pastor Henderson was not content to only act in a reserve status. As time allowed, he returned to the academy,
first earning a permanent reserve license and then, when he
had completed the full 600 hours of training given in three
parts to reserve officers, he became a full police officer, except that he still did not get paid. "It made a difference in
my ministry," Pastor Henderson explained. "The men and
women would have looked at me differently if I earned a
salary as police chaplain. By not getting paid, the officers
knew I cared about them. They knew they were my primary reason for being on the street.

"I wasn't trying to minister to civilians. That happened
at times, of course. But I was concerned with the officers. I
was there for them, whether it was working alongside them
during times of danger or helping them through a particularly difficult time.

"Of course, when I first went on the force, I thought I
was going to save the world. That's why I began taking my
business cards with me showing I was a pastor when I pa-
trolled certain parts of Harry Hines Boulevard."

Dallas' Harry Hines Boulevard is similar to streets in
other major cities throughout the United States. It is the
area where "decent" men and women do not travel after
dark. The only people who walk a particular stretch are

prostitutes looking for johns and pimps looking to protect their "merchandise." Police officers working the area would periodically make sweeps, arresting the prostitutes and sending them to jail. Then their pimps would pay the $300 fines to return them to the streets.

The problems with fighting prostitution were familiar ones, no different for Pastor Henderson than any one else seeking to end the exploitation. First there were the pressures that kept the women on the streets. Some had low self-esteem. Some were drug addicts. Some were terrified of the men who controlled them. Some had no education, great expenses and could find no other job that would pay as well. Few, if any, of the women wanted to be on the street and none of them had the strength, the opportunity, the resources, the support system or anything else necessary to help them leave. They were trapped in a world they hated, carrying on a symbiotic relationship with the police whose arrests gave them a chance to get a night's unhassled sleep and whose fines were the price of doing business.

Pastor Henderson began taking his wife along with him when he was not on duty, talking with the prostitutes, inviting some into his home or taking them for coffee. He convinced some to come to church, but success eluded him. The women understood that he was caring. The women understood that he meant well. But the women also understood that no matter how often they had coffee or went to church, the fundamental problems of their lives were not going to change.

And then came Margaret Perdoe.

Margaret Perdoe was a prostitute who seemed to truly want to leave the streets. Like so many others, Pastor Henderson brought her into his family's life. She was an attractive woman, her body not yet shattered by the stresses of the streets. There was still a twinkle in her eye, a style in her non-working dress, an attitude that caused his own children to embrace her as a friend. When she went to church with some of her friends, there was no difference between Margaret and any of the young women who had been following Christianity all their lives.

It was a Thursday night when Margaret Perdoe decided

she was truly going to leave prostitution. First, however, she had to do something about her pimp. She had to work a few things out. But so far as she was concerned as she sipped coffee with Pastor Henderson, it was time for a change.

"I was thrilled. I knew how hard it was for her. I also knew that of all the women I had met, Margaret was the one who could succeed."

Friday night came and Margaret worked one last time. She walked Harry Hines Boulevard and when a john offered her money, she went off with him. She owed that much to her pimp, like a shop clerk giving one hundred percent on her last day on the job.

This time the john was different. Margaret had experienced many types of men in the time she had worked the streets. She had been with men who wanted to talk, men who wanted straight sex and men who wanted some variation they were afraid to request from a wife or lover. She had been with men who wanted to demean her in order to become aroused and she had been with men who wanted her to demean them before they could experience sex.

This time the john wanted to hurt her until she could hurt no more. On Saturday morning Officer Henderson was called to the morgue to identify the body of Margaret Perdoe. However, instead of making him want to give up his efforts, her death increased the pastor's passion for law enforcement.

Nevertheless, there were other frustrations. Officer Henderson was on patrol with a partner on a New Year's morning when they were called to a house where a man was holed up with a meat cleaver. The house belonged to his grandmother and several family members had already fled. He was drunk and when he was asked to leave, he pulled the weapon, threatening everyone who came near.

Part of an officer's training is an understanding of how people respond when shot. Television and movies portray gunshot victims as being blown backwards or crumpling to the ground. Reality is quite different. Shoot someone in the head and the hand will make a grasping action as the person dies. If a criminal is pointing a gun at an officer and the officer shoots him in the head, the officer will be shot by the reflex action of the corpse. At the same time, if the officer shoots someone in the stomach, the hand relaxes. This is true whether the person lives or dies.

Training films in most police academies explain the problem by showing an actor portraying a criminal attacking with a knife or other stabbing weapon. A person charging an officer who gets closer than nine feet away is likely to have enough momentum and post-death gripping action to stab or kill the officer even after being fatally shot. This is why police are given the nine-foot rule in many departments. If an attacker starts to get closer than nine feet, deadly force *must* be used.

The situation is worse if the attacker is coming down steps. The momentum will take the person farther, again creating great risk for the officer *after* the perpetrator's death.

It is this knowledge that has led to confusion in the public's mind. The average person looks at the age and physical size of the armed attacker, weighing that against the skills and size of the officer. They think of television hand-to-hand combat and cannot understand how an officer, perhaps skilled in martial arts and carrying a baton, can choose to shoot an elderly woman charging him with a butcher knife. The public sees a crazy old lady who could easily be disarmed. The officer has learned that if deadly force is not used, there will be a point of no return where he will likely be severely injured or killed.

Pastor Henderson decided to try and talk the drunken man into putting down his weapon while Henderson and his partner waited for backup. Henderson holstered his gun, knowing his partner had hers carefully aimed at the man threatening the two of them with the meat cleaver. Then he quietly removed his nightstick to use if he miscalculated, trusting his partner to protect him. Finally he began talking as the minutes passed.

Two other officers arrived. Pastor Henderson tried to move closer to the man. A second later, Henderson took a step forward and the man raised his cleaver to either charge or throw. Henderson's partner fired a round into the man's stomach, causing him to drop the cleaver before falling to the ground.

The attacker was not seriously hurt. He went to the hospital, went to jail and then was released on probation. That was when he left Dallas and went to California.

A year later, while on probation for attempted capital murder against an officer, the man returned to Dallas, where he was arrested again for another crime. He had been through the revolving door of punishment. Because of his own standoff with the man, Henderson realized how personal and frustrating police work could be.

Eventually Pastor Henderson, as Officer Henderson, brought the Bible into the Police Academy. He, like Patsy Day, would prove to be an instrument of change.

Pastor Henderson understood the frustrations of police work in Dallas, from the low pay—lower than in any comparably sized city in the state and, quite likely, the nation at that time—to the substandard equipment, from the hostility of some of the public to the hours of boredom interspersed with moments of absolute terror. He did not see how any man or woman could become a police officer if all it meant to them was having a job and a steady paycheck. That was why he was fond of quoting the first four verses from chapter thirteen of Romans.

"Let every person be subject to the governing authority; for there is no authority except from God, and those authorities that exist have been instituted by God. Therefore whoever resists authority resists what God has appointed, and those who resist will incur judgment. For rulers are not a terror to good conduct, but to bad. Do you wish to have no fear of the authority? Then do what is good, and you will receive its approval; for it is God's servant for your good. But if you do what is wrong, you should be afraid, for the authority does not bear the sword in vain! It is the servant of God to execute wrath on the wrongdoer."

It was shortly before the time of Carol Bryan's rape that Officer Henderson began working with Gil Moroney, a field training officer who was also a deacon in Henderson's church. Gil, who had been recognized as Dallas Police Department's officer of the year, was working on planning deployment.

Moroney was doing the type of crime scene analysis that had begun with Detective Crowder. Instead of trying to match rapes, he was trying to spot crime trends of all sorts.

Moroney's idea, based on a concept being used in several other cities, was to look for criminal patterns in the community. All of Dallas was protected by police patrols. However, on many nights all available units in one section of the city were extremely busy while officers in other areas were not. Over time it sometimes becomes clear why there are problems in some areas of the city and not others.

For example, the concern might be a cluster of bars, restaurants and clubs that had become the trendy "in" location for college students and young business professionals. They might spend Friday and Saturday night barhopping—going in and out of businesses along the way, drinking, dancing and eating. Unlike clubs that cater to couples spending their entire evening inside, the employees in bars and clubs where patrons stay only a short time cannot tell who has been drinking too much. If someone appears reasonably sober and is of legal drinking age, the person will be served. The fact that he or she is past a safe alcohol limit may not be apparent. As a result, such locations have higher than average incidents of injuries and fights.

Or a new youth gang may have been started in another part of town. When officers learn this is happening, they know there may be fights between the youths staking out their territory and those who feel they already have clearly defined turf.

Whatever the situation, some problem areas are predictable during certain days of the week or month. The profiling of periodic trouble spots and learning the reasons why problems occur in those places allowed the Dallas force to make a greater presence in those areas during the times of greatest risk for violence.

The profiling was also effective when looking at nonviolent crimes. The revolving door aspect of the state penitentiary meant that repeat offenders would be regularly working the streets until caught again. Professionals develop a comfort zone for their crimes. They have learned the rhythm of the neighborhood, the workers, the people who live there. They know when there are dog walkers on the street. They know when most of the people are at work. They have observed which driveways always have at least one car, implying that someone is at home, and which have no cars in the drive for some portion of the day or night. They have a sense of both the affluence of the particular neighborhood and also how proactive the residents are towards protecting their money. Some individuals—because of their age and experiences during such eras as the Great Depression or because of the way financial institutions functioned in their country of origin—keep all their money in the home. Some individuals convert a portion of their wealth into precious gems and easily marketed collectibles such as rare or gold coins. Whatever the case, the pattern is often consistent among neighbors and burglars learn where even modest homes might have large sums of money or quality valuables to steal.

The burglars also learn the way people in different areas hide their wealth. Some have wall or floor safes. Many more hide their valuables in refrigerators or freezers. Still others sew money into mattresses.

Once a burglar realizes that he can gain a solid return for the work involved in stealing from the houses in a given area, he is likely to return to the neighborhood. He learns to anticipate the type of alarm systems most commonly installed. He learns to break through the windows or doors, knowing that most of the homes, having been built at the same time in the past, would likely have similar handles and locks.

True, many of the burglars are caught and sent to prison. However, they often are career criminals who feel that the mistakes that led to their arrests can be corrected through careful study and what they learn from other prison inmates. And when released, most of them return not only to their old occupation, but also to the neighborhoods and communities where they committed crimes in the past. The areas are familiar, the risks known and they feel they can succeed more easily and quickly than if they have to learn the particulars of a new location.

Such a scenario of a career criminal's life assured that periodically a particular section of Dallas would experience a rise in crime. The area analysis of civilian victim phone calls to police and neighborhood complaints allowed the police to increase patrols as soon as problems arose. And because repeat offenders had often been jailed, some of the more astute officers were able to spot probable suspects, because they were men and women who had been arrested before.

Moroney's work, coupled with the quality of the Dallas Police Academy training, led Officer Henderson to be unusually vigilant wherever he found himself, both on duty and off. He noticed when something minor seemed to be out of place. He learned to make a note to himself of whatever troubled him, even though most of the times what he was witnessing, though slightly different from normal, would turn out to not indicate criminal activity. Nevertheless, Pastor Henderson was certain that one day his vigilance would pay off.

CHAPTER 15

FRIENDS AND LOVERS

THEY HAD BECOME friends. Carol and Gilbert were gradually filling important voids in each other's lives.

As Carol saw more and more of Gilbert, she became convinced that her first impression of him was correct. Gil was a decent man, church centered, caring. He was insecure, of course. That was obvious by the way he adorned his body with the jewelry and expensive clothes he wanted everyone to see and admire. She surmised that his desperate need to be liked by the people at church had led him to pay for the Sunday lunch outings after church on which she now joined. She felt badly for him, suspecting that he might never be truly comfortable within himself.

At the same time, she told herself, Gil's insecurities were not indicative of the real man. This was a man, she could see, who genuinely cared about others. He worked hard to build his business. He understood that you could prosper best by serving the needs of the public and he did so with a wonderful, caring attitude.

Carol knew that there was a touch of the excesses of Big D about him just as there was about her first friend, Marion. However, where Marion divided the city into the haves and have-nots, staying strictly with the haves, Gil, Carol

Even as a child, Carol excelled in art classes and displayed a creative, sensitive nature.

Shortly after graduating high school, Carol married and moved with her new husband to San Diego.

In a few short years, Carol found herself divorced, caring for two small children and struggling on her own.

Soon after Carol remarried, she had to say good-bye to her second husband, Jim, as he left for a fateful flying mission that changed their lives forever.

After her second divorce Carol moved to Dallas to be near her daughters who were becoming adults.

Through a neighbor in her apartment complex, Carol met Gilbert Escobedo, a devoted churchgoer with gentlemanly manners. She was impressed by the time, effort and hard work he put into his business and pleasing his customers.

Becoming close friends and business partners, Gilbert spent many nights at Carol's home talking about their business and his life problems.

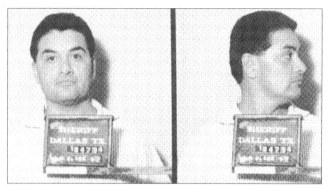

When a security guard noticed a suspicious man lurking near a house, he stopped the man and called Dallas police. Responding officers arrived and arrested Gilbert Escobedo, who repeatedly professed his innocence.

After Gilbert was arrested, Carol met and fell in love with Bob Cook. The two later married.

Just a few weeks after they married, Carol and Bob spent their first Christmas together.

Although she abandoned her artistic pursuits for years after the rape, through therapy, Carol has returned to art to express her creativity and feelings and to help other victims.

To help other victims cope, and as part of her own therapy, Carol created the Guy Gross doll, a faceless, symbolic attacker through which victims can express their anger and hurt. Carol also designed the heart, a pin for victims of violent crimes, to increase awareness of victims' suffering and the need for protective legislation. Carol hopes that one day the heart will be a unifying symbol for all crime victims.

ID Number: 551949
Date: 10/08/01
Name: GILBERT H. ESCOBEDO

551949
01/14/1999 003

01/14/1999 004

A recent photo of Gilbert Escobedo, taken by the Texas Department of Criminal Justice. In an interview, he was asked if he thought he'd rape again if he got out of jail today. Gilbert responded, "The percentage would be great."

A compassionate, artistic person before the rape, it has taken Carol years of therapy to return to her former self. Though she has come a long way, becoming a victims' advocate, life will never be the same for Carol Cook.

Attending a Victims Outreach fundraiser to increase awareness and aid for victims and their families, Carol is joined by famed author Dominick Dunne, whose actress daughter, Dominique, was murdered.

felt, was a victim of that kind of snobbery. His insecurity came, Carol believed, because he really had been put down over the years. His ethnic heritage, his ownership of a service business no matter how successful, his lack of education, even his mild dyslexia all were subject to derision within a community where too many sought the illusion of perfection.

Gil saw that Carol was bright, both college and self-educated. She was an artist, articulate and worldly. "Carol was just different," he later said, smiling. "She had a sparkle to her that was fascinating. I loved those things and she had them." She also had an understanding of business and the same dedication to serving the customer that he did. More important, she had the background to look at his business, understand it and perhaps help him to expand, both with her knowledge and with the cash she had brought to Dallas for investment.

It was February when Carol began to understand not only what Gil had created but how it could thrive.

The automobile detailing business was located in downtown Dallas, near the high-rise office towers where executives in banking, insurance, oil and other businesses had major office space, the police station, the library and upscale department stores. The car care work was handled inside a parking garage, assuring a steady stream of impulse and regular customers. In addition, Gil had aggressively sought work from companies that had need of specialized cleaning. The telephone company brought its trucks to him for cleaning, washing and general interior and exterior maintenance. Other companies maintained fleets of cars for use by their top executives, and these, too, began to use Gil's business, especially after he became a friend to some of the top executives. Other businesses would maintain the engines and replace tires as needed. His detailing operation recreated the "new car smell" experience, ridding the vehicles of the smoke, grease, grime and debris that accumulate from repeated use over time.

One of his friends was the vice president of a bank that repossessed cars. This proved another source of business. Dallas was an auction market within the state of Texas.

This meant that bank branches throughout the state would repossess cars the owners could no longer afford. The banks had received a down payment and monthly repayments for their loans when times were good for the owners. When times went bad, owners stopped making payments and the banks repossessed the cars. Then the cars would have to be cleaned and polished so they could be resold. This was where Gil's detailing business came in.

Gil had started his business during one of the roller coaster periods in Dallas. The bank repossessions often took the form of Cadillacs, Lincolns, BMWs, Porches, Corvettes and other luxury cars. The prices the banks resold the vehicles for was often far less than the book value, yet no matter what the resale price would be, the new owners of the cars were enthusiastic about car cosmetics. Many of the buyers knew nothing about engines, brakes and the hidden wear that could occur with improper or too limited maintenance. What they wanted was a car that looked good when they drove to the country club, drove to Austin to lobby the state legislature or drove to a nightclub where they hoped to find a partner drawn to the same hedonistic pleasures they valued. They wanted flash for their cash and the quality of Gil's work assured that the used cars would shine. No one but the buyers would know they were repos.

The quality of Gil's work assured a volume business. He employed his two brothers, a nephew and two other men in addition to paying himself a salary. His customers, especially the police officers who were grateful to get free car washes, recognized that the business was thriving and respected Gil's accomplishments.

However, Carol, who had innate business savvy, thought she could help him make the business grow. Gilbert had no tax number that would have allowed him to purchase his supplies at lower, wholesale prices. He only had a city license as required to do business. His suppliers and employees were paid in cash and that meant issues with Social Security and the Internal Revenue Service. His actions were not unusual for a first time entrepreneur who was growing a successful small business and the employees certainly benefited by being paid in cash. However, she knew, after surveying the business and checking the books, that three changes were needed.

First, her accountant confirmed that in the financial area Gilbert needed to start keeping better records. He needed to run the business properly so that he had a full accounting of every penny, met all legal obligations and obtained every possible deduction. With full access to his files, Carol could not find all the invoices, billing and employee records, purchase records and the like that were needed to completely understand and, possibly, revamp and expand the operation.

Carol felt Gilbert needed a full business plan, including developing more locations. A second one could double his business and after that the sky was the limit. Third, Gil needed to improve his hiring practices which until then often involved employing individuals who walked in off the street and then paying people in cash when he ran short of help.

There were other needs, but the business was essentially sound. It needed an infusion of capital and a firmer hand with the records. Carol decided to begin by investing $10,000, then getting involved with renegotiating a new lease for the business, creating a new bank account and getting all licenses. Gil made her a partner in the business.

At last Carol was part of a successful business venture, though not one she would have chosen for herself had she been starting out. Nevertheless, she had a friend and partner who respected her abilities and obviously admired her. This gave her more self-confidence though there were some nights she still awakened screaming. She remained restless, tired and fearful. Darkness was her enemy and she did not want to go out at night if she would have to return alone. She hoped time would remedy her problems, but there was a chance that the fears and the memories were never going to go away. She did not know if healing was possible. She did not know any other rape victims to ask when, if ever, the fear would recede and she'd begin to feel like her old self again.

The police were doing their best to help Carol, but their

services were limited. One compassionate officer, Detective Roberta King, kept checking on her. Detective King recognized the futility of all that was taking place as well as the absolute necessity of pursuing every lead if they ever were going to find the serial rapist who'd attacked Carol and many others and who was adding to his list daily. King knew that even if the police did capture the Ski Mask Rapist, he would not be the last sexual predator on the street. Still, she cared, making this case a priority and returning to see Carol, calling her, making certain that whatever help Carol requested, she would get.

The problem was that Carol could not yet confide in anyone. She was still amazed that she had called Norwood Dixon to take her to the hospital. He had arrived quickly, taken her without questioning and stayed until he was no longer needed. Then he seemed to disappear from her life. Perhaps the incident made him uncomfortable. Or, perhaps his disappearance from her life was due more to Carol's isolation than his avoidance. Carol never knew for sure, but she was certainly grateful for his kindness and compassion on that awful day.

The more Carol thought about it, she realized it was as though people were moving in and out of her world without rhyme or reason. But with the passing of time, she realized the two constants in her life were Detective King, who seemed to legitimately care about Carol's pain, and Gilbert Escobedo, the man to whom Carol was growing increasingly close.

During this period Carol's youngest daughter was experiencing her own problems, one of which was that her sister, with whom she was very close, had moved away from Dallas. At this time, communication between Carol and her daughter was difficult. They were in the awkward state of parent-child relations when the younger person is becoming an independent adult. They were working to understand their new roles in life, as so many other mothers with adult daughters must do as the years go by.

Carol's daughter had an added pressure. Her mother had always been a calm, all knowing, capable, stabilizing force in her life. Her mother had frequently been the only parent at home when the girls' father was overseas. Her mother had been the one who planned the moves, who helped the family pack, who oversaw the relocations. Her mother had turned the upheaval of their transient lifestyle into a series of small adventures, letting the girls explore the world as they pulled onto back roads, country lanes and regularly moved off the superhighways so they could see more of the United States than just toll roads and military bases.

Everything Carol had done when the girls were young children seemed natural. Many moms could and would do the same. But now her daughter was becoming independent and, though on one hand her childhood needs had ended, on another her more grownup ones were just beginning. Suddenly she could relate to her mother on a deeper level. She was in awe of the woman who had raised her and horrified by the intense personality changes she now saw in the mother who had finally discussed being raped with her daughters. Every time the girl looked at the frightened, withdrawn shell of her mother's former self, she wept bitterly and uncontrollably. It was as though she both mourned the loss of the woman who once was and feared a future where she, herself, would have to be stronger than she ever thought possible. She understood she now needed to be her mother's adult daughter. However, the young woman did not know how to cope with this shattered individual so unlike the strong, nurturing woman the daughter experienced all her life.

Gil provided stable friendship as Carol began her recovery. They were friends and business confidants and it was good for Carol to be able to focus on something other than her attack, though it was never far from her mind. Still, it surprised Carol that despite her agitated mental state, she was able to clearly analyze Gil's business problems. And he appreciated her efforts and listened closely as she outlined the problems created by the haphazard way the business was being run. He needed to screen his potential employees, to make certain they did not have criminal histories or personal problems that would make them difficult to work with. He was dealing with cash and supplies that could easily be taken. The quality and honesty of his employees was important.

Carol showed Gil that he needed more than an accountant who did his taxes. She met his brothers, met his employees, then together they saw an attorney as the business partnership came together. "I made plans to leave my job and we worked out a business deal. I would change things to make sure everything was set up and done legally. I made contracts with people, I hired and fired people and used job applications as my screening method. Several applicants refused to give me Social Security numbers or show me their green cards allowing them to work in the United States. I wouldn't hire them." Gilbert acted as if he didn't understand this method of screening and seemed surprised that it worked. He obviously had been smart enough to pull together a successful business with little knowledge of what he was doing. Carol had a larger vision. She showed him how they could open a second, a third and a fourth shop together, expanding into other areas and types of business.

They talked about franchises, publicity and public relations, as well as selling businesses on the idea of contracting them to care for the company's vehicles. Carol outlined her vision for the company's future and Gilbert seemed to embrace it. "I also acquired more respect for him. Gil knew his car business inside and out. He was good at what he did. I was good at what I did. We made a good team. He spent many hours teaching me and his knowledge was extensive, but there were things about current business practices he just didn't know. We both knew that before I sold a product I had to know what it was and why people needed it. Soon I was going to school to understand his part of the business. I went to class to learn as much as I could. I didn't tell Gilbert what I was doing, because I didn't think his ego could handle it. I couldn't tell him that my thirst for learning, my need to know literally everything about a business before I got involved, made going to school important." He seemed proud of how fast she was learning and it did not hurt their relationship that she let him think he had taught her everything.

Carol and Gilbert began spending time together during the day and late into the night most of the week. After work they went to Carol's condo and enthusiastically discussed any problems with the business and their plans for the future. When the hour got to be eleven or twelve, if he was too tired to drive, Gil slept in her guest bedroom or on the sofa.

As she became closer to Gilbert, Carol met more of his family. She found great pleasure in spending time with Gilbert's daughters. He had been a teenager, not quite seventeen years old, when he and his girlfriend at the time discovered she was pregnant. The situation was not unusual in the low-income neighborhood where they grew up. Sexual relations began at an earlier age in parts of Mexico and boys were able to get the same jobs as men, supporting their families despite limited education. Girls had usually stopped going to school in their home states in Mexico, but in Dallas, many of the girls felt that education was important. They had their babies and stayed in school, letting their extended families nurture the children when they were in classes. Many of the boys did the same, the infants being raised not so much by the children who were their parents as by extended families where others had the maturity to guide the young people.

Gilbert told Carol his girlfriend never had a formal marriage. "Gilbert said they had a common-law marriage. They signed their names as Mr. and Mrs. Escobedo, but they never had a church or civil marriage. I don't know if that was the same as a legal marriage in Texas, but I later learned that many states recognize common-law unions and require a formal divorce. Some of the Federal agencies, such as Social Security, apparently recognize such unions as well, provided the couple establishes their common-law marriage in at least one state where it is recognized."

There was a second child after the first and by the time Gilbert wanted Carol to meet them and his first wife, the girls were sixteen and seventeen years of age.

The first time she met his family, Carol immediately noticed Gilbert's ex-wife was nothing like the women he always commented upon as being so attractive when they were in church, eating out or when women came into their shop. "The women he was drawn to were always petite, trim, athletic, usually blonde and obviously had style and money. Gilbert's ex-wife had an attractive face, but was short, somewhat overweight and modest. However, she was always pleasant and quite happy to have me involved with her older daughters. Gilbert regularly visited them, paid for their support and was seemingly as good a father as he could be."

The girls were fun loving and sweet. Their mother had remarried and had several younger children in addition to the girls. The family was close. There were always nieces, nephews and cousins running around, but most of them were at least four or five years younger than Gil's daughters, so the girls liked to get away sometimes.

On a few occasions, the girls stayed with Carol at her condominium. The pretty, older girl was intelligent, but at times angry and hurting. "I don't know if it was her parents' divorce that caused her problems or if something else was bothering her. She seemed to like me and though we talked about many things, she never revealed that she had suffered or why she could be pleasant one moment and so hostile the next.

"The younger girl was petite and beautiful with lustrous dark brown hair cascading down her back. She was friendly, very sweet and outgoing and you could see where she might get more attention than her older sister when the two of them were together."

Spending time with Carol seemed to buy the girls freedom and a little privilege over their half-sisters and brothers. The family was not poor. Their mother worked as a clerk in one of the government offices and her husband had regular employment. Nevertheless, despite Gil's help, they had to stretch their limited budget and there was the need to skimp on clothing. "Though Gil never noticed the condition of the girls' clothes, I quickly noticed that the girls' undergarments were well worn. They were always clean, but they had been using them long past the point where I would have replaced my daughters' things. I took them to a store and bought them what they needed, along with other things, such as sweaters. I liked giving the girls experiences they would otherwise not have.

"Sometimes they wanted to spend an evening with me and we'd cook dinner or go to a restaurant. Sometimes they just needed to have fun in a safe environment away from adults. That's when I would loan them my car and give them the money to go to the movies. They loved the fact that I trusted them with my car. They thought it was fun and so did I. It helped me realize that life goes on, that other people could help me heal and that I could be important to others."

Gilbert's hours were irregular. At times he napped, left and returned to Carol's apartment at two or three in the morning. Other times he rested and then left after an hour or two. "I have nightmares," he explained, "and I have trouble sleeping."

"I can certainly relate to that," Carol told him.

She understood his insomnia and knew the presence of a friend was comforting, but Carol's own nightmares continued. She had difficulty staying focused at night on anything or anyone. "I buried myself in reading, sometimes devouring a thick novel in two or three nights." Many nights she cried out in her sleep and if Gilbert was there, he would come running in to hold her and tell her she was safe. It was on one such night that she first told him she had been raped. She shared as little as possible about the frightening attack and was thankful that Gilbert asked no questions.

"I felt separated from the world, my family, even my daughters who were nearby. I felt I could not contact old friends in the city I had lived in before. I didn't trust anyone, not even myself, because I couldn't seem to make decisions about my own well-being or rationalize the awful things that happened to me when I came to Dallas."

Until she and Gilbert began working together, Carol felt she had no direction and just lived day to day. "I did not know I needed help. I just knew I was different than I had been in the past and I wanted my old self back. I kept thinking I could fix myself, but I didn't know all that was broken."

Because she was such a loner and kept mainly to herself, never sharing her secret with anyone but Gilbert and her daughters, Carol did not know she also had legal rights she could have exercised toward the leasing company who managed the condo complex where she lived. Instead, she began to rely on Gilbert's presence to ease the days and nights of terror. She felt she was making progress in pulling herself together, but her agony did not end.

That Carol and Gilbert would become intimate seemed inevitable. They were friends who had become integral parts of each other's lives. They were together all day and for many nights. To Carol, Gil was both safe to be around and a man she could trust to go out with for lunch or dinner, to church or just to relax.

One night, Gilbert was rubbing her back, easing the tensions of the day when one thing led to another. They kissed, caressed and gradually made their way to the bedroom.

CHAPTER 16

GOOD SIDE/BAD SIDE

IN THE NEXT weeks, their intimacy created a new relationship between Carol and Gil, one neither expected. He began talking more personally than he had previously, revealing things Carol had never known. The good side of Gil was always evident. She appreciated his kindness and caring, but Carol felt, for her, though his lovemaking was quiet and gentle, it was not very satisfying. In truth, she had little desire for sex so soon after the attack. Her emotions were numb and the horrible flashbacks she continued experiencing were so unsettling that it took all her energy and determination to keep functioning on everyday things, no less form a serious personal attachment. She wanted comfort but not passion; passion she was unable to reciprocate.

However, Gil didn't seem to notice her reticence. When they were intimate only a short while, he confided, "I want a wife; I want to be a married man. We get along so well, we should get married." His words startled Carol. She didn't know if he was joking or not, but it was then she knew she had to reveal her own feelings.

Carol blurted out, "Gil, I can't. All I want is to be your friend and to have our business be successful. I never want to marry again."

He looked hurt but said nothing. After her announcement, Carol threw herself into work. They were planning to soon open a second location and she knew this was only the beginning of a successful partnership with the man whose friendship she had come to value so much.

Gil seemed to value her relationship with him as well. "Gil tried to establish some sort of new life with me. He seemed to want the intimacy of a female friend." Even when their time of being lovers was over, he continued to spend many nights in the guest room of Carol's condo. Insomnia plagued him. Late at night he watched television until he was finally tired enough to sleep.

"The orderliness of my home, the elegance of the objects I had collected over the years seemed to bring him comfort." And, of course, having him there made her feel safer. Nevertheless, she could not pretend that she felt more for him than she did and so she was relieved when Gil confided that he'd started dating other women again.

They were once again business partners and personal confidants. But as their friendship deepened, to Carol's surprise, Gilbert began revealing a far different side of himself than the gentle, genial man she had first known.

"Gil began criticizing others. He still talked about goodness and love. He seemed to genuinely believe that we are all called to care about other people, even those with whom we may be uncomfortable. Yet increasingly he complained about one person or another."

For Carol, the new part of Gil's personality was jarring. "Sometimes Gil reminded me of a cat the way he was now watching people. We'd be driving in the car and he'd be constantly observing, often making comments that told me where his eyes had strayed. Or we'd be in church or a restaurant and he'd start pointing out people's flaws."

"Look at that woman in the red dress," he said one evening when they were having dinner out together. "Doesn't she know how ridiculous she looks being so fat and wearing that fake jewelry?" On another occasion he commented, "Send that man back to school to teach him how to dress." And on another, "There's a good-looking woman! That Piaget watch, the diamond brooch, those clothes.

She's got money. Look at the fabric. Look at the quality of the setting on her ring." Carol was concerned that he seemed obsessed with the material and the superficial.

The strange part of Gil's obsession was that he did know quality. It surprised her that with a seemingly casual glance he could tell good jewelry from well-made costume. He could look at what seemed like precious gems from a distance and have a pretty good sense of whether the stones were real or fake, quality pieces or of low value. He had a better eye than Carol for some things and she owned some excellent pieces, especially among her crystal, some of which she obtained in England.

When Carol thought objectively about his critical comments, there seemed to be common targets. "He didn't like men who were taller, better educated or more successful than himself. He didn't like women who were too independent, especially if they were financially successful, dating or married to men taller than he was. He mocked superficial families we both knew from church, good families, decent people who previously he seemed to like."

Carol was shocked by Gil's harsh and increasingly frequent remarks. She tried to talk to him, to reason with him. She kept telling herself it was just Gil's terrible insecurity. "He kept telling me how he wanted to be powerful." Carol joked with him about it. "Power will be easy. All we have to do is perfect our business, then franchise the idea to individuals in areas similar to the ones where we find success. That will give you all the power you could want."

Gil couldn't seem to joke or accept her help. He constantly talked about what he had to do at church. "I have to get to the right people," he insisted. He wanted to be a desired intimate of those with top incomes who drove expensive cars and lived in the best homes. The congregation was so big that people from the same socio-economic strata tended to blend together and form their own groups. They were not being snobs. If you were involved with missionary work, a Bible study, fundraiser or something similar, it made sense to talk to people you met at your country club, business office, hair salon or specialty boutiques. They were not trying to be exclusionary. They never thought that what was convenient for them was sometimes difficult or impossible for the merely moderately successful.

Part of the problem, Carol felt, was that Gil hated being a Mexican. She noticed that he even bought blue and green contact lenses to change his eye color.

"His anger towards Mexicans carried over into his own family," Carol observed. "He frequently spoke against his brothers, yet at the same time, he was very good to them. He had his brothers working with him."

As for his parents, most of his negative comments were directed at his mother. Gilbert's parents had been unable to sustain their commitment to marriage when he was a child and it was clear to Carol that Gilbert still had angry feelings over that fact as an adult. Carol saw in Gilbert what she guessed was ongoing depression over the break-up of his parents and anger against his mother for leaving his father. Often he said that he felt his father was the injured party, that his mother had been the cause of the split. He told Carol that he thought his mother had cheated on his father, though there was no proof of that claim. Having met her a few times, Carol did not get the impression that Gilbert's mother was the type to commit adultery. Instead, Carol suspected that when Gilbert was young, he tried to justify in his own mind why his parents could no longer live with each other. Since he went to live with his father, it was probably easier for him to blame his mother. Carol felt that his parent's divorce made Gilbert somewhat bitter towards women, at the same time seeking their approval and telling many people that he wanted a relationship with a woman that would be "forever." Still, Gilbert treated his mother well and visited her regularly. By contrast, he only occasionally visited his father and stepmother and kept those visits brief as his relationship with his stepmother was strained. It seemed to Carol that Gilbert was torn between what he felt was the right way to behave toward his family members and the separation from his cultural and ethnic roots he felt he needed to maintain to be accepted in North Dallas.

As time went on, Carol's discomfort grew. "Gil was as against making Mexican friends as Marion. They were both bigoted in the same way, something I doubt either of them could have imagined."

What made Carol feel even worse was that she felt some of Gil's estrangement from his family seemed to be the result of her being his business partner. There was a lot of hostility between Gil's brothers and Carol. Though she tried to ignore anything negative, even going out to dinner with Gil's brothers and their girlfriends could not seem to alleviate the tension. They seemed to resent her role in the business and their lack of participation in the decision making. She told herself that Gil had the right to make any decision he wanted concerning their partnership in business and if Gil had not consulted with his brothers before making the business arrangement, that was his concern, not hers. The brothers did not own the business. They worked there. So far as Carol knew, though they provided much needed help, they had not, according to Gil, ever been promised partnerships.

Nevertheless, the tension grew. Increasingly, Gil talked against his family. His ethnic heritage bothered him, as did the unresolved issues about his parents' divorce. To listen to him, you would wonder whether his brothers were from the same mother and father as he was. It was angry talk, not based on fact and it troubled Carol that a grown man would have such serious unresolved issues from his childhood.

Soon the problems spilled over into their business lives. "At this point he became frustrated over little matters— mislaid paperwork, minor errors by the employees that were easily corrected before the customer picked up his or her car and similar nuisances. At times he threw temper tantrums, at others he was reduced to tears, frustrated with whatever was taking place.

"I'm just a failure," he said over and over, becoming angry, then getting angry with himself for having such strong feelings. He didn't drink or smoke, but Carol was becoming convinced that Gil had serious emotional problems and needed counseling in much the manner of an alcoholic needing AA. She tried tactfully to bring up the subject with him, but he became annoyed and brushed the suggestion aside.

"I began to worry about whether his change in personality could be my fault. I began to wonder if Gil was embarrassed by the sex between us that went nowhere, by the lovers we were obviously never meant to be. Even though he shared his dating experiences and seemed eager to tell me about this woman or that, I wasn't sure he had forgiven me for what he must have perceived as a blow to his ego. And his assessment of other women, which was sometimes positive but other times terribly derisive, made me uncomfortable. At the time, I didn't appreciate his critical attitude toward the women he was dating, but that was not so troubling as the way he reacted when I had guests in town. One time, I had friends—a husband and wife—who visited. We went out to dinner and then they spent the night at my home. Later, Gilbert told me he followed us out to dinner and said my friends were snobs and phony. I was stunned to learn he had followed us and would make such insulting comments about my friends.

"Another time, I had dinner with my stockbroker. Don was a well-dressed, financially successful, sophisticated and upbeat man. There was no romance. We were just friends and business associates talking over dinner. I was glad to get out of the house and be social in ways that seemed safe. At last I was not running scared from every man I met, though I was still experiencing periodic bouts of severe, almost crippling depression. I was still having flashbacks about the rape. I was still far from healed, but I knew I needed to get out more."

But to Carol's consternation, Gilbert mocked the men Carol saw. "They all seemed to be taller than me. Gil was shorter and that always bothered him. I tried to explain that I viewed a man's stature by what he was inside, not his physical attributes. Still, he was hostile, especially when I was not interested in the men with whom he wanted to fix me up. Some were from church. Some were from our business. None of them or, for that matter, anyone else interested me, and I suspected his primary concern was having me date someone he knew so he could keep an eye on me. I tried to tell him that my relationships were all platonic and I was just trying to get out of the house on occasion, but he didn't listen."

Then one night after Gil had mocked her dinner companion again, Carol had a particularly frightening dream. She awakened sweating, crying as she had so many nights from the flashbacks which would not end. She must have screamed out. She opened her eyes to find Gilbert, who had decided to stay overnight, standing in the doorway of her bedroom, knocking on the open door. The light from the television and a lamp in the other room silhouetted him. "He was obviously concerned, but I didn't recognize him for a moment. All I saw was his shadow, a shadow like the one I had seen on that horrible night. For a moment I thought the rapist had returned and I screamed. Then I realized it was Gilbert, the man who was doing more to help me recover than anyone I knew."

The next morning Carol contacted Detective Roberta King and told her what had happened. "I don't know if the extra information will help. But last night I had a flashback and in it I saw the rapist again. That was when I realized the rapist must have had a similar build and similar height to my business partner, Gilbert Escobedo. The rapist was dark, short and stocky. I think he was probably Mexican."

Carol wasn't bigoted like Marion. Everywhere she'd ever lived, there were always groups of people who looked quite similar. "When I was in Ohio, the steel towns like Cleveland had first generation immigrants from Eastern Europe whose limited nutrition left them short and squat. Their children were tall, but not the parents. I've seen a similar situation in San Diego with Japanese whose children tower over them. In the southwest, there often is a difference in body build and height between the reservation raised Native Americans and those raised in the cities.

"In Dallas, I found that the somewhat older Mexicans were built like Gilbert, though younger men and teenage boys usually were several inches taller. That's why, when I remembered that my attacker was short and stocky, I thought he probably was a Mexican. That's what I told Detective King."

The policewoman understood. The police had good relations with many of the residents of the low-income areas like Little Mexico. They all knew the men and women were low paid, but they worked hard to raise good families. Criminals came from all elements of Dallas society, whether Anglos, Hispanics or African-Americans. Detective King seemed glad Carol called to tell her her thoughts. She now had two more characteristics to add to the police profile of the Ski Mask Rapist. Hopefully they would help narrow the suspect list.

That night as she was getting ready for bed, Carol suddenly remembered the rapist's last words to her. In her mind she heard him saying, "I will keep watching you and I'll kill you if you call the police." She began crying and was unable to stop. Gilbert was there again and seemed deeply moved by Carol's distress. He gently held and reassured her, though she did not tell him why she was crying. She had learned well the code of silence taught the military wife, the old code by which she had lived. She was still trying to recover on her own. And Gil did not ask questions. He just made certain he was there when she needed him. She appreciated his concern, still, as if in return for his attention to her, he now began making demands.

The problems seemed to reach a peak a few weeks later when Carol was in her condo, talking on the telephone to a friend from church. They were organizing their next Bible study session when Gilbert came to the door. "Just a minute," she called. "I'm on the phone with Joanna."

"I need to see you," he shouted, banging on the door.

"Just a minute, Gil," she called to him, knowing he could hear.

But Gil had no patience. He pounded harder, then began kicking the wooden door like a man run amuck, venting his inappropriate rage and frustration. In moments the wood splintered and the friend on the telephone could hear the commotion. Joanna told her to hang up and dial 911. The operator would see her address and send the police. Shocked and frightened by Gilbert's rage, Carol followed Joanne's instructions.

At that moment, Gilbert broke through the door, certain

there was a man in the apartment. He was angry and a little embarrassed when he realized he had overreacted. Then he heard the siren of the police car. "You have to hide me. I'll be sent to jail." He ran to a closet and closed the door behind himself. Through the closet door Carol listened to Gilbert first beg her not to tell the police where he was, then begin crying, saying he was afraid they'd send him to jail. Jarred by his reaction but feeling a surge of pity, Carol promised Gilbert that she wouldn't press charges and she would ask the police not to make a big issue of the incident.

Carol was true to her word. There was no arrest. The police, treating it as a domestic dispute, left after talking to Carol, but not Gilbert. Gil emerged from his hiding place contrite, upset with the scene he caused and humiliated. With the initial shock worn off and seeing Gil's apparent remorse, Carol felt he had learned a lesson and forgave him. She told herself he had just been out of control for the moment and tried to remember that he was usually a calm, collected and caring individual. She couldn't stay mad at him; he was, after all, her best friend.

CHAPTER 17

STRANGE REVELATIONS

NOT LONG AFTER this incident, Carol began noticing problems with the company. "We were a cash operation and receipts often did not match the cash on hand. One day I asked Gilbert about this." She sat him down and made him go over the books with her. She showed him the discrepancies between the cash on hand and the receipts.

Gilbert started yelling. He hit things, threw things. He reminded Carol of a frustrated child having a tantrum. He claimed he was innocent of any wrongdoing and vowed to catch the culprit.

The next day, Gilbert came to Carol cursing his brothers. He was sure they had stolen the money from the business. "They are terrible people, untrustworthy no matter how much I do for them." The outbursts went on and on and became more frequent. Other days he cursed the employees, making the same arguments. Sometimes he broke down in tears.

Each time, Carol noticed that gradually his mood changed after the initial outburst. He became contrite. He admitted that he had used the money without telling her. Or his brothers had taken the money with his knowledge and agreement. "The fault was with no one but himself, yet he could not bring himself to be honest about it or talk to me before taking things from the business. Finally, I took the business checkbook home with me. If it wasn't available in the shop, at least he couldn't misuse the funds in the checking account."

Still the tantrums continued in other ways. Gilbert began leaving the employees unsupervised when he had promised to be at the office while Carol worked on expansion and sales. "It wasn't that I didn't trust the employees. It was just that they had different skill levels and needed one of us to make certain all the work was done correctly and on time. At other times, Gilbert was the last to leave the company at the end of the workday, as we had agreed, but he failed to lock up. Things turned up missing and there was no way to discover what happened or who took them.

"And always there was great hostility between Gilbert and his brothers. At times they all seemed to hate one another. Certainly they often were openly hostile to me. There were vicious rumors spread about everyone, including me, and the situation was getting out of hand."

Then one day after a particularly nasty argument between the brothers, Gil's brother waited until Gil had stormed out and then strode over to Carol.

"He's going back to his old self," he said bitterly.

"His old self?" she repeated, uncertain of what he meant.

He nodded. "You do know Gil has a criminal record, don't you?" She stared at the brother, silent and unbelieving. With all the accusations flying between the two men, it had to be just angry words, Carol thought. Nevertheless, the words made her uneasy. And it was a feeling she could not seem to shake. Carol began to have more flashbacks in which the shadowy form of the rapist returned. Even more frightening, each time he looked more and more like Gilbert.

Her calls to Roberta King became more frequent now. "Can't you please look for a man who looks like my business partner?" And King, unable to reveal the details of the police investigation or possible suspects about whom there was not enough proof to make an arrest, could only promise they would.

Though he had begun to date others, Gil was still spending many nights in the guest room of Carol's condo watching television until late and then trying to sleep. Many nights he knocked on her bedroom door at two or three o'-clock in the morning needing to talk. She understood how anxiety escalated in the darkness and he was a friend after all so she got out of bed and joined him in the living room to discuss whatever was bothering him. Though she didn't tell him what his brother had told her, he seemed to know and began to talk more of his past. "I feel so safe with you," he confided.

"I was a thief," Gilbert said quietly late one night. "I started stealing when I was a little kid. My parents never said anything. My brothers never said anything. It was something I was good at, something that got the other kids to look up to me."

He went on telling her how good he was. "No one will ever catch me."

"Catch you at what?" Carol asked, taken aback.

He laughed. "Pretty much anything I want to do. That's how good I am. I even know how to fool a lie detector."

"But your brother said you've been to prison."

Gilbert admitted that he had and more than once. Neither jail sentence was very long by prison standards, but he had been in the Texas State Penitentiary.

Carol was shocked. "I was raised to think that being in prison was the worst punishment you could have. A person has to do something really terrible to go to prison. It isn't something that just happens in life." She paused, stared at her friend and went on agitatedly, "Did you rob people at gunpoint? Did you go into their homes? Did you . . ."

She didn't really want to know any of this. She didn't want any more surprises. She didn't want to think about her friend and business partner being a criminal. He kept making excuses. She lost track of what she heard or didn't hear that night. She just knew it was too much.

Later, while Carol was still trying to understand and come to terms with what she had learned about him, Gilbert announced he was going on a weekend prison ministry program with an outreach group from church. He came to Carol's house when he returned, his face flush with joy, his look like that of a little boy on Christmas morning who had gotten every toy on his list from Santa and a few for which he had forgotten to ask.

"I have just given testimony. I'm not a thief, Carol. I was a thief. People change. I have changed."

He explained that the inmates liked the idea of talking with someone who had been where they are, who had turned his life around, who had become a success despite his past.

After this, Carol began to feel better. Gilbert had a right to be proud of himself, didn't he? Here was a man whose education was limited. His parents lived in Little Mexico, because they were not welcome in the better neighborhoods even though they could afford to live in them. He was a short man in a city that bragged about its tall Texans. He was stocky in a world that prized the lean and trim. He was merely financially comfortable in a city that worshipped economic excess. He had become a criminal for reasons that, while not good, were at least understandable. He had been a kid who had spent his life in the midst of "things" that would be the proud possessions only of other people, "better" people. It was obvious to Carol that he stole because just having some of the valuables made him feel that he was as good as everyone else.

Gilbert continued his confession. "Eventually I sold everything I stole. I had friends, men and women, who loved showing off their quality jewelry." They were Dallas rich, Dallas ostentatious—Dallas tacky, in Carol's mind— who wore expensive watches, rings, necklaces and bracelets so dazzling they could blind you in bright sunlight. The gemstones would sparkle like spotlights shooting in all directions, always flashing money.

"I had an arrangement with a jeweler—his name was Kevin—whose car I often detailed at the time." He is upscale—North Dallas—a man who would be responsible for crafting the Super Bowl rings one year.

"He knew I could sell expensive jewelry. I would come into my shop or meet with clients deliberately flashing a diamond encrusted gold Rolex or a necklace that probably wholesales for several thousand dollars. If I sold whatever it was, then he would give me a percentage." It was like one of those restaurants where there are models wearing expensive clothing from a local boutique moving among the tables at lunch, trying to get you to buy what they have on. The arrangement struck Carol as odd, but so did the people who flashed that kind of jewelry. She chalked it up as just one more eccentricity of Big D.

"The men I met during the ministry this weekend in prison look up to me," Gil said. "Most come from backgrounds no worse than mine." Most of them felt put down by society, by their "betters." They all knew that they would be out soon, that they would have another chance. And here was this Christian businessman, financially successful, a member of a prestigious church, an ex-con who loved them so much that he returned to the same place all of them were anxious to leave. They were deeply moved. They were inspired to succeed in their own rights and they were reinforced by his presence.

They also, Gilbert said, reinforced his feeling about how much his life had changed since he had gotten out of prison. "I could never do anything wrong now," he insisted. "I've become a Christian." Followers of Christ could forgive thieves but they didn't become thieves.

For a short while things seemed to quiet down a bit though Roberta King was calling Carol all the time now. Strangely enough, Carol thought, Detective King was asking more questions about Gil. It made Carol nervous when she was around him. And the end of Carol and Gil's brief love affair had been complicated by many things—both business wise and personally—that grew in importance. There were Gil's temper outbursts, his jealousy and the thefts from the company. Then Gil injured his ankle and said he could not work for six weeks.

Since Gilbert could not do the outside work because of his injury, Carol wanted him to cover the business at the shop while she went out selling new accounts, but she found she couldn't count on him. "I didn't know if the limited movement from the injury made him unusually restless or what. I just knew that he often left before the business day was over and when he could drive, he some-times took one of the bank cars and used it as a personal car for a few days, thinking either he would not be found out or they would not mind."

The situation darkened. Gilbert began following Carol day and night. She would drive to the mall or go some-where else and there he would be. "He insisted that he needed to protect me. He insisted that he needed to meet any man I considered dating. He was like a strict older brother whose kid sister just reached puberty and, for the first time, the brother's friends noticed the girl was be-coming a desirable young woman. It would have been flat-tering by some of the macho standards of Texas, but I wasn't a Texan and to me the standards were pathetically chauvinistic."

Carol tried joking with Gilbert about his behavior, hop-ing he would stop. He was serious, though, and said he had no intention of stopping. "I only want you to date men of whom I approve." In fact, on several occasions he chose men for Carol and had them come to meet her at work. Gilbert had told them that Carol wanted to meet them. Carol was upset not only by the inference, but by Gil's continued jealousy and his distrust of her ability to handle her own life. She tried to see his attention in a good light. She tried to tell herself he was worried about her. She tried to tell herself that her own emotions were on edge since the attack and perhaps she was overreacting. In reality, Gil's actions only served to intensify her fears.

"I told myself that my anger was misdirected. Gilbert didn't know much about the rape. Gilbert didn't know the number of times I returned to my apartment to check the locks on the doors and windows. Gilbert didn't know how often I got up in the middle of the night frightened by my dreams. He didn't understand the fear, the insecurity. He also didn't know when he had gone too far.

"I knew that Gilbert had friends in my complex from that first day when we met in the laundry room. I never met any others nor did I question him about them, because our relationship was such that we either were at work, at church or dining out. We weren't lolling around a swimming pool, we weren't partying at the complex or gossiping with neighbors. But I didn't like the fact that when I had some friends visit from out of town—a couple one time and a single woman another—he not only knew when they arrived and how long they stayed, but the places where I took them to eat, shop and sightsee.

"One night when I was trying to get him to stop joking about his constant surveillance, he told me that Detective King and some of the other officers connected with the Crimes Against Persons unit were talking to him. I didn't tell him that they were talking to me as well."

Carol knew that once you've been in prison, the police always want to talk to you. "It's not just that you might be committing a crime. It's that you also might have old friends from prison who are doing something wrong. They figure you're a good source. However, I felt it was my words to Detective King that had set off the alarm. I felt guilty that I had involved Gil, but a twinge of some unknown fear came over me. I pushed it away and forced myself to ignore it. Instead, I told him more about the rape, the details of which I had for so long kept to myself. I told him about the constant flashbacks. We had become so close despite the problems that were creeping into the business and our relationship, that I felt he needed to understand what had happened to make me the way I was, just as his telling me about his childhood, his time in prison, his allowing me to know his father, his brothers, his wife and daughters, all helped me to understand him. And Gil spent the rest of the evening comforting me. But we never discussed it after that one time. I didn't tell him so he could comfort me. I didn't expect him to help me recover other than just being my friend."

Over time Gil began revealing more and more to Carol. One night he confided the story of his former girlfriend, someone who had left Dallas after being seriously involved with him.

Apparently Gilbert's feelings for the young woman were strong, because when it was obvious that his romantic relationship with Carol was not going to last, he began trying to call the woman at her new home in Tennessee. He wanted to get back together with her, but she wanted nothing to do with him.

Carol wondered why the woman rejected Gilbert so she asked his brothers. "It's because he hit her," one of Gilbert's brothers confided to her a few days later. "Hit her nose and made it bloody." Carol didn't take what he said too seriously, because she felt the brother was jealous of Gil and trying to make him look bad. Yet she was jarred by his words.

She could not help asking Gil about it.

To her surprise, Gilbert told Carol his brother had told her the truth. Shamed, he said, "I never should have hit her. It was the wrong thing to do." He confirmed that the violence was bad enough for her nose to be injured and shortly after that she and her mother moved to Tennessee. No matter how much he apologized, no matter how much he wanted her back, she made it clear the relationship was over.

Carol was shocked that Gil had a violent side with women, although he swore that he had only lashed out that once and it would never happen again.

His revelations about his past were becoming more and more unnerving. Carol had tried to understand his past delinquency, rationalizing it as youthful indiscretion. Many people made mistakes and Gil had long made them right by changing his life, becoming a born-again Christian and helping others. But here was another instance of a worrisome character flaw in the person she thought of as her best friend.

Carol was almost relieved when Gil announced one day, "There is only one more step for me. I need to get married." Carol felt he was obsessed with marrying someone "respectable" and with securing his place in the church and the community. "He registered with dating services, lying about his background to attract the right kind of woman. He wanted in a woman what Marion admired in a man—the trim, blonde, upwardly mobile, personally secure person who kept herself in good physical and mental shape—someone like me. Although I had told him about the rape, he didn't know how much I was falling apart. He didn't know I had never recovered from the attack. He didn't know that, at times, our arguments provided emotional release that kept me from breaking down and crying. Not that I was using the fights. I never wanted them. It was that there was a fine line between anger and sadness and I constantly fought to keep from crossing it."

A few weeks later Gilbert announced he had met a woman he described as his future wife. She was a divorcée, the former wife of a prominent area professional. "She had blonde hair, the trim figure, all the features that mattered to him and when I saw her, I realized that she and I looked quite similar. Gilbert still spent occasional nights at my place, using my guest bedroom when we worked late or sometimes showing up quite late, because he had been unable to sleep. But he said he was planning on marrying this woman and they began sharing an intimate relationship. She lived not far from my complex so he was able to easily see us both, me for business purposes and her for nurturing what I assumed was a growing love between them."

The woman's name was Rosemarie. Gil confided, "I've finally met the person I've been searching for. God has given her to me, because I met her in church, she has money, a good job, owns a beautiful home and her parents have money she will inherit one day as their only child." Marrying her would leave him set for life. In fact, he told Carol he didn't feel he needed the business anymore. "Rosemarie has everything. Together we'll move away from Dallas where I have such bad memories."

"Just wanting to be married is not a good reason for marrying someone," Carol objected, but Gil didn't pay attention.

Gil told Carol the woman was unaware of his criminal background. She eventually found out, though. They were driving to meet her parents and they got stopped for speeding. Gil was driving and when his license was routinely run through the national computer system used by law enforcement officers throughout the country, his record was discovered.

A ticket for what most people see as a minor speeding violation, one in which the driver is acting safely for the road conditions, endangering no one else, but driving faster than the posted limit, is actually not usually treated as a major crime. However, the wrongdoer can be arrested and an officer can have the driver jailed.

The police officer who unknowingly had stopped the ex-convict had Gil get out of the car and began questioning him. The officer looked in the front and back as much as he could, knowing that if he found anything illegal within his line of sight, he could have the man arrested. There was nothing there. There were no warrants out on the man. There was no reason to hold him. However, the extra time and questions had been so unusual that Gilbert had to tell his girlfriend about his past. By the time the couple reached her parents' home, Rosemarie was aware that he had been a thief. Like Carol, she also forgave him, accepting that he had changed. And she stayed in the relationship after they returned from her parent's home.

Of course, Carol was unaware of what had happened between Gilbert and Rosemarie. Nevertheless, as they opened the second location for their business, Carol saw Gilbert becoming more fractured and emotional. There were days he didn't show up at all and others when he left in the middle of a transaction leaving whoever was there to finish up. The tension at the office was palpable. And as she confided to Detective King, Carol's nightmares about the man who raped her were becoming more, not less, frequent.

CHAPTER 18

MORE VICTIMS, MORE QUESTIONS

I entered the residence through the window, same pattern as previously. I knew where the bedroom was located and I was aware that there might be other people in the house, because it was a big house. I never did know for sure if there were other residents there, but I knew the other bedrooms were on the opposite side of the house. Anyway I took the screen off and opened the window, which was unlatched. Then I climbed through the window and I went into the bedroom. She didn't hear me come in.

I put something over my head like one of her T-shirts or something. Then I put on another T-shirt to cover my mouth at the same time, so she could only see my eyes.

Then I approached her. She was on her stomach. I covered her mouth and told her, "You make any noise and I'll have to use the pistol." I had the Derringer again . . .

I felt her and had her feel me. She was on her stomach when I approached her. And I injected her. In other words I made love to her, dog style, and this probably lasted for about ten to fifteen minutes. Then

I heard something in the house. I assumed somebody heard me or was coming in. They had a dog, but I believed the dog was in the backyard or he was up front and he wasn't around. So anyway I heard something. It was a clear noise that caught my attention. And then I left immediately through the same entrance that I came in. I had a cap that I'd left in the trash can in the back behind the residence. I had parked the car near Marsh Lane. There's a church there on the corner where I parked my girlfriend's red Nissan. And by the time I got to the car it dawned on me that I left my cap behind. I went back and got it out of the trashcan, then I went back to my car.

It was dark when Officer Henderson arrived at the entrance to Marsh Lane Baptist Church—dark and quiet. He had been on routine patrol, but it was already 3:00 A.M. on Sunday and in a few hours his parishioners would be coming for Sunday services. He needed to prepare, to review his sermon, collect his thoughts and switch from being a police officer to a pastor.

"I drove in and circled the parking lot and the building," said Pastor Henderson. "It was just a habit I had picked up from being an officer. You look for anything out of the ordinary, not that I was expecting anything.

"This time I saw a red car. I shined my brights on the car and it was empty."

Pastor Henderson thought little of the car parked in the lot. It could have been someone using the lot as a convenience while visiting someone down the alley that led to the homes on nearby Dutchess Trail. It could have been teenagers who stopped to park and then left to go somewhere. There was nothing suspicious about the car. Routinely, he took down the license number of the car that was parked where it did not belong. Then he went inside the church to his office.

It was only a few minutes later that Pastor Henderson heard a chopper overhead. He thought, *That isn't normal.* Immediately, he left his study and went out to the church parking lot. The red car was gone, replaced by patrol cars checking the area. One of the drivers, Officer Shirley Hobbs, came over to talk with him. That was when he learned about the rape. He went back inside and got the license number of the car that had been parked in the lot and they ran it. It was registered to a woman in Richardson.

Richardson, Texas is a suburb north of Dallas. The area was popular with electronics firms and the builders of up-scale housing. Developments for the wealthy were constantly under construction, the residents either working locally or taking the freeway for an easy commute to the adjoining major cities.

There was no proof that the car Henderson had seen in the parking lot was connected in any way to the rape that had just occurred. However, they were suspicious, because there didn't seem to be another logical explanation for the car's presence before the rape and its sudden disappearance afterwards. Pastor Henderson had not checked to see if the hood was hot, a sign that the car had been recently driven, but the officers felt they might have a lead.

Pastor Henderson returned to his police role and rode with the other officers to the address in Richardson listed on the car registration filed with the state motor vehicle division. There, in front of an upscale apartment building was the red Nissan. This time the officer checked the hood. It was hot. The car had definitely been recently driven. One of the officers turned to Henderson. "This could be our man."

They walked to the right apartment and knocked on the door. It took quite a while for a response. Finally, an attractive blonde woman in nightclothes answered. She said that the car parked outside was hers. "But I haven't been driving it." She added, "It's right where I left it several hours ago."

"Is there anyone else living here?" the officers wanted to know. "Is there anyone else who might have used the car?"

She brushed back a wisp of hair that had fallen in her eyes. "My boyfriend is spending the night, but I know he hasn't been using it, because I'm a very light sleeper. Every little sound awakens me. If he had gotten out of bed to go driving somewhere, I would have known about it."

She was annoyed to be needlessly awakened. However, she understood that something was wrong and was quite willing to cooperate. The woman was friendly, helpful and obviously telling the truth as she knew it.

But the real truth was quite different . . .

It was April, it was still kind of cool outside and I had a jacket and I wore gloves. When I got back home, I dusted myself off around the swimming pool and got a wash towel and cleaned myself good so I could get rid of the evidence. Then I entered my girl-friend's apartment or my apartment—it was our apartment—and she didn't hear me. She didn't hear me when I left either. She was a heavy sleeper. It was probably about fifteen or thirty minutes later when they came banging on the door. My girlfriend said, "It's the police." Then I said "Yeah, go ahead. Let them in," because there was no way I could exit any-way. They were going by the license plate. They said that the car was still warm when they felt the hood. So they came in and I acted like I didn't know what was going on. And honestly my girlfriend didn't know that I left and came back and got in the bed. Like I said, she was a heavy sleeper so she didn't know and wasn't aware of any of this.

The moment the man came out of the bedroom, Officer Henderson and the other Dallas Police Officers were suspicious. He was short and stockily built just as Carol Cook had described her rapist to Detective King and was corroborated by other victims of the Ski Mask Rapist. Not that there was any proof that this was the man they sought. What they had was a car that had been in a church parking lot at the same time that a rape was taking place a short distance away. The car had been driven from the church parking lot at a time that seemed to be between when the rape was reported to the police and when the police began scouring the neighborhood. And the car had been returned to the parking space used by the woman who owned it, a woman of money and prestige. But had her boyfriend been the driver? The woman was convinced she was a light sleeper and would have heard her boyfriend if he arose from their bed. That was all the information they had. That and the man's name and enough information about him to learn that he had prior felony convictions for which he had served the sentence demanded by the court.

If this had been a television script, there would have been several things happening immediately. First, twenty-four hour surveillance would have been placed on the man. This would have meant a rolling surveillance involving from two to three unmarked cars, all using special tactical radio frequencies allowing them to communicate with one another without someone listening to their conversations on a scanner. This would have meant two officers on a stakeout of the home whenever the man went to bed. And, in a television movie, but not in the real world, there would have been a search warrant immediately obtained, then executed while the prime suspect was away. The girlfriend would argue. She would be tearful. But she would cooperate, feeling that if she told the truth, if she let the officers look everywhere and at everything, including her most private possessions, the man she loved would be exonerated.

Again, in the movie, there would be the discovery of an object or objects linked to the crime. "May I have a closer look at the ring you are wearing, Ma'am," a detective might say.

"This ring? Isn't it beautiful? My beloved gave it to me."

"That ring has a unique setting and the initials MC engraved on the back."

"Yes, for Monroe Cartier of the Cartier jewelry family. My beloved showed me a book of their specially designed mounts and told me how the person who makes the jewelry always puts his initials there like an artist signing a painting."

"I'm sorry, Ma'am," the detective would say. "These initials are those of Monica Charles, one of the victims of the Ski Mask Rapist. Everywhere he went he would steal something. We're pretty sure he pawned most of it, but it looks like you have the misfortune of having been given

Ms. Charles' ring. I'm afraid I'll have to take it with me for evidence."

"My ring? The one my beloved gave me? Officer, how can you say that? How can you think such a thing? This is a genuine Cartier. My beloved wouldn't lie to me. He wouldn't! I know that. I . . ." And then she would break into tears, sobbing uncontrollably as she realizes the terrible truth.

Of course, there would be more evidence, perhaps a diary. It would be confiscated by the police and a warrant quickly issued for the man's arrest.

That's how it works on television. Real life was and is quite different.

The police had nothing conclusive. They had a man with a criminal record who was not wanted for so much as a misdemeanor traffic ticket when the officers confronted him around 4:00 A.M. that April Sunday. They had a highly believable "witness" who, though admittedly asleep between the time her boyfriend might have left the apartment and when the police came knocking, was convinced she would have fully awakened the moment the man beside her stirred from the bed. And they had another victim who could not recognize her assailant's face.

As bad as the lack of any meaningful evidence, except a woman's car that a competent defense attorney would show could have been stolen, was the fact that the department could not set up a twenty-four hour surveillance. Manpower shortages and equipment limitations left the police in a reactive state. They would do what they could to watch the man. They would go to his place of business. They would try to find and talk with his friends. But as soon as some other, unrelated major crime, like murder, occurred, it would be labeled a bigger priority. And the man they believed might possibly be the Ski Mask Rapist would be able to continue to violate women, because any judge who issued a search warrant based on the flimsy evidence the police now had would be liable for charges by the Bar Association. The police felt helpless.

Later, when Pastor Henderson went to see the latest distraught victim and tried to comfort her in his dual roles as pastor and police officer, he felt he could not just walk away. He gave his card to the victim's mother, telling her that he was available to anyone in the family who needed help. Then, after church on Sunday, Pastor Henderson and his wife returned to the home to meet with the victim and her mother. He was a man acting from two callings and his actions showed how important both could be to people within the terrorized city of Dallas.

NOT LONG AFTER this, Detective King began stopping by to see Carol. "She never told me if they were close to having some answers and, hopefully, being able to gain enough evidence to make an arrest. I didn't know if she was trying to reassure me that my nightmare would soon be over or if she was worried about me and the other victims, because the rapist was still on the loose. He had found us all once. Perhaps she felt we were at risk of his returning and making good on his death threats since our testimony could put him in jail."

CHAPTER 19

UNRAVELING

TIME SPUN PAST. It was in December that Carol's relationship with Gilbert began to deteriorate more. He had been distant and withdrawn in the previous two months. Then in December, he was preoccupied with his role in the church choir, which was preparing for the annual Christmas pageant. "The previous Christmas season, Gilbert asked me for help during the weeks prior to the pageant. He had difficulty reading and asked me to work with him on Bible passages. We went through similar work with the music he needed to practice. He could neither sight-read the notes nor readily read the lyrics. Some of the songs were familiar carols, of course, the type of thing everyone learns in school. Other songs were unfamiliar, more difficult, and that was where I came in.

"I supposed this year he was having his girlfriend help him, because he stopped asking for my help. On the increasingly rare occasions when I did see or speak to him, Gil seemed agitated and disturbed. He had not come to work most of November and did not work at all the entire month of December because of the church pageant. Aside from the physical absences, Gil also seemed to have lost interest in the business. He said on several occasions we should sell it and one time he told me I did such a good job running the business that he would gladly sell his half to me.

"Gilbert's relationship with his girlfriend also seemed strained. He said he was only going to marry her for her money, though I had the impression that either she truly cared about him or he believed that she did. We had met a few times and she was a very nice person. She certainly had the looks, the style and the intellect that I knew he was drawn to. Since she did seem to care about him, I suggested that he give the relationship more time. I knew that he had been anxious to get married from the time that we had ended our sexual relationship. I didn't think he understood how much one needs to nurture a relationship since he had been small when his own parents divorced. Maybe Gilbert and his girlfriend were right for each other, but I didn't think he could know that at this point. Besides, I hoped he was not serious about marrying her only for her money, though knowing what Gilbert had said in the past, that certainly was a possibility. And I worried about what he'd told me about dropping the business in which I had now invested so much time and money. Though his remarks about getting out of the business always seemed offhanded, I decided to take them seriously and do something to protect my investment. I contacted a lawyer to have papers drawn up for Gil to sell his half of the business to me. When I told Gil, he seemed relieved and promised he would sign the papers. I realized Gil no longer seemed driven in business the way I was. He didn't have pride in the long-term work, even though he delighted in pleasing a new customer the way he had pleased me the first time he cleaned my Cadillac. When he began talking more and more about moving to California and never having to struggle again, I was glad to have taken the step to contact the lawyer."

While Carol waited for a telephone call from the lawyer's office saying the papers were ready to be signed, Carol continued to struggle with the business. "Our company was going downhill because of Gil's failure to do his share of the work. He seemed to always have a lot of money, which I attributed to savings I knew nothing about. I was not so lucky. I had to tap into my savings for living expenses."

Other problems cropped up. "I found a business account check for over a thousand dollars that one of Gilbert's brothers had cashed. This was totally inappropriate, though I didn't blame his brother. I knew if I confronted Gilbert, he would likely say that his brother had stolen the money from the account. If I confronted the brother, he would say that Gilbert gave him the money. When I still trusted Gilbert completely, I would have believed that one or more of his brothers might be a thief. Now I assumed that Gilbert would lie, that he had given his brother the money."

Carol could not stand it anymore, especially in her fragile emotional and mental state. Rather than try to have it out with either Gilbert or his brother, Carol called to make another appointment with the attorney. The receptionist scheduled her for a morning meeting in a few days.

One day shortly before Carol's meeting with the lawyer, the tension at the business reached a boiling point. The employees had become extremely upset with Gilbert lately and his temper had grown worse. On this day when he walked into the shop, there were no more problems than normal. There were no questions that needed answering that should have been uncomfortable. Yet all of a sudden he strode over to Carol and exploded. "What have you done with the money?"

Gilbert was a small but powerfully built man. He grabbed Carol, twisted her arm behind her back, lifted her in the air and, while holding her painfully helpless in his grip, threw her over the desk. "I landed on a chair that was thrown back against the wall by the force of my body. Then I bounced off the chair and fell to the floor. Gilbert grabbed my handbag, jumped in his car and drove off.

"People who worked for us and others in the garage came rushing over to help me. Everyone was upset, worried about my injuries, talking about how he was crazy. Someone called 9-1-1 and a patrol car came immediately. Statements were taken, the information was broadcast and

Gilbert was arrested soon after that over at the site of the other shop."

Carol was too dazed to think about anything right then. "Everyone was angry and frightened for me and concerned about why such violence had happened. I immediately went to the doctor, who found bruises and a strain requiring my arm to be kept in a sling."

The day's shocking events took a toll on Carol's already frayed nerves even as she tried to sleep that night. After waking from another nightmare about the rape, Carol called Roberta King telling her again of her fears of being stalked by her rapist. "Please, can't you look for someone who looks like my partner?" Carol tearfully begged once more.

Once again, Detective King revealed nothing, but promised the police were doing everything they could to catch the Ski Mask Rapist. After a fitful night, Carol dragged herself to work the next morning.

Customers who came in that day asked questions. Some had heard what had happened the day before. Others noticed Carol's arm was in a sling and asked what happened. Many of them told Carol that they were loyal to the business because of her, not Gilbert. "Even the long-term customers he had had before I became his partner had come to dislike him. It was information that shocked me, though I was touched that so many people cared about my feelings and injuries."

Now afraid of the man who had been her friend and partner, Carol agreed to press assault and battery charges against Gilbert. Then he could be held in jail while the police obtained a warrant to search his home, the company, perhaps his girlfriend's home, all in pursuit of whatever other crimes he might have committed. It was extremely upsetting for everyone, but Detective King was adamant about wanting Carol to pursue this. "She kept saying it was important and I kept thinking about how Gilbert had talked about all ex-cons being harassed no matter what they did.

"I had been hurt and physically injured by his violent attack. Gilbert had done something terrible. Yet would my pressing charges result in a punishment greater than the crime just because of a past he seemed to have overcome?"

Carol was still pondering the question when she returned home from the police station. Suddenly the telephone rang and when Carol picked up the receiver she heard a man's voice she did not recognize. "Drop the assault charge on Gilbert or you're dead."

The next day she called the police to drop the charges. "Detective King begged me not to drop them, but she wouldn't give me any particularly compelling reason other than she wanted Gil held longer for investigation." Despite Detective King's pleas, the threatening phone call made Carol fear for her life, so she dropped the charges. "I wasn't certain of my decision or what would happen next. I just knew I had to get away from Gilbert. I would leave the business forever. I would have nothing more to do with Gilbert as a business partner or a friend. I had had enough."

With the charges dropped by Carol, Gilbert was released from jail. He immediately went to California.

Two days later, Carol met with her lawyer. He had the papers for sale of the business ready but now Gil wasn't even in the state to sign them. She told the lawyer about the problems with missing money and the attack on her. The lawyer recommended she work her way out of the business as quickly as possible and write off whatever she couldn't sell as a loss.

Gil's absence not only prevented Carol from legally taking over the company, it grounded business to a halt. All work at the shop stopped and Carol's physical and emotional well-being continued to decline. "My nerves were frayed from all the stress. I realized I needed to see a doctor. In the weeks immediately after the rape, I had lost a lot of weight. I had regained some of it, but now I was back down to 107, a weight that was still way too low for my height and build. I was sleeping only three or four hours a night. I was falling apart, though I would only admit to myself that I needed to regain the weight and get more rest."

A few days later, Gilbert called her on the phone. They

talked about the future of the business. He told Carol, "I am definitely going to marry my girlfriend. Soon, we'll move everything permanently to California to live. Now I'll definitely sign the papers to sell my half of the business to you if you want it."

Carol did not believe him.

By February, Carol was exhausted, frustrated, scared and uncertain about everything. A couple, both artists, she had met at her new church and had become friendly with noticed Carol's withdrawn and lonely appearance. The woman kept asking Carol to join her and her husband at social functions. She especially wanted Carol to meet a recently divorced friend of hers. After two weeks of hearing what a wonderful person this friend was, Carol finally agreed to meet the man at the couple's home. And so she met Bob Cook, a well-known artist and owner of an established and highly regarded architectural rendering studio. The first thing Carol noticed about him were his mischievous blue eyes and good looks. She also liked his infectious laugh and his happy, self-confident personality. She learned that in addition to his architectural renderings, Bob was a specialist in Corvette paintings. The Corvette is Chevrolet's high performance sports car that has almost a cult following among some drivers and collectors, including Carol. His images of Corvettes in a wide variety of conditions and settings were enormously popular with collectors and enthusiasts of the cars. "I was impressed with what he was doing and, though I had not been involved with my own art since the rape, when he saw some of my earlier work, he told me how much he liked the quality of it. I didn't know if he was just being nice, though I was impressed with his discussion of the technical side of what I was doing. But, most important, he had a great sense of humor. It was only when I began laughing that I realized how long it had been since I enjoyed even a simple conversation."

By March Carol had found even more terrible problems with the business accounting. There were bills for a variety of products and equipment, all paid for from the business checkbook, yet none of the items were in stock. "I didn't know if the books had been padded in order to steal the money or if the items had been purchased, then diverted."

It was also in March, long after their original discussion, that she again brought up the subject of her rape with Gilbert. He was back from California and despite her lack of trust in his word, Carol had the lawyer prepare a new set of papers for both she and Gilbert to sign to sell off the business. She had known for quite some time there was no way they were going to continue in business together and even though she hated to give it up, Carol felt selling it seemed the most sensible action they could take. Carol telephoned Gilbert and asked him to meet to sign the papers. She would no longer allow him to come to her home, so they met at a nearby restaurant for lunch. Though she only wanted to discuss the business, as they sat there, Carol could not help reliving the rape in her mind.

"Seeing him again in the restaurant reminded me of the night he had slept over when I had a bad dream about the rapist and Gil had come to my bedroom door." She remembered the alarm she had felt when she'd seen his silhouette. She'd thought in that moment the rapist had returned. Now, sitting across the table from him, Carol began experiencing what she told herself was irrational paranoia, but she couldn't stop the images that flashed across her mind. Without thinking, without realizing what she was about to say, she suddenly blurted out, "I have to ask you something, Gilbert. I have to know: Are you the rapist?"

Gilbert looked at her dead straight, took her hand in his and said, "Carol, I would never hurt you. I love you and you are the best friend I've ever had. I didn't do that."

"But the police are asking questions about you when they call me," she said, confusion in her voice. Of course, she didn't tell him about asking the police to search for someone who looked like Gilbert.

Quietly but passionately, he told her what it was like to be an ex-convict and always be under suspicion. He said it was hard enough dealing with the distrust of the police and strangers, but to have a close friend like Carol suspect him of a crime was doubly painful. Despite herself, she found he aroused her sympathies.

"The police don't believe that anyone can change. They even questioned my brothers. They don't believe that a man can serve his time, recognize his mistakes and move in a new direction with his life. The police always come back again and again to see if they can link someone who has a record with a current crime, even if the person has his own business, goes to church and keeps out of trouble."

At that moment, looking into his eyes and hearing his claims of innocence, Carol believed Gilbert. She told herself that it is hard for people to think differently about a person who made some mistakes in his past. She knew there were men and women who, when young, had gone to jail, then moved on to productive, respectable lives. Now she hoped the man across the table whose eyes were filled with compassion was sincere. Overwhelmed by her emotions, Carol said good-bye to Gilbert and left the restaurant without even bringing up the subject of selling the business.

Despite Gilbert's words at lunch, in the days that followed, doubt seeped into Carol's mind as she kept returning to her memories of the night he stayed in her apartment. Once again, she saw him back-lit, the mirror image of the rapist standing in her doorway. Despite his assurances and her momentary belief in his innocence the afternoon they met for lunch, when Carol later thought again how the two silhouettes seemed so similar, she was deeply troubled.

She tried not to obsess. "At the same time, we had customers who were police officers. We had a man who was a police helicopter pilot. We had some of the patrol officers with whom Gilbert had gone on ride-alongs. One was his friend and we even had gone out together. Why would policemen befriend someone they were trying to put in jail? It made no sense."

Carol talked again with Detective King. "I asked her more pointed questions about my case. I asked her specifically about Gilbert. I told her again that when I juxtaposed the silhouette of the rapist with Gilbert's, the similarities were striking. I felt sure she would somehow understand my fears."

A few days later, Detective King visited Carol at the shop. This time, she asked Carol very specific questions about Gilbert. "Do you know where he was on Wednesday, three weeks ago? Do you know where he obtained some of the jewelry he wears?" It bothered Carol, because she asked so many questions that seemed totally irrelevant. She wondered what Gilbert's choice in jewelry had to do with anything. It was as though he was suspected of stealing, something Carol felt sure he no longer did.

After Detective King left, Carol thought about the questions and felt a twinge of guilt. She was reminded of what Gilbert had told her over and over: the police are always suspicious of ex-convicts, never believing such people can live respectable, crime-free lives after time spent in prison. Besides, though Gilbert had lost some friends when he attacked Carol at the shop, she just could not believe that police officers would continue coming in if Gilbert had been committing major crimes.

A few weeks later, Detective King visited Carol again. Finally, King asked the question Carol dreaded hearing: "You don't think Gilbert could be the rapist, do you?"

Even though she had asked herself and Gilbert the very same question, Carol was shocked to hear it from a police officer. Despite her fear, deep down Carol wanted to believe Gilbert was innocent. *This has to be the police fishing for information against an ex-convict*, she told herself. She knew that Gilbert and his brothers had been questioned by the police about a variety of things over the years. They had talked of it in front of her before. They were outraged about it, even though there was no love lost among the brothers. To them, the ongoing police interest truly was harassment and Carol had to agree.

She had overheard the men talking of it at work one time and the conversation stirred Carol's memory of reports she had seen on the news or read in the newspapers. It seemed that every city she had ever lived in, men who were part of a minority frequently had problems. In some cities she read newspaper accounts in which men were arrested for an "offense" dubbed DWB—Driving While Black. A black male either alone in a nice car in a predominantly white neighborhood or a group of black males out at a time the police thought was inappropriate, would be stopped. The license would be run, the car checked as much as legally possible and then the person would be let go with a "warning" instead of a ticket that would leave a paper trail. And this was done without probable cause and without meaningful results.

In some cities, Asian males were stopped. In others, men of Hispanic or Middle Eastern appearance were subject to the same inappropriate, casual checks by police.

In Dallas, Texas, a man could be stopped because a victim said that the criminal was "Hispanic short, stocky build, with a mustache and black hair." Since many, many first generation Mexican-American males fit that description, the police had carte blanche to stop all Hispanic males. The better officers knew the description was meaningless except to maybe eliminate whites, blacks and most Native Americans as suspects. Yet they would stop a man with such a description serving as their probable cause. Other officers justified their stopping every male with such an appearance, no matter how ridiculous that might seem.

Though she didn't give an answer to Detective King, later, as she thought about Gilbert, Carol's mind cycled back and forth as fear turned into rationalization and rationalization turned back into fear. "I thought back over the months I had known Gilbert. I remembered all the good Gilbert had done. I remembered that he had become active in church, studying the Bible, trying to limit his friends to those who were not only Christians but those who would encourage his walk on the side of what was right. I remembered the pleasure he got from helping others, whether that meant buying a lunch or volunteering to do work others did not want to handle. He was right. A man could change.

"Then I thought about the day he had attacked me in our office. And I thought about the times he had done mean things to others, including talking in a hostile manner about them and I had scolded him for not practicing what he said he believed."

Not knowing where to turn, she called Gilbert and asked him to stop by. When he arrived, she brought up her doubts about his kindness to him. Gilbert turned serious. "I never meant to harm anyone, though I realize from what you are saying that I have, even if they never heard the words I was using. I wonder if God will forgive me?"

Forgiveness, Carol was beginning to think, was one of his magic words. "He wanted forgiveness, needed forgiveness, wondered where he stood with God."

As Carol talked to him, Gilbert broke down and started crying. "Lately I have been having old feelings. I have been thinking about stealing something or robbing someone. I did it all in the long-ago past. I had put it out of my mind, but now I am coming back to such thoughts."

Feeling a surge of sympathy, Carol patted his hand. "Thoughts are not deeds, Gilbert. God will forgive thoughts."

"Where can I turn for help?"

Carol talked to him about the possibility of therapy. He paused and looked at her. "What if I told you I killed someone, Carol," he said softly. "Will God forgive me that?"

Carol was speechless, her face ashen.

Abruptly Gilbert started laughing hysterically as if he could not stop. Finally he got hold of himself. "I was only kidding and I know God will forgive me. I only have to ask."

After he left, Carol thought about their conversation. One of his problems, Carol decided, was that Gilbert came from a Baptist theological position in which the thought was equal to the deed. The most famous example was an interview Southern Baptist President Jimmy Carter gave to *Playboy* magazine when he was running for election. He was asked if he had ever cheated on his wife, Rosalyn, and he said that he had. He explained that he had committed adultery in his heart, because he had occasionally looked at other women with lust in his heart. He had not flirted with the women. He had not touched them or kissed them. In all likelihood they never experienced treatment any different than they witnessed when Carter was with others, both female and male. However, many fundamentalists believe that Jesus taught that to think about an action can be as serious as taking the action. Nevertheless most people accept that all of us are human. All of us find people other than our spouses to be attractive. All of us may wonder what it would be like to kiss someone, have an affair with the person, perhaps marry the person, despite the fact that we are already in a committed relationship.

Most people do not think that the thought equals the deed. They feel that to think but choose to not act is a mature process. They point out that biologically we can be attracted to many people and, in the course of our lifetime, undoubtedly will be so attracted. That is the reality of being human. But because we do have a choice, the right choice is to not even hint at our interest in anyone other than a spouse.

Still, Carol could not forget their conversation. *Does Gilbert need forgiveness for thoughts that did not become deeds? Or, worse, thoughts that had?* Carol wondered. Perhaps in his theology he did. Certainly there were times when he told Carol that he had paid dearly for his "sins," how he had been forgiven and born again.

Carol's ambivalence in all this was obvious to Detective King during her visits over the next few months.

"What if I told you that Gilbert was a suspect in the rapes?" she asked Carol one afternoon, again casting the shadow of suspicion on Gilbert.

A sick feeling seeped through Carol, pushing away any indignation she would normally have felt over the police unfairly targeting ex-convicts. She shook her head no and said, "It couldn't be him."

King said nothing more.

The Ski Mask Rapist's next attack occurred very soon after this when the cunning criminal entered the apartment of a twenty-two-year-old woman living near Carol. It was 4:00 A.M. when he placed a towel over his victim's face before awakening her at gunpoint.

The area seemed to be a favorite of the man. Police suspected it was close to where he lived, the proximity to his home making it easier for him to commit his crimes without being caught. They were right; the rapist's home was never more than five miles away from wherever he struck. However, the police were frustrated that they were never able to catch the criminal. They didn't know he had moved several times.

A few nights later on April 24, a security guard was carefully checking the grounds of the same complex where Carol had been attacked. There had been a burglary earlier and he knew that his job would be on the line if he couldn't find a way to protect the property he was guarding. The burglary it later turned out, had also been committed by the Ski Mask Rapist, but since no one was assaulted, the police didn't realize the connection.

As the guard walked the complex, he spotted a man lurking in the shadows. The man might have been a Peeping Tom or a burglar, about to steal whatever valuables were inside. He might be the rapist, though he wore no disguise as he stood partially obscured by darkness near a window. Whatever the case, the man did not belong there. The security guard drew his gun, ordered the man to put up his hands and then called for a patrol car that quickly came racing to the scene.

The patrol officers frisked the man, read him his rights and handcuffed him. Then they called for the detectives in case the man was a suspect in one the crime sprees that had been plaguing the area.

"What is his name?" asked a detective.

The uniformed officer replied, "Gilbert Escobedo."

CHAPTER 20

BETRAYAL

GILBERT ESCOBEDO. HIS name was familiar to the officers who now arrested him. He was the man about whom Carol Cook had been telling Detective Roberta King. He was the man living with the woman whose car had been found near the scene of a rape that occurred just down the alleyway from Officer Henderson's church. He was the man who had come to the door, who had denied being out, who had been given an alibi by a woman considered highly credible. Once again, they seemed to have nothing that could *legally* link this man, possibly a Peeping Tom or a burglar, to the rapes.

Gilbert Escobedo's only known crime was being caught as a Peeping Tom and, because of proximity, the suspicion that he had committed the burglary of the nearby apartment. Those facts would probably assure that a judge would issue a search warrant for the places where he lived and worked. But there still remained nothing to link him with the rapes terrorizing the city. But the detectives felt there were too many coincidences between Escobedo and the Ski Mask Rapist. The only way to prove that they were one and the same was to utilize DNA.

DNA analysis seemed to be the one methodology that

could prove as reliable as fingerprints in identifying the perpetrator of a crime. Links that had been impossible to make in the past were now becoming routine—in places where DNA testing was being utilized. Dallas wasn't one of those places at that point.

Nevertheless, the detectives talking with Gilbert explained how DNA testing worked. "We'll be able to match genetic cell patterns from evidence gathered at the scenes of the rapes to the cell patterns of the suspect. You, for instance, Gilbert." Gilbert thought he had been so careful and had meticulously removed all traces of his presence, but obviously he must have slipped up. Gilbert, not realizing he was being bluffed, confessed. Detective Steve Hatchel and Detective Robert E. Rommel recorded his statement.

> Today is April the twenty-fifth. It's now about five minutes till six in the morning. We're at 106 South Harwood in Crimes Against Persons, Room 300. We're talking with Gilbert Escobedo, who's thirty-eight years old. Gilbert lives at 6565 McCallum, apartment number 182. We have advised Gilbert of his rights, Miranda Warnings. My name is Hatchel, S.K. Hatchel, I.D. 2140. With me in the room also is Detective Bob Rommel. His badge number is 4609. We've been with Gilbert for several hours now. He was arrested last night on a charge, on a burglary charge, an attempted burglary and Gilbert has voluntarily written out in his own hand, a couple of statements, one regarding a rape case up on Arapaho and a couple of burglaries that he admitted to and Gilbert's wanting to tell about all his sexual assault cases and his escapades and so the next voice you hear is going to be Gilbert, so Gilbert I'm going to turn it over to you and just turn loose please.

> Gilbert began to speak: Well basically this first started when I was released from TDC, that's where it started. The number of rapes that I have committed right now is countless. . . ."

His confession continued on and on. Gilbert Escobedo was, in fact, the Ski Mask Rapist. He did not detail all the rapes. Even those that came most quickly to mind—twelve to fifteen of the more recent acts of violence—were not necessary for the police. They were dealing with just two concerns. One was getting enough information to put Gilbert in prison for as many years as possible for the rapes committed during the period before the statute of limitations ran out. The second was getting enough information so that they could close out the books on crimes for which they might not be able to charge him.

All police forces are judged, in part, by their ability to solve crimes. Gilbert was likely involved with hundreds of burglaries and rapes for which it was too late to charge him. If the officers could get him talking over the next few days and weeks, they might be able at least to clear their records. They felt that the man might brag or he might feel that his attempts to follow Christianity would cause him, once caught, to be willing to admit to what he had done, to clear his conscience. That belief was further strengthened when Gilbert said, *I've been going to church previously the last three years and I had one foot in church and one foot out of church and so I've had a problem all these years concerning this weakness for females and it just started, when I was a little boy and it led up to this . . .*

Shortly after his arrest, Gilbert made a phone call.

He had not yet gone before a judge and been formally charged so perhaps he had the right to make a local call without prior censorship. Perhaps he convinced someone that making the call was the "right thing" to do. And perhaps no one thought that he would continue such actions from jail. Whatever the case, Carol Cook picked up the phone to hear Gilbert's voice, a sound almost as terrifying when he spoke his first words as the touch of the gun had been when she was first awakened to her living nightmare.

"Carol, this is Gilbert," he said, paused and then went on. "I wanted to tell you that I am the one who hurt you and I want to ask you to forgive me."

Carol was stunned to have her deepest fear, the one she had tried so hard to push out of her mind, realized. The man she befriended, her business partner and one-time lover, the man who had proclaimed innocence when she had asked him point-blank if he was the rapist, now confessed to the truth. He had violated her home, her body and her trust, betrayed her in a way she never thought possible and now asked for forgiveness as easily as he asked for change for the soda machine when they first met. She took a deep breath to steady herself and replied, "No, Gilbert." Her voice was soft but had a steel edge.

What was even more troubling to Carol was that even though he was confessing, Gilbert failed to admit what he really had done to her. He told her, "I am the one who *hurt* you." He could have been talking about the business or the violence at work, not the rape. He was in denial, perhaps always would be. "Don't ever call me again," Carol said without hesitation and quickly hung up. Then she wrote a letter to Gilbert at the jail telling him to have no further contact with her.

The next call Carol received was from Detective King. "She gave me all the details. Her call was both professional and compassionate. Nevertheless, I don't think she understood how horrified I was by all this. I don't think anyone could. This was the man who had befriended me when I was reeling from the violence of a monster. This was the man who had helped me rethink the spiritual side of life. This was the man who had become my business partner, my friend, my lover and this was the monster who had invaded my home, pressed a gun to my head, threatened me with death and raped not only me but scores of other women."

The first wave of publicity about the case hit next. "Police Say Man They Suspect as 'Ski Mask Rapist' Confesses," read one headline. "Series of Bold Attacks Began in Spring of 1985 and Continued Till the Time of His Arrest," read another.

The *Dallas Morning News,* in the first few days after Gilbert's arrest, released a timetable of the rapes to which Gilbert had been linked (though the date of Carol's rape and her home address were not listed with the others). They produced a chart showing the dates, the times, the ages of the victims and the methods of entry. The earliest rapes, aberrations from his later pattern, occurred at 2:45 P.M. and 3:00 P.M. Most were in the late evening or early morning, with 5:00 A.M. being the closest to sunrise. Although some thought Gilbert was a genius at burglary, the rapes were done in homes where there was usually a fairly simple way inside—"Broke a locked living room window," "An unlocked laundry room window," "An unlocked door," "An unlocked window," "An unlocked side window" and on and on, seventeen in all.

The newspaper stories also brought out a seemingly simple but frightening fact. Even when detectives strongly suspected that Mr. Escobedo was the rapist—although they had declined to say how they knew or how long they had suspected him—there wasn't enough evidence to charge him.

Carol didn't realize the impact the unfolding stories were going to have on her life. She was still trying to understand the magnitude of the betrayal she had experienced. She wanted to confront Gilbert, to look him in the eye and ask him the simple but agonizing question, "Why?"

The days passed swiftly. On May 10, newspapers headlined "Ski Mask Rapist Indicted." Three weeks later, without being forewarned, Carol saw in the papers to her horror that Gilbert had plea-bargained. " 'Ski Mask Rapist' Assessed Ten Life Terms in Plea Deal." The day before, Gilbert had gone into court, pleaded guilty to five rapes and five burglaries with a deadly weapon, all first-degree felonies. His punishment was ten life sentences to run concurrently. In Big D and the State of Texas, that meant he would be eligible for parole in twenty years. There was no trial because of the confession.

Had Escobedo been sentenced to life in prison on each case by a jury, state District Judge Faith Johnson could have ordered the sentences to run consecutively. That would have meant Escobedo could have been required to serve at least twenty years on each of the older cases, then a minimum of fifteen years on those crimes committed since 1988. The Texas law had changed in 1988, reducing the minimum penalty for rape in the state by five years.

According to an article on the *Dallas Morning News*, ". . . Mr. [John] Vance said the State went along with the plea agreement partly because the victims were so traumatized by their attacks that they were afraid to testify in front of a jury.

" 'This is something the victims wanted to do,' Mr. Vance said."

On the contrary, Carol was one victim who vehemently objected. "I was never notified of any plea arrangement and later learned neither were any of the other victims. I was never asked whether I wanted to testify against Gilbert. I was never asked if I wanted him to have a sentence less than the maximum penalty for what he did. Because the truth was I wanted him to serve every day."

Later Carol was told many things—that Gilbert participated in a sting operation against jeweler Kevin Cook (*no relation to Carol or Bob Cook) who was convicted of receiving stolen merchandise. Apparently, Gilbert went to see Cook wearing a wire. He was recorded explaining that Cook would be offered some expensive stolen merchandise that could be obtained inexpensively. Cook was interested, an undercover officer brought the items to him, making clear that they were "stolen," and when it came time to pay, he was arrested.

Gilbert apparently cooperated in other ways. "They said Gilbert also talked about as many of his past burglaries and rapes as he could remember. These were cases for which he could no longer be prosecuted, but closing the cases helped the police. Somehow it was felt that the plea arrangement was worth destroying the peace of mind of both the victims and other Dallas women who were familiar with the revolving door policy of the state prison." Carol talked with the District Attorney about the plea bargain, voicing her vehement objections. "But I will always feel as though we were betrayed. Maybe the D.A. thought it was for good reason and I'm sure it did help the police, they wanted him off the streets as much as I did. They knew, as I would learn, that a serial rapist never stops. There is no way to put him into some form of therapy that will keep him from raping again."

One rumor among individuals formerly in the DA's office hinted that because the District Attorney John Vance was retiring, he wanted to leave office with the Ski Mask Rapist behind bars. The plea bargain agreement allowed District Attorney Vance's office to clear one hundred rapes and one hundred fifty burglaries from their books. What is chilling is the fact that the two hundred fifty major felonies reflected only those crimes Gilbert could remember in enough detail so that there was no question he had been the perpetrator. The plea deal he received made it probable no one would ever know what the real number was.

There would be no trial, no appearance before a jury, no opportunity to be confronted by the victims whose lives he unalterably changed. Instead Gilbert Escobedo was "tried by affidavit and information."

What this meant was that a series of written confessions were presented to the court under Judge Faith Johnson. Each was marked "The State of Texas vs. Gilbert H. Escobedo." Each began:

JUDICIAL CONFESSION

Comes now Defendant in the above cause, in writing and in open Court, and consents to the stipulation of the evidence in this case and in so doing expressly waives the appearance, confrontation and cross-examination of witnesses. I further consent to the introduction of testimony orally, by affidavits, written statements of witnesses and other documentary evidence. Accordingly, having waived my Federal and State constitutional right against self-incrimination, and after having been sworn, upon oath, I judicially confess to the following facts and agree and stipulate that these facts are true and correct and constitute the evidence in this case . . .

Following this general opening to each confession were descriptions of each specific incident. The cold terms used to describe the attack on her wounded Carol again. The confessions, one for each incident for which he was being tried, were signed and dated.

There was also a plea bargain agreement that was highly misleading. It stated:

> **TO THE HONORABLE JUDGE OF SAID COURT:**
> Comes now Defendant, Counsel for Defendant and Counsel for State herein and would show that a plea bargain agreement has been entered into between the undersigned, and that under the terms of said agreement the defendant agrees and requests that a presentence investigation report not be made and both sides agree they will waive their right to a jury trial and agree to and recommend the following . . .

Checked on the form were the facts that the Defendant would plead guilty, would testify and would accept confinement in Texas Department of Corrections for Life with No Probation, the conviction listed as a felony. What went unsaid was that not enough law had changed in Texas for Life to be the sentence the victims desired. Gilbert would one day walk free a relatively young man, strong enough and angry enough to return to hurting women.

None of the victims could anticipate the disparity between the sentence handed down and the actual time to be served. What mattered to the police was that a violent, potentially deadly criminal was taken off the street. What mattered to some of the victims was for the moment, they had a sense of safety knowing the Ski Mask Rapist was behind bars. And then there was Carol, the victim/survivor who now vowed she had to find a way to do something for herself and the other rape victims, something that wasn't a quick or fleeting antidote to the recurring, lifelong pain they all shared. She had to find a way for victims to not only survive but to gain a lasting peace. She wasn't sure how or what that could be.

Carol decided she had to confront Gilbert face to face. Detective King, to whom she spoke, felt such an action was appropriate. She learned from Detective King that one of the privileges Gilbert was given after he cooperated with authorities was a chance to say goodbye to his two daughters and Rosemarie, the woman he had planned to marry. Carol called Gilbert's girlfriend and asked if she could come by while Gilbert was there. Rosemarie, as dazed and upset as Carol, agreed to allow Carol to be present.

Gilbert was escorted from the Dallas County Jail by two plainclothes officers, a privilege given to him because of his confessions. They drove in an unmarked car to Rosemarie's home. Detective King alerted the two detectives accompanying Gilbert that Carol would be coming as well. "When I arrived, the detectives and Gilbert were already there. Rosemarie and one detective answered the door. Poor Rosemarie still looked dazed and shocked.

"Gilbert's daughters were sitting on the couch, crying softly. I wanted to reach out to them, tell them something that would help, but there was nothing to be said. Their father was a serial rapist. Their father had terrorized women for years. Their father was a man who, if they had only read about him as a stranger, might have been someone they felt should be condemned to Hell. Their betrayal was, at least, as great as my own and there was nothing to say."

Gilbert sat on a chair wearing civilian clothes and full manacles. A chain encircled his waist and was locked to the cuffs on his wrists so he could not raise his hands. Another chain went down his front and held leg cuffs in place on his ankles. He could move with short steps, but any attempt to run or even walk normally would cause him to fall. His movement was also restricted so much that he could not take hold of someone in a manner that might render the other person helpless.

"The detectives were shocked to see me there, but Gilbert's girlfriend accepted the situation. She just stared at me. We were sister victims and we both knew it."

Carol asked to speak with Gilbert privately. He was allowed to shuffle into the dining room with her. Two officers standing at the far end of the room were ready to grab him if he tried anything. "I knew they were probably watching me as well, concerned that I might be carrying a weapon, seeking revenge. I wasn't though. I just wanted an answer."

"Why did you do this to me?" Carol asked Gilbert.

He avoided her gaze, instead staring at his hands in his lap. Finally, he said almost in a whisper, "I love you, Carol. I've always loved you. I didn't mean to hurt you. You are the only friend I've ever loved."

Carol stared at him. He was still trying to con her. This man had raped her and betrayed her. Then he befriended her and betrayed her again. This man had confessed to a series of horrendous crimes. This man had been given a life sentence and was bound with leg cuffs, handcuffs and chains. Yet still he lied.

"Perhaps in your deranged and strange way you cared about me, just as you cared about your daughters at the same time that you frequently neglected them. I don't think you realized how much you really did harm me, how much you have harmed your daughters. When you hurt us, you must have meant to hurt us, wanted the power that came from harming others."

Suddenly, she understood. Carol believed he still needed power. He wanted to prove to himself he could always have power over people. He wanted to do whatever he wanted, break people down or get back at all the people or things he hated so much. He knew his shortcomings. He knew that people looked down upon him and he could bring himself above them by harming them. It was the harm that gave him power.

"Can you forgive me?" he begged. Carol knew "forgive" was one of his favorite words.

"You seem to feel if you ask for forgiveness for anything, it is all right. You can do it again and again. All you have to do each time is say, 'I'm sorry. Forgive me.' Well, it's not enough, not nearly enough."

Carol stared at him. She knew forgiveness was part of the church's teachings. She believed in it. But perhaps forgiveness for such inhumane savage deeds as this man had done was best left to divine not human sources. She could not offer it, not now anyway. She stood up to leave.

"Can you forgive me?" He asked again.

"No, Gilbert, I can't."

"Will you visit me?"

Again she said, "No."

Almost in a whisper he said, "I'm sorry. I didn't mean to hurt you."

He kept his gaze fixed on the floor. Carol shook her head in a mixture of pity and disgust, then she walked away. Approaching the detectives on the other side of the room, Carol softly said, "Thank you." Gilbert's girlfriend appeared to be in a trance. She was staring, unseeing, obviously in shock. His daughters remained on the couch, crying. Carol said, "I'm sorry," to Rosemarie and quietly slipped out the front door.

As Carol slowly walked to her car, thoughts swirled through her mind. So many lives had been shattered by him. The anguish and pain his victims felt would be with them forever, some having pain even greater than Carol's. The embarrassment and hurt his family felt was beyond description. His daughters were devastated, not wanting to believe. Carol felt, for her, it was finally over. Of course, she did not know that though unexpected happiness awaited her, there also would be one more betrayal to come.

CHAPTER 21

LOVE AND FEAR

CAROL HAD KNOWN Bob Cook only a few months when Gilbert was arrested. She had come to admire his skill as a watercolor artist and the quality of his architectural renderings. She learned he was a nationally recognized, accredited, fine watercolor artist whose works hung in corporate collections worldwide. He had come to Dallas for the opportunities it offered during a massive growth phase, then stayed even when it went through economic hard times. He and his staff of twenty-six employees were turning out eighty-five renderings in one month, a massive number Carol later learned. Then, as the economy soured and savings and loans which were improperly financed and run began to fail, all construction stopped. Losses were being written off. Loans were ended or called in.

One firm, HKI, that was run by Harwood K. Smith, brother of newscaster Howard K. Smith, had between 500 and 600 resident architects. Business was so good that the company was profitable despite overhead that ran one million dollars per day.

It took just two months in the sour economy for HKI to have to layoff all but about fifty architects. Bob Cook lost almost everything in the economic downturn, but had the courage to not give up. He also never lost his sense of humor.

As their relationship developed, Bob had no idea why Carol seemed so troubled and tense at times. He did not ask. He had a feeling she would tell him when she was ready. Eventually, she felt safe enough to tell him a little about the rape that she had endured. She was surprised by his compassion and understanding. Bob was available for her whenever she wanted him and the two were becoming closer by the day. She seemed to have found the relationship which she had thought hers and Dennis' could have been and which his death had ended.

However, Carol's circumstances had changed with the loss of both the income she had been making from Gilbert's and her business and the fact that the apartment in which she had been living had increased in rent and was now too expensive. Adding to the expense, her immune system was low from all the stress and her medical bills were mounting.

Carol tried to delay moving. She hated where she was, but moving would be added stress which she hoped to avoid. She sold several pieces of jewelry and original art, as well as an antique desk. She was able to get fair prices, but the money was only a stopgap. She knew there would come a time when she would have to sell more and more. That was when she made her decision and moved to a less expensive location. This was a temporary move as far as Carol was concerned. As soon as she could dissolve the business, she would leave Dallas.

Within days of the move, however, someone broke into her new home. They took jewelry, along with clothing, silver, leather and fur coats and a VCR. However, the strangest item stolen was her address book. Carol was not home at the time, the only good thing about the crime.

Because of the theft of the address book, her insecurity intensified. *Was this someone connected with Gilbert? Was this a warning that she would always be vulnerable?* All Carol knew was that she was emotionally shaken. Bob was furious. He was not about to let the woman he increasingly was coming to love risk being alone if it might mean another rape, a beating or her life. "I own a four bedroom home, Carol, please move in with me."

Carol was hesitant. "I'm not trying to take advantage of you," Bob said. "You'll have your own room and bath, sharing the rest of the facilities. I just want you someplace where you'll be less vulnerable."

At first, Carol rejected his offer. She had never lived with a man out of wedlock. It was just something she felt was wrong. However, as she looked at the risk of staying alone and when she realized she really would have privacy in Bob's home, she agreed.

After Carol moved in, the couple acted like two teenagers breaking curfew and terrified of punishment. Bob knew he could not tell his family what he was doing. Carol realized she had to keep it all a secret from her children. Neither side would believe they were living together as roommates, not lovers sharing a bed.

Except . . .

In a short time, Carol and Bob discovered they held the same values, same family ideals and same interests. They were both artists. He confessed that he had fallen in love within days of meeting her the first time, but did not dare say so. Bob proposed marriage.

Carol sighed, unsure that she was ready to make such a commitment. One day she would have to confess to him that she was still having flashbacks of the rape and still suffered emotionally. But she realized for the moment she was living again, loving again, laughing for the first time in months—and it was all because of Bob. They decided they would marry in early December.

Still, despite her newfound happiness, on numerous days and the dark nights that followed, Carol fixated on Gilbert's attack and her own feelings of anxiety. "I kept asking myself how I could not have known that Gilbert was my rapist. I kept thinking there were signs I should have seen. I kept thinking that anyone else would have known. I kept feeling that I must have either asked for what eventually happened or was so stupid that I was worthless."

Finally, Carol confessed her inability to return to normalcy to Detective Roberta King. King, trying to comfort

Carol, pointed out the fact that she and the other members of the Crimes Against Persons squad were highly trained professionals. "We've spent many years studying the men who commit violence through rape. We've talked with criminals after they've been arrested. We are able to go through the criminal records of men whose pasts make them suspects for similar crimes committed after the men have been released from jail. Yet with all our training, we were unable to get the Ski Mask Rapist." Carol's calls and flashbacks had been significant. Gilbert became a suspect because of his history, but there was so little evidence of possible guilt legally obtainable by the police that he remained one of several suspects.

The reassurance by Detective King and the loving support of Bob Cook seemed enough to make things right at least for a time. The couple married. They honeymooned in the Caribbean. They returned to laughter and art, to love and involvement in special interests.

Carol took a job selling advertising for an area newspaper. She was a skilled businessperson with an eagerness to learn whatever she did not know. The couple lived in a nice home. Bob's business was increasing as the construction industry slowly rebounded from the problems of the past. Life was good.

And then Carol started crying uncontrollably at odd times. There seemed no particular reason for her despair. There were no triggers. She just developed overwhelming fears, saw shadows everywhere, was startled by every noise and then the tears flowed.

She had headaches. She had never had headaches before. Sometimes they were minor, almost like the dull pain you get for a day or two after you stop using caffeine heavily. At other times they were so intense that Carol became nauseated. Light bothered her. Sound bothered her. She had to lie down and could focus only on the pain inside her head. Nothing else mattered and as time passed the symptoms got more severe. Bob did his best to help Carol, but there was little he could do to ease the pain. He was concerned about her physical symptoms and emotional instability, having no idea why the woman he married seemed to change overnight.

Once again, Carol began losing weight. "I had a normal appetite and looked forward to eating. Then I found myself throwing up. I wasn't doing it deliberately. I wasn't bulimic, trying to binge eat, then purge. It was more like what happens when you unexpectedly come down with the flu, one moment feeling normal, the next moment heaving uncontrollably."

There were other problems as well. Sometimes Carol's heart beat so rapidly she could hear it and she felt dizzy. Other times her body ached from tiredness, though she had done nothing to warrant such exhaustion. She was extremely nervous, began to have panic attacks and could not sleep.

She found herself losing things, forgetting things. "I was a highly organized person, able to focus on any project I started. Yet suddenly nothing was right. I was confused, disoriented. I could become preoccupied with concerns that made little sense, checking the same thing over and over again. I was increasingly comfortable being alone, isolated in body and mind. Yet, I was also frightened at home, frequently making certain doors and windows were locked, the alarm was on. I still had nightmares. I still had flashbacks. Nevertheless I refused to admit I had a problem."

Bob didn't know what was happening. He knew about her past, from the losses in her life to the trials and tribulations of being a military wife then a single, working mother. He admired her for how far she had come, her ambition and her strength. He assumed this vibrant, capable woman had gotten beyond the trauma of the rape. Certainly she hadn't told him she was depressed or having difficulties. In fact, she seemed very happy when they were first together. She appeared lively, open and interested in everything they were doing together. She even seemed to bounce back from the robbery of her apartment pretty quickly. It was natural for him to assume that the rape and betrayals no longer dominated Carol's life.

"Bob wasn't aware I would always be affected to some degree by the violence I had endured. No person who experiences such trauma ever forgets it. But I know now you can get beyond it, get on with your life, accepting the fears that come from knowing there is evil in the world and that good people can become victims of it through no fault of their own. However, for many of us, perhaps most of us, it takes help and I never asked for any."

Instead, Carol let the pain and trauma fester below the surface. And, as time went on, Carol's instability only worsened. Bob watched helplessly at the unexplainable changes in the woman he loved: she avoided watching on the television news programs or reading in the newspaper any story of violence, cried easily, displayed dark, depressed moods, suffered from severe headaches and other maladies, acted nervous and frightened, was always on edge and generally seemed to be falling apart. He tried to talk with her, to ask her what was wrong and how he could help, but most of the time Carol shut him out. She was near a complete nervous breakdown.

Bob was on the right track; Carol did need to talk to someone. What Bob did not understand was that Carol badly needed counseling. She needed to sit down with a therapist and deal with all the issues she had not really faced. Yet how could he possibly know that when Carol herself didn't realize it?

Bob finally became horribly frustrated with the situation. "I want the old Carol back. I want the Carol I married. I want the woman who was laughing and fun to be with. You have to get over whatever it is that is bothering you. We are married. You are safe now."

" 'I know,' " I told him. But all I did was feel depressed and cry."

Finally Carol told Detective King what had been going on.

"I'm falling apart. My weight is dropping drastically. My health is bad. I can't sleep through the night. My marriage is in trouble."

Detective King was shocked by what Carol had to say. There had technically been a protocol for handling rape victims at the time Gilbert attacked Carol. This included providing victims with information about their rights and where to get the psychological help they needed. The state had prepared the information, including the fact that under the Texas Crime Victims Compensation Act, Carol could receive payment for a medical exam and referral to social service agencies that would provide counseling. However, neither the District Attorney's office nor anyone from the police department had ever shared this information with Carol.

The truth was that Dallas was just beginning to change the way the police handled the aftermath of rape and many officers either did not know what to do or still did not care. Carol never received the counseling she should have.

Fortunately, Detective King had become involved with an organization called Victims Outreach. "You are still in shock, as much as a soldier who comes home from intense combat and can not adjust to civilian life. The only change will come through counseling." King explained how to get in touch with Victims Outreach. Though she was terrified by her own actions and the way she was feeling, it took Carol a few days to gather the courage to call the organization. She was so afraid to admit that something was wrong that she couldn't even tell Bob she was thinking of calling Victims Outreach. Thoughts raced through her fragile mind: *Who will find out about the rape? Will they think I was stupid? Will they look at me as less of a person for associating with a man who had a criminal background? Can talking to the people at Victims Outreach really help ease my fears? Can they really help me get back to being the person I once was? Will anyone ever understand what I feel? Can these people tell me what is wrong with me? More importantly, can they help me fix what is wrong?*

By chance, on the day Carol finally called Victims Outreach, they were short-handed. One of the counselors, a female therapist in her forties named Sharon Ross, was covering the telephones. "I could barely speak, barely tell her what happened. It was obvious that I was falling apart. Somehow she convinced me to leave my house and come to see her.

"In my despair I reached out to the organization, because there was no other place to go. I was giving up on life. I was letting my health deteriorate to a degree where I ultimately might have died."

The Victims Outreach office was located in a nondescript office building in the North Dallas business district. It was just off the LBJ Freeway and set between the upscale Valley View Mall and the equally expensive Galleria. The location was critical. Low-income men and women in need of the therapists' services could easily reach the area. At the same time, the wealthy individuals in crisis who had once thought that violence could not affect anyone in their neighborhoods also lived and shopped nearby.

The unspoken class prejudice in much of Big D did not pass through the entryway of the Victims Outreach office. Shared pain destroys all walls, all artificial barriers. A struggling laborer living in the barrio whose grocery clerk daughter is murdered in a bodega robbery experiences the same grief as a wealthy North Dallas mother whose teenager is killed during the carjacking of her sports car. Suffering is based on the horrifying vagaries of life, not social position, bank account or the size of someone's home.

Carol tentatively stepped inside the office and looked around. It was sparsely furnished but comfortable. There was a sofa, some chairs and a desk in the entrance. One wall had all the certification papers of the staff members, each carefully framed. There were a few framed prints, pastoral scenes and abstracts. Both there and in the small offices where the therapists met with their clients, there was nothing of a personal nature. There were no photographs of happy children at play. There were no pictures of a therapist's spouse or other family members. There were no drawings made by their children. It was as though no one working there had a life she or he was living outside of that environment. Carol later learned the sparseness was deliberate. Personal pictures would have been too upsetting for many people whose own families were falling apart.

How do you show a picture of your child to someone

who has just lost hers? How do you exhibit a picture of your boyfriend when you are trying to help someone just raped and battered by hers? The photograph of the strapping young Marine whose parents are so proud is emotionally shattering to the parent of the child shot in their driveway after returning home from getting supplies needed for his first semester of college. Every person's worst nightmare would come through the doors of Victims Outreach in any given month.

Dallas was experiencing a continuing crime wave. What Carol didn't know the day she first went to Victims Outreach was how many different types of violent crimes were shattering people's lives.

Carol learned of several widows, widowers, parents and children who were trying to deal with driveway shootings occurring in expensive areas of Dallas. This was an extraordinarily brutal way to burglarize a home with an attached garage and the added security of a locking remote garage door. The robber would wait outside a targeted house. When the homeowner drove up and opened the garage door, the robber would go to the car, shoot the person, then go inside the house through the garage for a leisurely opportunity to steal everything of value that could be removed.

Carjackings were also common. There were many ways these occurred, though all of them involved the stopping of an expensive car whose driver looked rather passive. Sometimes two cars would block in the target. At other times an accident would be staged, the carjackers' car being used to lightly bump the target. Whatever the case, the end was always the same. There would be a shooting and then the targeted car would be driven away. Sometimes it was stolen to order, the identification numbers altered, the vehicle given new paint, and then the vehicle would be turned over to someone willing to pay cash. The selling price would be a fraction of the car's value, but several cars could be stolen each week in this manner, bringing huge sums of money to all involved. Sometimes the car was stolen for parts. It would be taken to what was called a chop shop where it would be completely stripped.

Then there were victims of violence between friends or neighbors or caused by robberies in homes, stores, hotels and elsewhere. Carol met people who were victims of violent relatives, gang shootings, child molesters and, of course, victims of the Ski Mask Rapist.

The staff also lived with their own tragedies. Founder of Victims Outreach Patsy Day's fourteen-year-old daughter was kidnapped from the doughnut shop where she worked part-time and murdered. The case was never solved. The receptionist had also experienced a violent loss, as had others in the organization.

Victims Outreach was not a place for victims to help victims, though such experiences did occur. Rather, it was a reflection of the city itself that so many people in the community, including a percentage of the organization's staff, had known a loved one who was violently assaulted or killed.

Sharon Ross, the therapist Carol saw, had not experienced personal violence when she began her internship at Victims Outreach. She had been a schoolteacher right out of college, but stopped teaching a few years later when she married and had children. Once her children were older, Sharon divorced and chose to return to school to become a licensed therapist and work with trauma victims of all types. By chance she was answering the telephones when Carol called for an appointment. She was able to convince Carol to stop in just to talk.

The therapist welcomed Carol and brought her to her office where they sat down and talked. "Carol, the most important point I learned to stress in my training is the fact that the victim is never at fault," explained Sharon Ross. "Rape victims often blame themselves for the violent crime they experienced. I had one woman who told me that she had four locks on her door and a rapist still came in and attacked her. She rationalized that the assault would not have happened if she had had one more lock."

Sharon could see that Carol was on the verge of a nervous breakdown when she came into the office. The first thing Sharon had to convince Carol of was that the crime wasn't Carol's fault. She said to Carol the same thing she told many other victims: "You did not cause the crime committed against you. You could not have prevented it. It is not your fault." Sharon told Carol she could expect to hear the same thing in each session. "You'll eventually get tired of hearing me say it, but it often takes several sessions before the truth of that statement sinks in."

"It's so difficult for me to forgive myself for not being able to protect myself from this cunning and creative con man," said Carol. "If I had recognized him sooner, I could have saved many other women. I could have saved myself further pain."

Carol gripped the side of the chair and paused, then went on, "I still feel foolish, stupid, ashamed, guilty and sometimes very alone, because I can't share myself with others anymore. I don't feel like I have a single friend anymore, because I can't trust my feelings, my thoughts or my judgement. I have no one to tell my hurt to."

At first Carol was barely able to explain what had happened. Telling the details of her rape and its aftermath was, at that point, nearly impossible.

The problem was that she was going against everything she had ever believed to be right. Military wives could handle any crisis. After all, a woman whose husband was making a career in the armed forces knew that she had a good chance of being widowed. She knew that under the best of circumstances, most of the first twenty years of marriage would involve extended periods of separation. She knew that she would have to face the world more alone than a single parent because single parents can date, they can have a normal social life. A military wife has no such comfort. She is in a community where she must be faithful, loyal and supportive, filling a role as patriotic as that of her husband. To do less is to be ostracized by the community.

Carol's daughters reinforced this image. Carol was the strong one. Carol could handle anything. Carol was the role model for what a woman should be within her family.

Hadn't Bob Cook been impressed with Carol, after all? Hadn't this wonderful man, skilled artist, successful businessman able to pull himself out of financial trouble and triumph after the economy went sour, told her how much he admired *her* strength and independence?

And now Carol was a wreck of her former self. The daughter who had remained in Dallas could not see her without tearfully wondering where the mother she knew had gone. Bob was dismayed that the woman he married seemed to have vanished. Carol herself realized that she was a shell of the person she had once been and she felt guilty. She feared telling Sharon her true feelings, because it might mean that Carol was a failure. She feared Sharon and the rest of the staff might also tell her she was a failure.

But Sharon kept reassuring Carol, telling her the crime she had suffered and could not forget was not her fault. She could not have prevented the rape. She could not have known that her trusted friend, lover and business partner was the man who had not only terrified and devastated her, but also had done the same to dozens and dozens of other women.

CHAPTER 22

THE HEALING PROCESS

CAROL'S THERAPY WENT slowly in the beginning. New victims often came to the program once a week for counseling. Carol went twice a week and continued with that pattern for a full year.

It was not that Carol's experience was somehow more horrible than what other victims of violent criminals had endured. Rather it was a matter of her delay in seeking help. More than two years had elapsed since her rape. In that time, Carol had tried to suppress emotions she needed to release. She had tried to create a normal life and, when she had found her first happiness, she tried to convince herself that she could heal completely without help. She had never even told Bob everything and he was the most trusted person in her life. She needed to talk and at Victims Outreach over time she found the words she needed to deal with the pain she felt. Perhaps most importantly, she heard and began to believe what her therapist said to her over and over: "You did not cause your rape. You could not have prevented being a victim. You could not have known."

Not only the staff but Detective King reinforced this fact whenever she talked with Carol. If trained professionals talking to Gilbert could not find evidence that he was the serial rapist, how could someone who had never before encountered this sociopath?

After a period of intensive one-on-one therapy, Sharon convinced Carol to try group therapy. The group met in Presbyterian Hospital, just one mile from Carol's home. Carol was hesitant.

"It was one thing to talk to a therapist. It was quite another matter to speak before a group." Despite her fear, Carol finally agreed to attend the group therapy sessions, under certain conditions. "I refused to speak or even wear a nametag. I also made certain that I left before dark. But I went. At first all I did was listen to others talk about the crimes committed against them, what the crimes had done to them and their feelings. Many felt pain and anger, some felt dirty and shameful and others simply felt lost. A few people were or had been suicidal. This really jolted me. It was sad to see these people were feeling so hurt and hopeless that they wanted to or even had tried to commit suicide. I began to see the crime against me as small and insignificant compared to what these people had experienced. Yet the therapist convinced me my crime had done just as much damage, taken away just as much, had shattered my sense of safety and self-esteem, just as the other victims had happen to them. I learned it wasn't a competition; each person's pain and loss is his or her own."

Carol was unsure of what to say to Bob during this period. She was not yet ready to disclose all she had suffered and was feeling. She couldn't share her experiences in therapy. Bob was left in the dark. "Yet I felt that he should bear with me, be understanding and supportive. Going through therapy, dealing with my pain, seemed an impossible burden for me in much the same manner that Bob's lack of awareness of what I had been through must have been a terrible burden for him. We each had unrealistic expectations of the other and neither of us knew how to break through the barriers that had gradually come between us. It was a difficult time."

Nevertheless, Carol was making progress and somewhat to her surprise, much of her progress came about through group therapy.

After attending group therapy for about a month, Carol mustered the courage to wear a nametag and, more importantly, to speak about her experiences. Once she shared her story, she began to see that as different as they all were in group therapy—male, female, young, old, black, white, Hispanic, educated, uneducated, rich, poor—they were all the same. "It was in group therapy that I began to realize I was not unique. All of our senses of safety, direction and security had been changed, our faith tested, lost or changed and our family values, trust in others and goals had changed. We all felt vulnerable and looked at the world with different eyes than before we experienced the horrible crimes committed against us."

When it came to the rape victims, Carol saw that there were others who were much more troubled than she. "My trauma was horrible. The series of betrayals that occurred afterwards were overwhelming. But I was physically without scars. My intellect remained intact. I had been able to experience the joy of physical intimacy for the first time in a healthy manner as a young woman and a wife in a loving marriage. There were young women in group therapy who had their first sexual experience with a rapist and knew only terror, horrifying pain and intense fear. I had experienced the gift of deepest intimacy, both for the creation of children and for the joy of loving and being loved. And I was lucky enough to have found a gentle, giving man in my new husband with whom I planned to create a fulfilling life."

Carol had found Bob, let herself be vulnerable to him and been rewarded for the effort. Some of the victims at the group meeting did not date. Some of the others became involved with violent men who brutalized them with demeaning demands and language. They did so because they were so filled with self hate that they felt they only deserved such individuals. Others had involved themselves with the most passive men they could find. Passive men made no demands. Passive men brought them no pressure. Passive men were safe. Though such relationships might not have had any pain, they also had no pleasure.

As time went on and more facts about Carol's case unfolded, legal questions were addressed and she began to see the many betrayals: how badly her case had been handled, the broken justice system, the lack of laws protecting crime victims, the ease with which criminals could avoid punishment, the monetary cost of the crimes and the emotional toll the crimes took on the victims. These were not betrayals against Carol alone. They were betrayals against all victims of violent crimes. From her own therapy and her group therapy sessions, Carol knew how hurt and angry crime victims were and how helpless and hopeless they felt over the justice system's failures. "I had compassion for the men and women in group therapy, knowing what I had endured and seeing what they were trying to overcome. I realized I wanted to do something to help others; I needed to do something to help others."

It had been five years since Carol's rape. For five years she had not touched her art supplies. For five years she had not considered drawing or painting or making jewelry. For five years she had let the skills that once mattered to her most lay dormant.

"The problem was that I knew the rapist had touched my art supplies, as he had touched all my personal underclothes. The image of that touch had festered in my mind. It was as though I was living in one of those horror movies where a disgusting ooze seeps from the ground and slowly destroys all that it touches.

"The lingerie, panties, bras, silk bathrobe, silk night clothes and the like were all washed and bagged within days of the rape. I took them to a Goodwill drop center and left them for others. There was nothing wrong with the items. I did not believe that the rapist's touch would linger, infecting his poison on woman after woman whose only connection was obtaining what I had to discard. I just could not be reminded of what occurred."

Her art was a different matter. She could not discard it, did not want to discard it. Knowing of her own angry feelings, and seeing the anger and hurt in others, Carol turned back to her creative mind to find ways to express her strong emotions. "That was when I created the anger doll for victims, Guy Gross."

For centuries anatomically correct dolls were used in China for providing healthcare for women. Doctors were men in a culture that did not allow women to be examined by them. The women could only be naked in front of their husbands.

When a man's wife was sick or hurting, he would come to the doctor in his wife's place. Then, using a small anatomically correct nude figure of a reclining woman, the husband would show the doctor where his wife was having the problem. He would describe whatever pain or other symptoms she was suffering. Based on that alone, the doctor would make a diagnosis, then prescribe a course of treatment. It was all quite primitive, but it was the way things were done in that culture.

It has only been in the last two or three decades that dolls have been widely used to help abuse and rape victims identify what happened to them. This is especially helpful with children who may be too young to have the appropriate vocabulary. The children show investigators and therapists where and how they were touched. Adults who are unable to discuss what happened to them do the same.

The doll Carol created was different in that it is for use when the victim is trying to heal, not in the aftermath of when she is first attacked. It is meant for therapy, to vent anger, frustration and hurt. It is meant to help the victim reclaim a sense of power and control, to get beyond the sadness and the undeserved guilt.

The doll is now extensively in use throughout Texas and other parts of the country. Carol receives no financial benefits from her creation. All the money goes to Victims Outreach. The Guy Gross Anger Doll is either twelve inches or eighteen inches in size, with multi-colored yarn hair. "It has a detachable head, arms, legs, genitals and a yellow heart. Velcro holds each piece onto the torso of the body. It is a washable cotton fabric with polyester fiberfill. There was no definition of the eyes or mouth, leaving it faceless. This is because some of the victims subconsciously want their perpetrators to be faceless, while others never saw their attackers' faces.

"I call him Guy because most of the victims refer to

their attackers in such a way. They say, 'The Guy' or 'That Guy.' I made the body green because 'Green Monster' is often used figuratively to describe something fearful, terrible or unknown. The lack of a definable race or ethnicity in the green body and multi-colored hair allows victims to associate the doll with their attackers no matter who they were or what they looked like.

"The doll comes with a one and one-half inch pin, because many of the victims or their families like hurting a surrogate, a little like a Voodoo doll. I used Velcro to hold all the parts in place so the person can 'hurt' the doll where they've been hurt." Carol found that some people tear off the penis. Others twist the arms and rip out the heart. Some victims sit with the doll, poking it for a while as if to torture it. Then they begin ripping off each limb, one at a time, until finally, they decapitate the doll. "The action fits what many victims feel, that we want to inflict a painful or violent death on the perpetrator, even if it is just symbolically."

Working on the doll was very fulfilling for Carol. Once she finished, however, she began to feel she was no longer making progress in her recovery. She continued struggling in therapy and was disappointed with the results. She felt it was taking too long and was concerned about her ongoing sadness and fears. Citing her recurring feelings of hopeless despair as an example of her failure, Carol shared her concerns over her poor self-evaluation with Sharon Ross. Again, Carol's therapist came through for her. She informed Carol that she, like millions of others, has an illness as the result of the violent crime committed against her. She told Carol she shares the same wounds of mind and soul that veterans of war suffer—post-traumatic stress disorder. "You and all other victims of violent crimes have wounded and broken hearts," Ross added.

With her newfound understanding of post-traumatic stress disorder, Carol's feelings made more sense to her and she began to heal. She also continued to get a lot out of group therapy. "The healing messages I heard and struggled to grasp, from both the therapist and through group therapy, were the beginning of rebirth. I learned and saw firsthand that I wasn't alone, nor was I crazy. Others had greater pain, greater challenges, yet were making positive strides in treatment and recovery. All shared broken spirits, a torn soul and wounded hearts. Nothing else about us mattered, for as different as we were, we were all alike.

What Carol learned and realized in those days from her caring therapist and what she heard in group therapy from other crime victims reawakened her creativity and need to do something for others. Carol once again returned to the idea of utilizing her talents to create. "There was no crime victim's symbol, something to acknowledge our wounded hearts, a symbol to recognize and support victims of violent crime, recognize the need for changes in laws to protect us and changes for stronger punishment for criminals who destroy our communities."

So, Carol set to work on a symbol for the victims of violent crimes. Within months she had created a heart logo to represent the wounded hearts of crime victims. She hoped somehow it could become the symbol so needed to make a statement about violent crime, to force people to look carefully at the justice system, to fix it and to admit that violent crime destroys people and communities. The logo consisted of a lavender heart with a purple ribbon at the top tied in a bow.

"When I created the Heart, I wanted to make sure it would exhibit hope to all victims of violence, so I chose the colors in the Heart for reasons everyone will understand.

"I selected lavender, because it is attributed to flowers and peace. I believe crime victims are like flowers, because they grow with each day and search for peace in a world torn with violence. The color purple was chosen to symbolize valor and strength, because a crime victim exhibits strength as they struggle to survive a crime and its aftermath. The purple ribbon at the top of the Heart ties us together, making us stronger as we unite and work to overcome violence, work to have our lawmakers recognize the desperate need for stronger laws for violent predators."

At the same time, Carol's therapist asked her to write as part of her therapy. Carol took her feelings, her fears, her thoughts and her dreams and put them down on paper. She gathered all the notes and diary entries she had written following the rape and, along with the writings she was currently doing in therapy, used these materials to write poetry. "In one year, I wrote about fifty poems, some very dark and disturbing, but healing and cathartic as well.

"Next, I began to write about children's fears, because my therapist noticed my fears were very childlike and I often regressed to childish, fearful behavior during therapy. At that time I began writing children's books. I created ten stories and two dozen characters, all relating to dealing with and overcoming fears."

Throughout this period, Carol also performed volunteer work at Victims Outreach as part of her healing process. Sharon Ross left the organization, though Carol continued seeing Ross in her private practice. Slowly Carol was willing to share all her experiences with other victims and, eventually, spoke to groups in the community. Each time she was terrified to speak. Each time she had to remind herself that she did not cause her rape; she could not have prevented it. She was a victim in recovery. There were other victims who were not so far along. There were other victims whose families did not understand. She could make a difference for those people—and for herself.

Gradually Carol spoke to larger and more diverse groups not only in her community but in the surrounding states and, eventually, across the nation. Again and again she encountered others' prejudices that evolved from the same biases that had shaped her early feelings about herself. Men and sometimes women looked at her and said, "You don't look like a rape victim."

"I knew what they meant. I knew that some people, even well-educated ones, think that rape victims are sluts. They think rape victims must have worn revealing clothing, had come-on looks or were trolling for men who could give them sexual pleasure. The thinking is that rape victims obviously have loose morals and, though they may not have wanted to be raped, they certainly were partly responsible for dressing and acting in manners that were clearly invitations to rapists.

"I wanted to say something to these people who were so ignorant as to say I didn't look like a rape victim. I wanted to tell them there is no stereotype, we can all be victimized." Finally, Carol learned to turn to the person and say, "Well, what is one supposed to look like?"

One man she said this to was stunned. She decided to ease his shock and her anger by saying, "I didn't think I would ever be one and neither does your wife, mother or your pastor's wife.

"Sometimes you can change a person's thinking. Sometimes you realize that he or she just doesn't hear your message. They never hear it. They never get it."

Carol talked with some of the law enforcement officers in her city about rape, though most of the changes taking place in the Dallas Police Department were coming about as a result of Patsy Day's work. She was teaching at the Academy, trying to influence the newest officers so they would have compassion and understanding. Carol also spoke at the medical school, trying to affect the young doctors who would be treating the physical and emotional aftermath of rape.

Soon Carol was invited to her first fundraising luncheon for Victims Outreach. The fundraiser was held to bring about awareness of violent crimes and the toll they take on victims, families and communities. Civic leaders were there, police officials attended and Patsy Day spoke. The guest speaker was Marla Hanson, the New York City model who had graced the pages of dozens of national fashion magazines for years until an attack that almost left her dead. She was attacked by a stalker, her face so horribly slashed with a knife that it required over 200 stitches, numerous reconstructive surgeries and years of recovery. "She told us about the assault that nearly ended and forever changed her life. She said that there were few laws in place to protect her or to punish her attacker. She still battles the emotional scars of the crime. I empathized with her and realized again, despite superficial differences, how much we victims have in common."

The following year Carol again attended the Victims Outreach fundraiser luncheon. This time the guest speaker was Terry Anderson, the American journalist on assignment with the Associated Press who was kidnapped in

Lebanon by armed terrorists. "He described how the terrorists held him captive and tortured him for seven years. To hear him speak of what he endured, the effects the trauma had on him, the toll the experience took on his life and the harrowing recovery he has made left an audience of 600 people utterly spellbound. I knew then that I had to push harder to get the crime victim logo the attention it deserved so that more people would listen and understand we who have been so harmed by the evil that befell us and see the changes needed in our justice system."

By 1996, the Heart Carol created to symbolize victims' plights was being used by crime victims organizations around Texas and requests to get it acknowledged as a symbol for crime victims everywhere was being frequently asked. At that year's annual luncheon, Carol had 1,000 pins made and placed on the tables for each attendee. The guest speaker was famed author Dominick Dunne. "When Mr. Dunne described what he and his family endured after their twenty-one-year-old daughter was murdered by her boyfriend and the lack of laws in place to punish the man responsible for her death, we gained more support for getting a symbol of our suffering recognized. Later, Dallas Police Chief, Ben Click, introduced me to Dominick Dunne. I was so happy to see that we were all wearing the heart pin."

The healing began moving swiftly once Carol decided to become more open. "As I spoke out more and more, I saw and heard the same things over and over: how people suffered, how so few laws were in place to protect victims and punish perpetrators. This kept me going, encouraging me to continue speaking at workshops, seminars, health fairs and to civic groups and medical school students. This was cathartic and I believe it helped move me closer to recovery, because I was using a terrible crime to heal myself and help others. I learned so much from other victims, the people and the families from all ethnic and social levels who were disillusioned at the lack of punishment for violent criminals. I learned about the similarities in our anger and pain, our entire existences changing or being altered, our struggles to come to terms with the violence committed against us and the violent world in which we live.

"The Heart I created came to symbolize this struggle. The Heart has been given to Senator Kay Bailey Hutchinson of Texas so we can get it recognized as a crime victims symbol everywhere."

Then her healing was interrupted. Carol was horrified to find out what, for her, was the most chilling betrayal of all. She knew she was safe from Gilbert only so long as he was behind bars. She was safe from Gilbert only if "life" in the Texas penitentiary meant that he would die behind bars. Yet she learned in Texas a life term is not literal. Gilbert will be up for parole in 2005 and no later than approximately 2010. He will still be a relatively young man. He will have had the opportunity to improve his health, increase his strength and gain greater knowledge of how to break and enter during the years spent with other convicts. He will also be fiercely angry about being caught. It is likely, as he has admitted when filmed in an interview at the prison, that he will rape again rather than restrain such impulses. It is more likely that if he rapes, he will murder his victims than he will leave them cowering as in the past. In fact, in front of a reporter he knew would air his words on national television, he stated, "I think I would be a threat to society if I got out today. That's what scares me."

The reporter gasped. "You think you'd rape again if you got out today?"

Gilbert shook his head. "The percentage would be great."

EPILOGUE

BETRAYAL FOR CAROL began in a small way as it does for so many of us, when a neighbor child informed her that there was no Santa Claus. Not that she believed him immediately. She had known Santa Claus all six years of her life. She had sat on his lap in the Southern Ohio department store, given him her wish list and received so many of the toys she told him about that he had to be real. Yet something about the boy's sincerity caused her to ask her mother if what he said was true. Was Santa just a nice old man in a costume and fake beard? Was Santa someone parents only pretend exists?

Her mother tried to ease the trauma, as good parents must do. She told her daughter that Santa was the spirit of selfless giving. She told her daughter about the real St. Nicholas. But all the words didn't matter. Carol had been betrayed and she didn't know if she was angrier at her parents for telling the lie or at the neighbor boy for revealing what they had done.

There would be other betrayals as she grew up, of course. "You can share your secret with me, Carol. I'll never tell another living soul. I promise!" "Tell me which boy you really, really like, Carol. I won't let him know."

"You have to have the shot to get well, but it won't hurt at all. Trust me." "Those vegetables taste wonderful. Just try them. You'll love them."

And there were the adult betrayals. "I'll love you forever, Carol." "I'll never leave you, Carol." "If you are a good person, attend church every Sunday and do what is right, the road of life will be straight and smooth."

Each betrayal seems the worst we can imagine at the time and each betrayal seems never so bad as the next.

As the years progress, we get older, mature and adapt to the betrayals of life. Sometimes we say we've grown cynical. Other times we say we've become realists. Whatever the case, we learn that parents and loved ones can die. Relationships can end. The government can be corrupt. And the police can't always keep us safe even when we're at home in our own beds.

Carol Bryan only thought she understood betrayal when she moved to a new home in North Dallas, Texas. She had experienced divorce and the premature death of a loved one. Her children were growing up, beginning to be independent and leaving home, two of them preceding her to that same city. Now she was at a time and place in life when she could build her own future in what was arguably the most flamboyant community in America. She had a dream and dreamers were always welcome in Dallas.

When Carol Bryan went to bed that warm April night, she knew that by Dallas standards she had it all. That was why she should have been able to rest peacefully. That was why she should have been able to sleep without worry. That was why she could not imagine betrayal so complete that it would shatter her trust in people, the government, the media, her faith and her ability to continue in a life she thought she understood.

The most momentous betrayal began with an unknown man watching her intently as she moved into the condominium. It continued as he kept tabs on her day and night until the shadow of a man entered her condominium at three o'clock in the morning. It exploded a half-hour later when she was startled awake by the pressure of a gun barrel pressed against her temple. And it came once more when she thought her life was incapable of spiraling any more out of control and found that those she thought she knew best were most suspect.

Though violence and betrayal are at the core of Carol's story, it is also the story of the triumph of the human spirit over adversity. Her ultimate victory over the evil that was and, by his own admission, continues to be Gilbert Escobedo has been in creating a rich, full life filled with happiness.

Today, Carol is a devout Christian who attends church, worships joyfully and has compassion for others. She does not forgive Gilbert, because she believes human forgiveness has always been his ultimate cop-out. He says he tried to absolve himself of the guilt of her rape by taking her to the upscale, prestigious mega-church where he was accepted. He thought that if he could be the vehicle for saving her soul, something never in jeopardy, then he would be seen as a good person and forgiven for his heinous crimes against Carol. It was as though he believed that you could sin throughout life and die at peace with God so long as after each deliberate act of violence and abomination you merely said, "I'm sorry."

Forgiveness, for Gilbert, has a magical quality. The term, when spoken aloud, can cleanse away all bad deeds so he can go out and rape again. To ask forgiveness in this way, Carol feels, is meaningless.

Carol works every day to move forward with her life and she has not been alone. "Detective King has always been wonderful. Sergeant Rommel has always been kind to me. They have understood that there was no way I could have known about Gilbert. They understood that even with their greater knowledge they did not know about him. They could not arrest him. They could not bring him to justice any sooner than they did.

"Other people in the law enforcement community have not been so kind. Sometimes in the police station I was treated with disdain. Some felt I was a dimwitted bimbo. Others thought that I was a fool or that rape is somehow an erotic experience that bonded me to Gilbert.

"Their demented thinking made me feel dirty, humiliated and stupid around them. There were days I didn't want to go on, didn't want to fight. But somehow, some way I found the strength to go on.

"And then there were the deals that were made. Gilbert was able to telephone me from jail, for example. I felt intense relief when his mask was torn away, knowing that the man who hurt me was where he could never touch me again. Then the telephone rang and it was him! It was as though I could never escape him, never have safety, never have peace. My stomach churned as though he might be able to ooze through the telephone and attack me once again.

The healing process was not an easy one and was not helped by some members of the news media who made hurtful comments in print and on the air. They incorrectly implied that the police could have arrested Gilbert whenever they desired. Carol learned that the police didn't know it was Gilbert all along, as some members of the media claimed, and even if they suspected him, they didn't have enough proof to arrest him before they actually did. Yet the media could not let go. They continued inundating papers and television with stories that hinted at police incompetence or corruption. Some stated important information was withheld from certain detectives, thereby stalling the investigation, a few claimed one or another detective had been a "cowboy," acting alone and others questioned and openly criticized the police over Gilbert's involvement with the police ride-along program.

"Perhaps the news media did the best they could under the circumstances. Perhaps they were trying to tell an effective story that would help others. Perhaps everyone was well intentioned. But it has only been the truth that has helped me.

"Until Ted Schwarz came to Dallas and asked them the questions that I had been afraid to ask, the whole truth did not come out. I blamed the police for not protecting me. Though I appreciated officers such as Detective King, who went out of their way to try to find some way to keep me from being hurt further, I was frustrated and angry with the police for not doing more. I know now that it took time to establish the facts that led to a conviction, respecting the fact that in our society, a person is considered innocent of a crime until the facts of his or her guilt can be presented in a court of law."

A conspiracy against the victim is the kind of story reporters like to break. An incompetent police department leaving the city's women helpless in the wake of a madman is a great story. But good people doing the best they can when understaffed, ill-equipped, overworked and desperately trying to protect the rights of all the city's citizens as they have sworn an oath to do is not a great story. Instead, that is exactly what the police did and what they do seven days a week, twenty-four hours a day. Some are better at it than others. Some are admittedly failures or a bad lot who hopefully will eventually be weeded out. But the vast majority were and are dedicated in ways that no member of the media has a right to smear. Worse, in recreating only part of the story, often inaccurately, some perpetuated the sense of fear and betrayal for the other victims and for Carol.

One thing that has helped to end some misconceptions about law enforcement and improve the justice system, as well as help Carol heal, is her public speaking on the subject. "Bringing my crime public, getting support from crime victims organizations, working as a volunteer to help those in power or in government positions see the need for stronger rights for victims and stronger punishment and longer prison time for perpetrators of violent crimes has helped shape a new agenda for criminal justice. Victims advocates, like Patsy Day and Raven Kazen, as well as several senators and congressmen and women began fighting long and hard for stronger laws, more prisons and longer punishment time for violent criminals. Their efforts finally paid off when legislation was passed under the governorship of George W. Bush. As a result, in Texas crime has now decreased, more crime prevention educational programs are in place and compensation for crime victims and their families has begun to aid victims.

"For us our final triumph is the truth. I have decided to tell the truth which, shall set me and, I hope, all of the others free."

AFTERWORD

CAROL COOK HAS triumphed over evil. She has moved forward with her life. She and her husband volunteer to help other victims and support a program that benefits battered and abused children. She is once again a working artist. She has a marriage as happy and emotionally intimate as those of couples successfully together for decades. Yet the reality for her and for all victims of violent crimes is that the event is never completely gone from the mind. It is like a wound that fully heals yet leaves behind an indelible scar. The scar might be ignored much of the time, but it is always there—a stark reminder of the pain that once was.

When I met Carol in person, I saw an attractive woman whose face is smooth and unlined. She has the strong, trim body of someone who is athletic and delights in physical activity. It is easy to see why Marion put her in the category of the Big D divorcée who could attract the most powerful, wealthiest and generous of men in Dallas.

Then we began talking about the rape. We visited the condominium where it occurred. We traveled only in broad daylight. We talked only in the morning when she felt safe enough to recall the bad memories. We covered the history of time past, not events that could still take place, because, for the moment, Gilbert Escobedo remains in the state penitentiary for what Dallas convicts laughingly call "life."

As we talked or visited the sites of past horrors, Carol's face changed. Her smooth jaw and lips took on stress lines. Wrinkles appeared. Her face had the appearance of alcoholics in AA, women who take what they hope will be the last sip of booze and last drags on a cigarette just before walking into the meeting. Heavy abuse of alcohol and nicotine create such lines and marks that often disappear when the alcoholic successfully stops drinking and smoking. In fact, the change to a more youthful physical appearance and the woman's vanity about how she has come to look often are all that keep her from going back to the addictions that were destroying her.

High stress and exhaustion can also cause such marks. Carol, at peace before we discussed the rape, aged each morning as we talked, then healed in the afternoon and evening and was young again when I met her the next day. The only exception was the day we talked through the afternoon. She was physically safe in the secure home she shared with the man she loved and who truly loved her, yet her mind remained on the event of long ago. That night, her sleep was restless. The next day, I saw that the stress marks had never left.

And so it is with victims of violent crimes. There are always triggers. There are always words or images, places or objects or odors that take the person back to the moment when life suddenly became an instant Hell.

Such momentary flashbacks are impossible to prevent. They may even be helpful in some instances, reminding the person that a particular location, lifestyle or attitude can be dangerous. They differ from the post-traumatic stress syndrome which Carol suffered in the aftermath of the rape in that they are not crippling. They do not create the fatigue, mood swings, physical and mental suffering, inability to function and other factors that force the sufferer to put his or her life on hold for what may be many years if effective therapy is not sought. But it is naïve to say that a victim can ever completely "get over it." Instead the person moves forward, the event an irrevocable part of the individual's life history yet no longer the emotional stopping point.

Carol has found and wants to tell other victims that there is life after being the victim of violent crime. There is joy. There are positive relationships. There is a future. Life may even have an added richness, the good days savored in ways that once were almost ignored, the bad days more acceptable, because the person has experienced far worse than the momentary problem or sadness.

This is not to say that to be a victim is a good thing. Only a fool would suggest that. What is important is that despite Carol Bryan Cook's savage experiences, her betrayals far beyond what any victim should have had to endure, she believes and teaches others that the ability to move forward can be attained by all who have suffered, whether as victims or the loved ones of victims. She believes that by standing together we can change the way criminals are perceived and victims are treated and ensure that the Gilbert Escobedos of the world will never triumph.

TED SCHWARZ, NOVEMBER 2001

* * *

This book is my version of times in my life and of a crime that altered the lives and existences of many people. There might be differences in facts and conclusions between my version and what others think, believe or want to believe, which does not surprise me. However, I know what I lived.

Writing what I lived has been difficult, painful and fascinating. Reliving the course of years, reliving the crime against me and the long road back from the devastation of violence was not something I could prepare myself for. Sadly, I learned that you cannot prepare for emotions that overtake you as you descend back into time.

Each day I worked on this book I felt sadness, fear and sometimes even joy. The reality of my life laid out before me on the pages at times brought about lingering questions, which was usually followed by the numbness of acceptance of what you can not change.

While no one chooses the kind of terrible events that engulfed me, I have much to be thankful for during the years of testing my limits. Today I have even more to be thankful for. I know myself, my strengths and my weaknesses much better; I know the depth and strength of love from family and friends; my faith is stronger and my outlook on the future is solid.

For me and for millions of other people who have lived through the violence of crimes against us, our world afterward was first seen through eyes of fear and hurt. With therapy to help us regain what has been lost, we may almost be startled by the return to life, new hope revealed and the promise of transformation and renewal.

Though I know how difficult this can be, I strongly urge crime victims to step forward, take a stand, make their attackers accountable and bring them face-to-face with the community. Also, work with the community, law makers and victim advocates so that we can all unite in helping to prevent the criminals responsible for such violent crimes from destroying more lives.

CAROL (BRYAN) COOK, NOVEMBER 2001

Appendix

Resources for Crime Victims

This section provides a list of resources, support groups, organizations, Web sites, state coalitions and other government agencies that offer support and valuable information to victims of rape and other violent crimes. The organizations and services are listed alphabetically under the following categories: Rape and Sexual Assault Victims, Violent Crimes/Victims and Their Loved Ones, Support Groups/Mental Health Services and a State-by-state/ Territory Listing of Coalitions Against Sexual Assault.

RAPE AND SEXUAL ASSAULT VICTIMS

The Brazos County Rape Crisis Center, Inc.
Web site: http://rapecrisis.txcyber.com
Though this is the Web site of a rape crisis center in Texas, it offers anonymous and confidential Internet support services to anyone who needs it. In addition, the site provides information for rape victims and their loved ones on a variety of subjects including rape awareness, what to do if you are attacked, the phases of rape trauma, regaining control and helping significant others of the victims.

Hope for Healing
Web site: http://www.hopeforhealing.com
This Web site offers a great deal of informative links on topics including advocacy, books, chat rooms, crisis centers, date rape, depression, eating disorders, flashbacks, healing, male victims of rape, myths, pregnancy by rape, post-traumatic stress disorder, romance after rape, stalking, statistics and survivors' stories. Designed for rape victims by a rape victim, the site fosters healing, hope and empowerment.

National Sexual Violence Resource Center
123 N. Enola Drive
Enola, PA 17025
Telephone: (877) 739-3895 ext. 105
Fax: (717) 909-0714
TTY: (717) 909-0715
E-mail: jwilt@nsvrc.org
Web site: http://www.nsvrc.org
A clearinghouse for resources, research and information, NSVRC supports sexual assault providers on the local, state and national levels; provides information to assist in improving sexual violence education and prevention; identifies emergency policy issues; works with a partner, the University of Pennsylvania, to promote awareness of important issues regarding sexual violence through investigation, research and review of current policies and practices. The organization's Web site offers medical, legal, statistical and public policy information as well as links to federal agencies and state and national organizations.

Rape, Abuse & Incest National Network (RAINN)
Telephone: (800) 656-HOPE
Web site: http://www.rainn.org
This nonprofit organization operates America's only national hotline for victims of sexual assault. The hotline offers free, confidential counseling and support twenty-four hours a day from anywhere in the United States. Calls are analyzed by computer and instantly connected to a rape crisis center nearest the caller. As of 2001, RAINN had almost 900 rape crisis center affiliates across America.

The Web site provides links to government reports providing the latest statistics on sexual assault and other violent crimes, helpful information geared specifically for women, men, children and college-students and facts on criminal profiles and the myths surrounding sexual assault. Through widespread celebrity support, including that of recording artist, rape survivor and RAINN founding member, Tori Amos, RAINN has been able to reach out to and help over 400,000 sexual assault victims across the country.

Sexual Assault Information Page
Web site: http://www.cs.utk.edu/~bartley/saInfoPage.html
The Sexual Assault Information Page is an information and referral service that provides links to sites on topics including counseling, law, literature, media, offenders, post-traumatic stress disorder, prevention, rape trauma syndrome, self-defense, survivors and both men's and women's resources. It also offers a listing of rape/sexual assault crisis centers throughout Canada, the United Kingdom and the United States.

Sexual Assault Resources Page
(Feminist Majority Foundation)
Web site: http://www.feminist.org/911/assaultlinks.html
This page on the Feminist Majority Foundation's Web site features an extensive list of other Web sites (including links and descriptions) devoted to sexual assault for care providers, on college campuses and for both male and female victims.

The Survivor's Page
E-mail: thesurvivorpage@home.net
Web site: http://www.stardate.bc.ca/survivors/
This Web site is designed to promote recovery and healing by providing an outlet for survivors of sexual assault and rape. It includes a list of related organizations, crisis centers, interactive chat rooms, newsgroups, a letters/poetry section and an area where users can post their own writing or read others' stories of sexual assault survival and recovery.

VIOLENT CRIMES / VICTIMS AND THEIR LOVED ONES

Communities Against Violence Network (CAVNET)
Web site: http://cavnet2.org
This Washington, D.C. based nonprofit organization started by a former prosecutor works internationally to address violence against women, youth violence and crimes against people with disabilities. CAVNET has developed an online database of information and a virtual community of over 950 professionals from North and South America, Europe, Australia, New Zealand, South Africa and the Middle East. In addition, using the Internet, the organization offers real-time voice conferencing with professionals and survivors from around the globe.

The National Center for Victims of Crime
2000 M Street, NW, Suite 480
Washington, DC 20036
Telephone: (202) 467-8700 / (800) FYI-CALL
TTY: (800) 211-7996
Fax: (202) 467-8701
E-mail: gethelp@ncvc.org
Web site: http://www.ncvc.org
The Center provides victim services and support including a toll-free help line, information on safety strategies, provider referrals, outreach materials, information on public policy and the latest news as well as assistance in contacting attorneys and other professionals for civil litigation. In addition, the center's Web site hosts a variety of resources including a virtual library—with literature on research, crime statistics and recommended reading for crime victims—and the Stalking Resource Center which offers an overview on stalking and an on-line newsletter. To improve services for crime victims, the center offers a training institute for professionals and the Last Step in First Response initiative, a campaign to encourage law enforcement professionals to put victims immediately in touch with the support and outreach services they may need.

National Organization for Victim Assistance
Web site: http://www.try-nova.org
This organization, focusing both on victims of disaster as well as crime, provides educational materials and training for crisis response providers, assists victims in getting the help they need, fights for public policies to aid victims of crimes, offers cutting edge services for crime and other victims and provides literature on psychological issues, services and victims' rights.

Office for Victims of Crime
Department of Justice
Office for Victims of Crime
810 Seventh Street, NW
Washington, DC 20531
Telephone: (202) 307-5983 / (800) 627-6872
E-mail: askovc@ojp.usdoj.gov
Web site: http://www.ojp.usdoj.gov/ovc
Under the U.S. Department of Justice, the Office for Victims of Crime (OVC) was established by the 1984 Victims of Crime Act to oversee diverse programs that benefit victims of crime. OVC provides substantial funding to state victim assistance and compensation programs and supports training designed to educate criminal justice and allied professionals. Their Web site provides resource links, information and facts on crime in the United States, links to help for victims and training information.

Partnership Against Violence Network
Web site: http://www.parnet.org
A Web site for violence prevention professionals, it provides a searchable database of violence prevention programs, information on funding, teaching curricula, data from government agencies and articles on topics including breaking the cycle of violence, children and guns, family violence and gang violence.

Victims Outreach
5327 North Central Expressway, Suite 305
Dallas, TX 75251
Telephone: (214) 358-5173

This organization offers a variety of services to crime victims and their families including emotional support—via trauma and grief counseling, crisis intervention, a twenty-four hour crisis hotline and peer support meetings, criminal justice support including accompanying victims to court, acting as a liaison with police and district attorney, case management through referrals and help with crime victims' compensation and raising public awareness. There are no fees charged for any services offered.

SUPPORT GROUPS/MENTAL HEALTH SERVICES

American Psychiatric Association
1400 K Street, NW
Washington, DC 20005
Telephone: (202) 682-6239
Fax: (202) 682-6850
Web site: http://www.apa.org
APA is a professional society of psychiatrists and medical doctors who specialize in treating individuals with mental or emotional disorders. The association continues to research and improve the diagnosis, treatment and rehabilitation of individuals through continuing education programs for psychiatrists. Individuals can contact the Association to locate a psychiatrist in their area for consultation.

The National Mental Health Association
102 Prince Street
Alexandria, VA 22314-2971
Telephone: (703) 684-7722 / (800) 969-6642
Fax: (703) 684-5968
Web site: http://www.nmha.org
Dedicated to improving the mental health of all individuals and achieving victory over mental illness, the National Mental Health Association (NMHA) works to achieve its goals through advocacy, education, research and service. NMHA was at the forefront of efforts that resulted in the 1996 Mental Health Parity Act, which bars insurance companies from plac-

ing annual or lifetime dollar limits on mental health coverage, and their National Public Education Campaign on Clinical Depression, begun in 1993, continues to inform Americans on the symptoms of depression and provide information about treatment. Their newsletter, *The Bell*, and other publications are available on-line.

Psychology.com Therapist Directory

Web site: http://www.psychology.com/therapist

This Web site offers a directory of therapists throughout the United States and parts of Canada as well as a helpful question and answer section that provides information like what to expect in therapy, how to learn if your insurance will cover sessions and how to tell what type of qualifications and educational background a specific therapist has.

Support-Group.com

Web site: http://www.support-group.com

This Web site allows people with a variety of health, personal, relationship and emotional problems or issues to share their experiences through bulletin boards and on-line chats. The site also provides links to support-related information on the Internet.

STATE AND TERRITORY SEXUAL ASSAULT COALITIONS

ALABAMA
Alabama Coalition Against Rape
804 S. Perry Street, Suite 100
Montgomery, AL 36104
Tel: (334) 264-0123 / (888) 725-7273
Fax: (334) 264-0128
Fax: (907) 463-4493
Web site: http://www.acar.org

ALASKA
Alaska Network on Domestic Violence & Sexual Assault
130 Seward Street, Suite 209
Juneau, AK 99801
Tel: (907) 465-2071 / (800) 520-2666
E-mail: acar@acar.org
E-mail: andvsa@hotmail.com
Web site: http://www.andvsa.org

ARIZONA
Arizona Sexual Assault Network
12 West Madison
Phoenix, AZ 85003
Tel: (602) 258-1195
Fax: (602) 258-7390
E-mail: info@azsan.org
Web site: http://www.azsan.org

ARKANSAS
Arkansas Coalition Against Sexual Assault
628 West Broadway, Suite 202
North Little Rock, AR 72114
Tel: (501) 801-2700 / (800) 818-1189
Fax: (501) 280-4501
E-mail: orcc@mail.cswnet.com

CALIFORNIA
California Coalition Against Sexual Assault
1215 K Street, Suite 1100
Sacramento, CA 95814
Tel: (916) 446-2520
Fax: (916) 446-8166
E-mail: info@calcasa.org
Web site: http://www.calcasa.org

COLORADO
Colorado Coalition Against Sexual Assault
P.O. Box 300398
Denver, CO 80203
Tel: (303) 861-7033
Fax: (303) 832-7067
E-mail: info@ccasa.org
Web site: http://www.ccasa.org

CONNECTICUT
Connecticut Sexual Assault Crisis Services
96 Pitkin Street
East Hartford, CT 06108
Tel: (860) 282-9881 / (888) 999-5545
Fax: (860) 291-9335
E-mail: info@connsacs.org
Web site: http://www.connsacs.org

DELAWARE
CONTACT Delaware Inc.
P.O. Box 9525
Wilmington, DE 19809
Tel: (302) 761-9800
Fax: (302) 761-4280
E-mail: ptedford@contact delaware.org
Web site: http://www.contact delaware.org

DISTRICT OF COLUMBIA
D.C. Rape Crisis Center
P.O. Box 34125
Washington, DC 20043
Tel: (202) 232-0789
Fax: (202) 387-3812
E-mail: dcrcc@dcrcc.org
Web site: http://www.dcrcc.org

FLORIDA
Florida Council Against Sexual Violence
1311-A Paul Russell Road, Suite 102
Tallahassee, FL 32301
Tel: (850) 297-2000 / (888) 956-7273
Fax: (850) 297-2002
E-mail: fcasv@nettally.com
Web site: http://www.fcasv.org

GEORGIA
Georgia Network to End Sexual
   Assault
659 Auburn Avenue, Suite 139
Atlanta, GA 30312
Tel: (404) 659-6482
Fax: (404) 659-6383
E-mail: gnesa@mindspring.com
Web site: http://www.gnesa.org

IDAHO
Idaho Coalition Against Domestic
   Violence & Sexual Assault
815 Park Boulevard, Suite 140
Boise, ID 83712
Tel: (208) 384-0419 / (888) 293-
   6118
Fax: (208) 331-0687
E-mail: domvio@micron.net
Web site: http://www.idvsa.org

INDIANA
Indiana Coalition Against Sexual
   Assault
55 Monument Circle, Suite 1224
Indianapolis, IN 46204
Tel: (317) 423-0233 / (800) 691-
   2272
Fax: (317) 423-0237
E-mail: incasa@incasa.org
Web site: http://www.incasa.org

KANSAS
Kansas Coalition Against Sexual
   Assault
220 SW 33rd Street, Suite 100
Topeka, KS 66611
Tel: (785) 232-9784
Fax: (785) 266-2874
E-mail: kcsdv@kcsdv.org
Web site: http://www.kasap.
   org

HAWAII
Hawaii Coalition Against Sexual
   Assault
741A Sunset Avenue, Room 105
Honolulu, HI 96816
Tel: (808) 733-9038
Fax: (808) 733-9032
E-mail: msshari@aloha.net

ILLINOIS
Illinois Coalition Against Sexual
   Assault
100 North 16th Street
Springfield, IL 62703
Tel: (217) 753-4117
Fax: (217) 753-8229
E-mail: icasa@famvid.com

IOWA
Iowa Coalition Against Sexual
   Assault
2603 Bell Avenue, Suite 102
Des Moines, IA 50319
Tel: (515) 244-7424
Fax: (515) 244-7417
E-mail: IowaCASA@aol.com
Web site: http://www.iowacasa.
   org

KENTUCKY
Kentucky Association of Sexual
   Assault Programs & Domestic
   Violence
P.O. Box 602
Frankfort, KY 40602
Tel: (502) 226-2704
Fax: (502) 226-2725
E-mail:msexton@vnet.vineco.
   com

LOUISIANA
Louisiana Foundation Against
    Sexual Assault
P.O. Box 40
Independence, LA 70443
Tel: (985) 345-5995 / (888) 995-
    7273
Fax: (985) 345-5592
E-mail: lafasa@I-55.com
Web site: http://www.lafasaorg.
    hypermart.net

MARYLAND
Maryland Coalition Against Sexual
    Sexual Assault
1517 Gov. Ritchie Highway,
    Suite 207
Arnold, MD 21012
Tel: (410) 974-4507 / (800) 983-
    7273
Fax: (410) 757-4770
E-mail: info@mcasa.org
Web site: http://www.mcasa.org

MICHIGAN
Michigan Coalition Against
    Domestic Sexual Violence
3893 Okemos Road, Suite B2
Okemos, MI 48864
Tel: (517) 347-7000
Fax: (517) 347-1377
E-mail: mcadsv@pilot.msu.edu
Web site: http://www.mcadsv.org

MISSISSIPPI
Mississippi Coalition Against
    Sexual Assault
P.O. Box 4172
Jackson, MS 38655
Tel: (601) 987-9011 / (888) 987-
    9011
Fax: (601) 987-9166

MAINE
Maine Coalition Against Sexual
    Assault
3 Mulliken Court
Augusta, ME 04330
Tel: (207) 626-0034
Fax: (207) 626-5503
E-mail: mecasa@aol.com

MASSACHUSETTS
Massachusetts Coalition Against
    Assault & Domestic
    Violence—Jane Doe Inc.
14 Beacon Street, Suite 507
Boston, MA 02108
Tel: (617) 248-0922
Fax: (617) 248-0902
E-mail: marewinters@earthlink.net
Web site: http://www.janedoe.org

MINNESOTA
Minnesota Coalition Against
    Sexual & Assault
420 N. 5th Street, Suite 690
Minneapolis, MN 55401
Tel: (612) 313-2797 / (800) 964-
    8847
Fax: (612) 313-2799
E-mail: mncasa@msn.com
Web site: http://www.mncasa.org

MISSOURI
Missouri Coalition Against Sexual
    Assault
P.O. Box 104866
Jefferson City, MO 65110
Tel: (573) 636-8776
Fax: (573) 636-6613
E-mail: Riehljd@aol.com
Web site: http://mocasa.missouri.
    org

MONTANA
Montana Coalition Against
  Domestic & Sexual Violence
P.O. Box 633
Helena, MT 59624
Tel: (406) 443-7794
Fax: (406) 443-7818
E-mail: mcadsv.mt.net
Web site: http://www.mt.net/mcadsv

NEVADA
Nevada Coalition Against Sexual
  Violence
P.O. Box 530103
Henderson, NV 89053
Tel: (702) 914-6878
Fax: (702) 914-6879
E-mail: tysonlow@aol.com
Web site: http://www.ncasv.org

NEW JERSEY
New Jersey Coalition Against
  Sexual Assault
1 Edinburg Road, 2nd Floor
Trenton, NJ 08619
Tel: (609) 631-4450 / (800) 601-
  7200
Fax: (609) 631-4453
E-mail: mail@njcasa.org
Web site: http://www.njcasa.org

NEW YORK STATE
New York State Coalition Against
  Sexual Assault
784 Washington Avenue
Albany, NY 12203
Tel: (518) 482-4222
Fax: (518) 482-4248
E-mail: info@nyscasa.org
Web site: http://www.nyscasa.org

NEBRASKA
Nebraska Domestic Violence &
  Sexual Assault Coalition
825 M Street, Suite 404
Lincoln, NE 68508
Tel: (402) 476-6256
Fax: (402) 476-6806
E-mail: administrator@ndvsac.org
Web site: http://www.ndvsac.org

NEW HAMPSHIRE
New Hampshire Coalition Against
  Domestic and Sexual Violence
P.O. Box 353
Concord, NH 03302
Tel: (603) 271-6105
Fax: (603) 228-6096
E-mail: mattern@nhcadsv.org
Web site: http://www.nhcadsv.org

NEW MEXICO
New Mexico Coalition of Sexual
  Assault Programs
4004 Carlisle, NE, Suite D
Albuquerque, NM 87107
Tel: (505) 883-8020 / (888) 883-
  8020
Fax: (505) 883-7530
E-mail: nmcsaas@swcp.com
Web site: http://www.swcp.com/
  nmcsaas

NEW YORK CITY
New York City Alliance Against
  Sexual Assault
c/o St. Luke's Roosevelt Hospital
411 West 114th Street, Suite 6D
New York, NY 10025
Tel: (212) 523-4185
Fax: (212) 523-4429
E-mail: hlessel@nycagainstrape.
  org
Web site: http://www.nycagainst
  rape.org

NORTH CAROLINA
North Carolina Coalition Against
    Sexual Assault
4426 Louisburg Road, Suite 100
Raleigh, NC 27616
Tel: (919) 431-0995 / (888) 737-
    2272
Fax: (919) 431-0096
E-mail: nccasa@nccasa.org
Web site: http://www.nccasa.org

OHIO
Ohio Coalition Against Sexual
    Assault and Sexual Assault
4041 N. High Street, Suite 410
Columbus, OH 43214
Tel: (614) 268-3322
Fax: (614) 268-0881
E-mail: ohiocoalition@aol.com

OREGON
Oregon Coalition Against Domestic
    and Sexual Violence
659 Cottage NE
Salem, OR 97301
Tel: (503) 365-9644 / (800) 622-
    3782
Fax: (503) 566-7870
E-mail: ocadsv@teleport.com
Web site: http://www.ocadsv.com

RHODE ISLAND
Rhode Island Sexual Assault
    Coalition
300 Richmond Street, Suite 205
Providence, RI 02903
Tel: (401) 421-4100
Fax: (401) 454-5565
E-mail: info@satrc.org
    Fax: (803) 256-1030
Web site: http://www.satrc.org

NORTH DAKOTA
North Dakota Coalition Against
    Sexual Assault
418 East Rousser, #320
Bismarck, ND 58501
Tel: (701) 255-6240 / (888) 255-
    6240
Fax: (701) 255-1904
E-mail: ndcaws@ndcaws.org

OKLAHOMA
Oklahoma Coalition Against
    Domestic Violence
2525 NW Expressway, Suite 101
Oklahoma City, OK 73112
Tel: (405) 848-1815
Fax: (405) 848-3469
E-mail: ocdvsa@swbell.net

PENNSYLVANIA
Pennsylvania Coalition Against
    Rape
125 N. Enola Drive
Enola, PA 17205
Tel: (717) 728-9740 / (800) 692-
    7445
Fax: (717) 728-9781
E-mail: stop@pcar.org
Web site: http://www.pcar.org

SOUTH CAROLINA
South Carolina Coalition Against
    Domestic Violence and Sexual
    Assault
P.O. Box 7776
Columbia, SC 29202
Tel: (803) 256-2900 / (800) 260-
    9293
E-mail: mosi@sccadvasa.org
Web site: http://www.sccadvasa.
    org

SOUTH DAKOTA
South Dakota Coalition Against
    Sexual Violence and Domestic
    Violence
P.O. Box 306
Eagle Butte, SD 57625
Tel: (605) 945-0869 / (800) 572-
    9196
Fax: (605) 945-0870
E-mail: sdcadvsa@cam-walnet.com
Web site: http://www.southdakota
    coalition.com

TEXAS
Texas Association Against Sexual
    Assault
800 Brazos, Suite 810
Austin, TX 78701
Tel: (512) 474-7190 / (888) 918-
    2272
Fax: (512) 474-6490
E-mail: taasa@taasa.org

VERMONT
Vermont Network Against Domestic
    Violence and Sexual Assault
P.O. Box 405
Montpelier, VT 05601
Tel: (802) 223-1302
Fax: (802) 223-6943
E-mail: vnadvsa@sover.net
Web site: http://www.ntnetwork.org

WASHINGTON
Washington Coalition of Sexual
    Assault Programs
2415 Pacific Avenue, SE, #10-C
Olympia, WA 98504
Tel: (360) 754-7583
Fax: (360) 786-8707
E-mail: wcsap@wcsap.org
Web site: http://www.wcsap.org

TENNESSEE
Tennessee Coalition Against
    Domestic and Sexual Violence
P.O. Box 120972
Nashville, TN 37212
Tel: (615) 386-9406
Fax: (615) 383-2967
E-mail: tcadsv@telalink.net
Web site: http://www.tcadsv.city
    search.com

UTAH
Utah Coalition Against Sexual
    Assault
220 East 3900 South, Suite 1
Salt Lake City, UT 84109
Tel: (801) 266-5094
Fax: (801) 266-5187
E-mail: ucasa@mcleodusa.net
Web site: http://www.u-casa.org

VIRGINIA
Virginians Aligned Against Sexual
    Assault
508 Dale Avenue, Suite B
Charlottesville, VA 22903
Tel: (804) 979-9002 / (800) 838-
    8238
Fax: (804) 979-9003
E-mail: vaasa@rlc.net
Web site: http://www.vaasa.org

WEST VIRGINIA
West Virginia Foundation for Rape
    Information and Services
112 Braddock Street
Fairmont, WV 26554
Tel: (304) 366-9500
Fax: (304) 366-9501
E-mail: fris@labs.net
Web site: http://www.fris.org

WISCONSIN
Wisconsin Coalition Against Sexual
  Assault
600 Williamson Street, Suite N-2
Madison, WI 53703
Tel: (608) 257-1516
Fax: (608) 257-2150
E-mail: wcasa@wcasa.org
Web site: http://www.wcasa.org

GUAM
Guam Healing Arts Crisis Center
790 Gov. Carlos G. Camacho Road
Tamuning, GU 96911
Tel: (671) 647-5351 / (800)-711-
  4826
Fax: (671) 637-6948
E-mail: csmau@mail.gov.gu

VIRGIN ISLANDS
Women's Coalition of St. Croix
P.O. Box 2734
Christiansted
St. Croix, VI 00822
Tel: (340) 773-9272
Fax: (340) 773-9062
E-mail:wcscstx@worldnet.att.net
Web site: http://www.wcstx.com

WYOMING
Wyoming Coalition Against Sexual
  Assault and Domestic Violence
409 S. 4th Street, P.O. Box 236
Laramie, WY 82073
Tel: (307) 755-5481 / (800) 990-
  3877
Fax: (307) 755-5482
E-mail: wcadvsa@vcn.com
Web site: http://www.geocities.
  com/wcadvsa

PUERTO RICO
Puerto Rico Rape Crisis
P.O. Box 9175
Caguas, PR 00726
Tel: (787) 756-0910
Fax: (787) 756-7840

REFERENCES

Romans 13: 1–4. *The New Oxford Annotated Bible With the Apocrypha*. New York: Oxford University Press, 1991.

Acheson, Sam. *Dallas Yesterday*. Dallas: Southern Methodist University Press, 1977.

Donovan, Jim. *Dallas: Shining Star of Texas*. Stillwater, MN: Voyageur Press, 1994. Reprinted by permission of publisher (1-800-888-9653).

Hill, Patricia Evridge. *Dallas: The Making of a Modern City*. Austin: University of Texas Press, 1996.

Leslie, Warren. *Dallas Public and Private: Aspects of an American City*. Dallas: Southern Methodist University Press, 1964.

Payne, Darwin. *Dallas: An Illustrated History*. Woodland Hills, CA: Windsor Publications, 1982.

ABOUT THE AUTHORS

Carol Cook is a spokesperson for Victims Outreach, an organization that provides grief and trauma counseling to crime victims and the community. An artist, she donated a percentage of her art sales to a home for abused and needy children. She resides in Dallas, Texas, with her husband and is the mother of three daughters.

Ted Schwarz is the bestselling author of more than ninety books and over two thousand articles. His true crime writing includes *Secret Weapons*, *The Hillside Strangler*, and other books frequently made into movies, including *Deadly Whispers* and *False Arrest*. He and his family live in Cleveland, Ohio.